What It Takes Master Climbers to Become Chiefs

What It Takes Master Climbers to Become Chiefs

Eugene E. Jennings, Ph.D.

VANTAGE PRESS
New York

FIRST EDITION

All rights reserved, including the right of
reproduction in whole or in part in any form.

Copyright ©2002 by Eugene E. Jennings, Ph.D.

Published by Vantage Press, Inc.
516 West 34th Street, New York, New York 10001

Manufactured in the United States of America
ISBN: 0-533-14188-5

Library of Congress Catalog Card No: 02-091902

0 9 8 7 6 5 4 3 2 1

Publications of Eugene Emerson Jennings, Ph.D.

The Mobile Manager
Routes to the Executive Suite
Executive Success; Stresses, Problems, Adjustments
Executive in Crisis
The Executive: Autocrat, Bureaucrat, Democrat
Anatomy of Leadership, Princes, Heroes, and Supermen

Publications after 1979:
Career Success—AMA Audio Cassette
Stress Intelligence, National Education and Training Corp.
    Audio and Visual two-hour cassette

Most recent publication:

How Managers Become Chiefs, 1997

To Marilynne
My wife for fifty-five years
My friend for fifty-nine years
My love forever

CONTENTS

Preface	xi
Foreword	xix
Prologue	1
1 The Fast Route to the Top	7
2 Corporate Sense	12
3 Advanced Fundamentals	18
4 The Superiority of Ordinary Behavior	27
5 The Formula	32
6 The Mobile Manager	42
7 The Invisible Climber	48
8 Getting into the Lineup	55
9 The Power of Lineups	62
10 The Crucial Subordinate	74
11 Bypassing Levels	83
Intermission: A Quiz of Your Climbing Smarts	92
12 The Promotable Manager	94
13 The Right Moves	105
14 Basic Moves: Away, With, Against (AWA)	116
15 The Rules of Moves	124
16 Relationship Sense	132
17 The Powerful Superior	144
18 The Sponsor	161
19 The Mind for the Climb	172
20 Conclusion: Efforts vs. Wits	190
Appendix A: The Origins of Chiefs	202
Appendix B: The Mobility Patterns of Chiefs	205
Appendix C: The Language of Mobility	209
Appendix D: Wit From A to Z	218

Appendix E: Rules of Moves 222
*Appendix F: Major Conclusions of the Fifty-Year
   Mobility Study* 225
About the Author 229

PREFACE

This book is predicated upon the single observation that managers who become chiefs leverage more advancements from their achievements than the managers they leave behind These passed-over managers often incur as good or better records of accomplishments. They may give as much to their businesses but in return get fewer or slower promotions in spite of their ambitions to go as high as possible. It is obvious that something more than achievements is at work to create a superior lift for chiefs. What it takes (wit) is most demonstrable in the mobility patterns of master climbers. The speed and ease of their climbs show the power of mobility when used widely and skillfully. (Please see Appendix F for more conclusions derived from the Mobility Study.)

Mobility is not a defining metaphor for moving ahead, but rather it is the very substance of climbing. I first wrote about this ubiquitous but underestimated power of mobility in *The Mobile Manager* (1967), *Routes to the Executive Suite* (1971), and *How Managers Become Chiefs* (1997), and mobility is herein featured again as the essential way that corporations spawn managers who become chiefs. (Please see Appendix B: The Mobility Patterns of Chiefs.)

This text is the logical extension of six books written in the 1960s and 1970s, based upon what has become the oldest, continuous study of the mobility patterns of chief executive officers of America's largest industrial corporations. In addition to this **Mobility Study** started in 1949, I started in the early 1960s the practice of confidential adviser to chiefs and their protégés, which accelerated in the late 1970s and continues to this day to augment the mobility study. This counseling experience provided the text of two books written in the late 1960s and early 1970s: The *Executive in Crisis* and *Executive Success*.

I did not publish during the 1980s. In 1997 in *How Managers Become Chiefs,* I presented the most salient and enduring ideas collected by my research and counseling and a glossary of over 100 items accumulated since 1949, when the Mobility Study began. *Master Climbers* is one of several books to be spun from the 1997 book.

However, the Mobility Study continues. Recently I came to the belief that the chief officers of the material supply chain in major corporations will become eligible for CEO positions. In 1996 I became affiliated with the Center for Advanced Purchasing Studies located at Arizona State University, Tempe, Arizona, under sponsorship of the Director, Phil Carter, Ph.D. With the lead effort by my former doctoral student Aaron A. Buchko, Ph.D., Associate Professor of Business at Bradley University, a major, long-term study was launched to investigate the mobility patterns of supply chain chiefs. Aaron uses the language of a computer program that I introduced in *Mobile Manager*. Available now is the first of several publications, *The Making of the CPO: The Mobility Pattern of Chief Purchasing Officers*, (CAPs, www.capsresearch.org.).

After this five-decade study of how managers become chiefs, I may appear to focus attention upon getting ahead as the end-all of business. Such is not my intention. Business does not exist primarily to serve the ambitions of managers who want to go to the top, contrary to what some ambitious climbers may believe. My concern is about results-driven, high-performance managers whose businesses fail to take advantage of their potential worth at higher levels because these managers do not know how to employ the power of mobility. Theirs is a deficiency of practical sense more than skill. (Please see Appendix D for Rules of Wit.)

If I have learned anything during this lengthy sojourn, it is that youth aggressively pressing upwards encourages superiors to perform better their managerial responsibilities. Climbers make managers better. In this context, I offer the examples of chiefs who excel at both managing and climbing, who go from the bottom to the pinnacle of a single corporation, who contrive the necessary support to ascend in record time, and who deserve the appellation, **"Master Climbers."**

And who, by the way, may serve to encourage managers who believe that they need two or more businesses to achieve their ambitions to rethink their career strategy.

The parlaying of experiences gained in one business into better opportunities in other businesses is called "leveraging,"* one of the

---

*Jennings, Eugene E., *Routes to the Executive Suite*, 1971, McGraw-Hill.

sequels to *How Managers Become Chiefs*. However, the largest batch of chiefs, which include the masters, needs only one employer to prove *what it takes* to get ahead.

Chiefs often complain that business is a tower of blather. In every decade since 1949, when the Mobility Study was started, chiefs have complained about managers who periodically bolt on this or that latest fad, accumulating a jerry-rigged contraption of management ideas and tools with all the current words to make these tinkerers appear fashionable. However, in the first three decades of this study, chiefs usually spoke with gentility and precision. They were respectful of language sufficiently to seek careful expression to avoid being misunderstood. They were wordsmiths of the first order, seldom seen among chiefs today.

In the last decade, chiefs have become more casual than usual, using words contrived for effect. They often create words and beg, borrow, or steal from the popular and fuzzy lexicon of the day. Many are given to throwing out bromides, as though they were dispensing prescriptions in a pharmacy. I never quite know what they may mean because often they cannot clearly define what they say. Flamboyant or pretentious words impede their explanations of how they ascended. Lately I must work harder than in previous decades to find among chiefs common meanings of the words they use. A five-decade study should not use words and meanings that are transitory and require translating from one decade to the next.

I am also aware of the growing reaction lately among some chiefs to this clutter of what they call useless, mindless verbiage that neither advances business nor careers. The last thing readers need is more of the same. However, the use of the language of mobility is not quite as foreign today as it was when I first introduced into the business world the book, *The Mobile Manager* (1967). To avoid blather, the words then and now are taken from standard dictionaries, usually *Merriam Webster's Collegiate* (Please refer to Appendix C, the Language of Mobility.)

One faddish word whose denotations are not commonly shared among chiefs is the word "culture," which for the first forty years of the study had not yet been misappropriated from social sciences. In interviewing and counseling managers who become chiefs, I ask for their practical meanings for climbing. Usually "culture" can be simplified by the word "ways." All corporations have characteristic, regular or habitual ways of believing and behaving by their employees. Ways are seldom uniformly present throughout the corporation and also differ by their formality and informality and by the recognition, value, and credibility accorded them.

The focus of the text is on *managers,* both by title and role, from first level above rank-and-file employees to the executive levels of the chief. The rules of mobility cannot be explained without putting the manager in a working context. For this reason, the reader will note that the words "superior," "manager," and "subordinate" are always used to denote the same hierarchical relationship throughout the text. When the text refers to a superior, it means one with responsibility for a manager who, in turn, is responsible for a subordinate. This prevents confusing the manager as the superior of a subordinate when, in the usage, superior is always over the manager, and the manager is the one to whom the subordinate reports.

This practice conforms to business use of a superior, manager, and subordinate as the minimum unit of the hierarchy. Managers oversee the work of subordinates under the authority granted by superiors. Because superiors also have superiors, I call the latter "extended," and the former "immediate" superiors. Also, because subordinates have direct reports, I call them "extended subordinates." When several managers report to the same superior, I call the latter the "common superior." Because manager is the focus of the text, I foil off superior and subordinate as needed. Over the many years of the Mobility Study, this lexicon has tended to minimize confusion, especially when *manager* is also a superior and subordinate. All master climbers are viewed from the title and role of manager.

Note also the meaning of "manager." It is one who has two or more subordinates other than clerical and support staff. Many soloists are called managers who simply are in charge of assignments and projects without supervisory responsibility. In this text, they are not classified as managers. The reasons for this definition of managers are several. One is that the title, "manager," was not generally given to soloists during the first thirty years of this study. Second, I cannot track nonmanagers because of their large numbers. For mobility-auditing procedures, I pick managers from the lists given by corporations of people with managerial rank. Third, the vast proportion of chiefs begin their ascents early in their careers as managers herein defined. To repeat this clarification, the protagonists are always master climbers with titles and roles of managers.

The use of "executive" is reserved for corporate officers. The board of directors elects them, and they may or may not sit on their boards. Executives are first in line to form and implement the responsibilities of the chief executive officer and have a fiduciary responsibility unmatched by managers as herein defined.

The word "climber" is used for ambitious managers who set out early in their careers to go to the top. In this sense, climbing is an intentional effort almost as purposive as achieving a record of high performance. This report does not use chiefs who later in their careers focus their ambition to go to the top or use more than one company. The ambition of masters sustains their drive from the bottom to the top of a single company. (Please see Appendix A: The Origins of Chiefs.)

The arrangement of the text is a foreword that alerts the readers to what generally may be expected to follow. Then a prologue follows that serves as a quick, concise summation of the mind for the climb, including the listing of the Masters' Rules. The chapters start with describing the barest ingredients of the fast route to the top. Chapter 19, The Mind for the Climb, brings together the wits for what it takes to defy the odds of making it to the top ahead of time for climbers who become chiefs (masters). After reading the Foreword, Prologue, and the first chapter, The Fast Route, the reader may benefit from Chapter 19 because it represents the salient ideas of the main body of the text. Then the reader may gain detailed explanations from the intervening chapters. The final chapter, Efforts vs. Wits, directs the reader's attention to the most likely competitors of climbers. They are not master climbers but rather managers plying the slow routes.

The appendixes are to inform the reader about the language of mobility used to discern the corporate ways that climbers use to get to the top. Appendix A, The Origins of Chiefs, shows the several general routes that chiefs take and the significance of the fast route of the masters. Appendix B describes the several specific mobility patterns. Masters are usually sleepers or shooting stars. Appendix C offers the language of mobility, which is necessary because the language of management is inadequate for separating the wits needed for climbing from the skills for managing. Appendix D offers the rules from A to Z of what it takes to think as a climber. Appendix E lists the rules that govern smart moves. It is smart moves that produce exceptional achievements and what sponsors look for in forming lineups. Appendix F concerns the concluding observations of the fifty-year study of *How Managers Become Chiefs,* excluding the observation upon which this text is based.

It is tempting to conclude here, because I do not wish to give the story line away in the preface. However, I want to encourage the readers to look for ideas available everyday to everybody. Behind the often bewildering, noisy, confusing, and ostentatious display of great corporate achievements are acts that are elegant because of their simplicity and powerful because of their precise focus and timing. Unfortunately, over the years of this study, scholars and practitioners have developed a set of practices of business management that are without foundation in elementary human behavior. This superficiality is why chiefs cannot explain what it takes to get to the top by the use of management language and why the language of mobility is necessary.

For example, a chief of an automobile company said in the late 1960s, "I use the same basic moves in my boardroom as at home with my family. The moves are for different purposes and uniquely focused because of different responsibilities." A former chief of another large industrial corporation said in 1990, "I did not cease to act human as I rose to become chief. All my noteworthy achievements were launched and completed by efforts commonly found among employees in our plants." And recently a chief explained, "How more elementary can one behave than to avoid or support or oppose somebody or something? What other choice do you have when it comes to making your moves?" (Please see Appendix E, Rules of Moves.) Over the years, I have come to label these practices "The superiority of ordinary behavior." They too are demonstrable in masters of the climb and help to explain their skillful use of the power of mobility.

Readers will not see these gifted climbers in the corporate showcases of fashionable management where other chiefs may be found. Masters occasionally practice gimmickry or tinker with exotic notions of the day. But for the most part, masters simply, adroitly, and inconspicuously mobilize in productive ways what is available to all people who want to get ahead. For this reason, master climbers usually blend with their surroundings to become known as well-respected managers.

In times when ideas seemingly have to be new or novel to be powerful, ordinary people with practical sense to embrace elementary practices are most likely to gain more advancements from their achievements. They are fundamentalists, using just plain wits to employ the simplest ways of human behavior consistent with corporate life. In this sense, masters are authentic representations of basic predispositions inherent and available to all people. They get their advantages from the superiority of simplicity. So the masters practiced fifty years ago when I started the Mobility Study of *How Managers Become Chiefs*,* and surely they shall for many years to come.

I wish to recognize a master climber whom I have counseled for over fifteen years. John Scales became the CEO of Vlasic Foods at forty-one years of age, more than tripled the business, and sold it for a substantial premium to Campbell Soup Company. John's career represents the qualities of mobility herein described.

I dedicate this book to "Pete" as Marilynne was called when I first met her in tenth grade in high school in Moline, Illinois. Marilynne has been of crucial assistance to our work and has never failed to assume an opportunity to assist me in over fifty years of the Mobility Study. No words may ring authentic of my abiding respect and gratitude for this true friend and colleague.

Eugene E. Jennings
Professor Emeritus, Business Management
Michigan State University

---

*Jennings, Eugene E. *How Managers Become Chiefs*, 1997, CAPS, Arizona State University, P.O. Box 22160, Tempe, AZ 85285-2160. www.capsresearch.org

FOREWORD

The reader may expect from the main text the answer to the conundrum, *what it takes*. Early on, I set the objective of the Mobility Study to discover how managers become chiefs. I thought managing was the way to the top. Then a close examination of master climbers showed that climbing, not managing, makes chiefs. In fact, to be precise, I do not know what makes chiefs. I know something about how mobility helps managers get to the point of their corporations, for whom anything less than total sacrifice is insufficient and incomprehensible.

After years of serving as confidential adviser to chiefs, I understand why a recently made master said, "Make not a mockery of the corporation by ignoring its potential to make the most of you. What do you believe this strung-out hierarchy, broad at its base and pointed at the top, is for: To repose in a niche that others have carved out for you? If someone stacks many levels of people between you and the point, are you going to sit there and imagine or pretend that you are the boss? The point of the pinnacle challenges you to get there, to aim your wits to make a run for it. If perchance your final effort falls short, you will harbor no regret. You did your best of what was expected. You followed the lead of the point. Anything else should have been pointless."

Also, the text shall affirm masters who say, "People who cannot justify a life devoted to the climb make room for those who cannot justify a life without the climb." Still plenty of contestants remain for whom getting there is as important as being there. And finally, ready to assume the point, the final victory comes to those found worthy of the climb that spans several decades.

These affirmations by true believers of the climb, no matter how often I hear them, I am still left with the question of what it takes ordinary people to become successful climbers. What is the magical elixir strong enough to endure the marathon that consumes the better part of an adult's life? Is it something as apparent as the ambition to become good at managing? Do good managers make good climbers? Is there something about the fast route to the top that completely changes the nature of the climb and of climbers?

Managing requires an organizing awareness that focuses upon getting results through the efforts of people. Climbing also requires getting things done through people. Except the people include more than subordinate staffs, and also a dense hierarchy of superiors pressing downwards and scrambling upwards through which climbers encounter formidable resistance from people who fear becoming passed up and over and who will often work harder to preserve their gains than to get promotions. They are not about to give quarter to anyone younger, less experienced, such as the masters.

Climbing also has an organizing awareness, but such alertness first makes a practical distinction between climbing and managing. More specially, the requirements for climbing from the bottom to the top of large industrial corporations are substantially different from managing people at each level. To pass through these many and varied levels presents substantial risks to the careers of those who try. A shrewd sense of how the corporation works and how to work it is required. Such smartness attracts powerful support from people above who serve as pathbreakers to minimize the hazards and to assure safe passage. This *wit* is most demonstrable in masters who make it to the top in record times with incomparable ease.

The next question is, if the *what* of *What It Takes* to climb is *wit* as herein described, what is the *it* that requires so much *wit*? Of course, I am not using "it" as an anticipatory subject as in "It is good to see you," but rather as a subject of the impersonal verb "takes" that expresses a condition or action of a master climber. In general, the "it" concerns climbing. However, this catch-all word begs the question about how masters gain the assistance of superiors above them, many of whom will eventually become subordinate to them, and how they use subordinates without being accused of climbing on their backs to get ahead?

One would expect to find among masters the usual relationships that prevail among superiors and subordinates; subordinates depend upon superiors for support for managing their responsibilities. But in climbing, masters behave as to cause the promotion of superiors to depend in a large part upon them. Ordinarily, climbers attempt to achieve exceptional managerial performance to gain promotions. By this practice, they play the management game, not the climbing game.

The climbing game aims for winning more than a promotion. The vast majority of people who get a promotion do not get another one, and those who do will spend, on average, more than three years of career time to get a second promotion. They are on the slow climb. Fast climbing requires the ability to sustain a progression of promotions. This feat is called "promotability." By attaching ability to promote, the idea is derived about the masters' power to gain promotions. Promotability is more than deserving promotions and waiting for superiors to grant them at their will and call. Masters do not simply wait to hitch a ride with a superior. They are not going to ride free in someone's car. They want to help build the vehicle. They contrive the means whereby the long-term value of their superiors is substantially enhanced. So crucial are their contributions that their superiors would not think of moving up without taking masters with them. Superiors depend upon them for maintaining their own future worth.

While many managers are preoccupied with becoming good bosses to their subordinates, in order to be favored by the superiors for promotion, masters are prepared to subordinate their careers to those of their superiors. And the people masters take with them practice the same crucial subordination.

After becoming chiefs, masters recall the number of former superiors and subordinates who contributed to their ascents. Some of them may be presently their key officers serving as their crucial subordinates. It takes a myriad of such "helpers" to make a single successful climber. How masters make productive and enduring relationships that have the power to carry them to the top approximates the meaning of "it," at least for now. Climbing takes special wits.

The *it* requires intelligence, but what kind? Does the *it* employ the same wits needed for managing? (Please see Appendix D for the rules of Wit from A to Z.) Usually I care not a whit for acronyms. But *wit* is more than alphabetical letters for the compound term, *what it takes*. It is a word. The old medieval Europe root of *wit* is *witen, wizzi,* which means to know and to see as in the adage, "You live and die by your wits." The wits of the masters are framed and directed by their sense of the ways their corporations work and how to work them. This sense of the corporation is unique to each master and cannot be transferred to other climbers except by careful adjustments and adaptations. How masters acquire their wits is directly related to the company they keep. They learn by watching and doing with others. Masters get smart to adroitly ply their corporations by achieving productive relationships with smart people who also have a keen sense of the corporation. Smart people grow smarter together. Relationships count.

Please note that the word "intelligence," often involves obtuse and misleading connotations. Chiefs use the word so diversely and connotatively that I wonder at times if either of us has the intelligence to understand what they mean. Formal intelligence may be defined as the ability to think abstractly, as in test situations, and is presumably measurable by objective criteria (IQ tests). The Mobility Study shows that formal intelligence does not differentiate between masters and the managers they pass up, probably because each group usually has above average and more than enough. What counts is how people efficiently use their powers of intellect. For this reason, I use "functional intelligence," to describe the ability to master practical situations, to set goals and achieve them efficiently, and to solve problems that are involved in both managing and climbing.

Many CEOs proclaim that they care not a whit about *formal* intelligence. Others maintain that people with high measurable IQ's give their corporations a competitive advantage. However, intelligence is illusive unless compared to something. The examples that chiefs give invariably describe people whose smart moves and exceptional results make it easy for them to run their businesses.

However, functional intelligence may be limited to specific activities. A business manager may be quite dumb about political and governmental affairs. Likewise, the smarts of a football coach may have little transfer value to surviving in a huge bureaucracy. This is not to say that someone cannot be a good coach and a good bureaucrat. But to label such feats intelligence does nothing to describe how to function in each of these modes successfully.

One who is quick-witted about managing may not be quick-witted about climbing. What I have found is that masters have a propensity for climbing more than other contestants, for which functional intelligence is the general mental facility that frames their wits.

The wits of the masters are often partly based upon knowing what they should know before they need to know it. They approach climbing the way smart students study together to take exams in college. They figure out what they need to know in order to know what to study. This takes a special wit that is not the subject matter of the professor's exam. Others find out after the exam what they should have known. They are not test-bright.

Likewise, the corporation will not instruct climbers about what they need to know to get ahead. (Please see Chapter 7, The Invisible Climbers.) The attempt to read the few fleeting and mixed signs that pop up now and then will easily mislead climbers if they do not know what to look for in the first place or do not have access to people who do. Unlike the classroom, no textbook or manual of directions or instruction, or training is provided. Besides, few things worth knowing about climbing are found in the classroom. Masters survive and advance primarily by combining their uneducated and untutored wits with that of others who, together, share a mutual respect for deciphering the corporate ways that work for climbing. They accumulate a keen sense of their corporate ways.

There are several sides to the wits of masters that are not told herein. One is their actual skills and practices. I refer to their exceptional performances without describing what these achievements are. For example, a division manager may have embraced a failed strategy in the marketplace. A management orientation will describe that strategy and why it failed. Since I draw a cleavage between climbing and managing practices in order to sharpen the reader's wits for the ingredients of climbing, little note is made of what it takes to be an effective management strategist and practitioner.

Nor do I directly refer to the skills of climbing. Climbers do the wrong things because they do not know the correct things. Of course, skill is important, but it should be under the direction of awareness, which is needed also to see and learn from clever skills in action and their consequences. What distinguishes masters is not what they do but what they know, what is in their heads. Most managers who want to get ahead have the necessary skills because the required practices are quite commonplace. They do not know what skills to apply, or when, or how. Knowing what they need to know should be the better part of their wits. As has been noted, this practical sense, in the first instance, is to make a useful difference between climbing and managing. This distinction, even if it is at first artificially or intuitively contrived, will force climbers to assess their skills differently.

Another side of masters is fortune. I do not know of a chief who has not been helped and hurt by good and bad breaks, which is why prediction of managers who become chiefs is not possible. My clients and I have spent years trying to identify qualities that reliably distinguish masters from managers left behind. There is none. Given any set of observable or testable qualities, masters as a group are just as diverse as managers passed up by them. The big unknown is fortune, because of which, finding winning qualities is like trying to tack Jell-O to the wall. (Please see Appendix F, Major Conclusions of the Five-Decade Mobility Study.)

I can only say that the skills to capitalize on good breaks draw upon the same wits that minimize bad breaks. I may also say that fortune seems to smile more favorably upon masters. This is partly because of what masters do as herein described. The histories of their experiences show several times the luck of the draw by assignment to superiors who are going somewhere and look for help to get there. Promotable superiors make others promotable. This is the climbers' prime rule.

The readers should not look forward to another item. It has been said that a fictional tale, however imaginatively contrived and artfully told, cannot exact the interest of a true report of an actual life. Whoever said this speaks as well of the lives of master climbers. But I am not sure that I am the one to bring to life the exciting drama their extraordinary struggles deserve. I shall not even try.

While the story of masters is not Spartan or Homeric in dimensions, it is often virulent and violent. Occasionally, surreal drama inserts itself into the climbs of masters that includes scheming people, ruthless spinmeisters, and desperate antagonists ready to wreak havoc; good will "ambassadors," who dissemble to protect themselves and others; informal saboteurs who know how to interrupt the momentum of fast-paced climbers; marginal managers scrambling simply to keep their turfs clear of invaders; poachers stealing the best managers and then using them as draw horses; predators robbing managers of their achievements and exploiting their failings;

and vamps seducing and beguiling managers into their debilitating clutches, much as blood suckers slowly drain the vitality of their victims. Sounds unreal. Well, that is what all climbers say until they realize that business is no more rational than the human beings employed by it.

The fact that almost every quality among "street people" will be found among corporate people except theirs will be more subdued and obsequious owing to the disciplined ways required of running a business. Many people have not the wits to use this perversity to advantage and, thus, tolerate with varying degrees of patience the claim it makes upon their lives. Their key to survival is to occasionally go into suspended animation where, by appearance and presence, they dry up to their former size, and once the danger has passed, they return to normal and waddle off as though not much has happened.

A Darwinistic view of the corporation is inadequate because surviving is not climbing. Masters want more than to survive. They want fast climbs, for which they are more apt to receive the brunt of corporate versions of skullduggery and mayhem from the dark side of corporate life, which is constantly present. However, the good side dominates their climbs, which will be the principal side described in this text. The conniving, manipulative, and deceitful practices for the most part will be reserved for "The Second Book of Wit: Maze Bright."

Lastly, I am not providing a cookbook of recipes and prescriptions about how to succeed in business. My objective is to describe the real world of master climbers. I shall attempt to be as clinically dispassionate as possible to explain rather than prescribe. I am not trying to proselytize people for climbing. As far as I am concerned, earning and living the good life at any level is, and I hope, always shall be respectable and fulfilling. However, after fifty years of living with an idea, I have not found it easy to withhold my sheer excitement and enthusiasm about how managers become chiefs, especially about master climbers.

Someone said, "Follow quickly the direction of your dreams . . . " to which one may reply, "But then, be sure to wake up. When you do, then you will see a mass of human beings stacked many levels high above you with ambitions no less than yours, more achievements recorded, and more advancements rewarded, whose dreams will not be sacrificed for yours to be afforded."

PROLOGUE

Masters' Rules of Thumb

The ways are many that trip up high achievers. The masters' rules that make climbing less difficult and slow are not easy to acquire or to apply. Ambitions to advance require more wits than exceptional achievements allow. These wits listed below in the form of rules of thumb are intended to serve as a platform for their explanation in subsequent chapters. The rules are arranged without priority and are followed by a brief rationale. The numbers after each rule represent chapters that deal directly with the subject. Chapter 19 revisits these rules in narrative form.

The Rules:

1. Use your corporate sense to devise a perspective for climbing that is not dependent upon your managerial skills and results. (2, 19)
2. Include in your corporate sense the various ways that relate to promotion, promotable, and promotability. (12)
3. Do not confuse what it takes to gain a promotion with a progression of advancements. (8, 12)
4. Aim your wits for the climb and not just for the next position ahead. (1, 12)
5. Direct your ambitions toward advancement rather than achievements. (5, 8)
6. Remember that you can ascend no faster than the quality of support provided by superiors and subordinates. (13, 9)
7. Develop relationships with superiors and potential successors for sharing and enhancing your perspective. (16, 19)
8. If necessary, convert superiors and subordinates who are ignorant of the ingredients of the climb or reluctant to use them. (18, 12)

9. Practice ideal subordination with your superiors and encourage it from your subordinates. (10, 11)
10. Devise opportunities to advance the promotability of your superiors first and yourself second. (12, 11)
11. Rely upon opportunities with the highest exposure and visibility with extended superiors. (11, 9)
12. Use practical distinctions between authority and power; rely more upon power and do not misuse or abuse authority. (18, 17)
13. Identify and discriminate between people who can help or hurt you, and use both to your advantage. (17, 14)
14. Gain power of sponsorship to hand pick your key subordinates and successors. (18, 17)
15. Make smart moves that are more conspicuous and valuable than the results achieved. (13, 15)
16. Do not select moves without understanding the basic options available. (14, 4)
17. Astutely judge your promotability, and if necessary, form your own lineup. (12, 17)
18. Do not invite into your lineup people who are not sufficiently promotable. (9, 12)
19. Encourage and rely upon the division of wits and efforts among members of your lineup to gain the benefits of informal organization. (3, 19)
20. Use the power to sponsor for making your lineup attractive and powerful to its members. (17, 8)
21. Never violate the silent code of lineups: Always be available for giving assistance to the members. (10, 8)
22. Win all judgments affecting credits toward your promotability and long-term future worth. (5, 12)
23. Be wary of false promotions that limit future advancements. Prepare to transfer or leave the company if necessary. (20, 17)
24. Do not be reluctant to attempt to displace unpromotable superiors to avoid wasting your career time. (20, 17)
25. Select successors who with their successors have the wits and skills to occupy and control key positions in their present and future levels. (9, 10)
26. It is ideal if your successors have future worth greater than required for the next level. (11, 9)

27. Keep your eyes on the climb, but never forsake exceptional achievements. They are your lifeline to prevent failing and falling. (3, 19)
28. Keep mobile by having available at all times optimal amounts of agility, flexibility, and adaptability. (6, 15)
29. Your ultimate master is not your corporation, but reality. You must see things as they are in order to take control of them. (20)
30. Use the wits implicit in the above rules to select and modify them as appropriate during your ascent. (1, 20)

The Rationale:

Some corporate ways make it difficult for managers to climb. These practices exert a downward force to keep managers at the lowest levels where most of the work is done. The ideal is to keep high-performing managers as close to their proven skills as possible. These managers represent the binder that gives business its stability and assure its viability. In contrast, other ways attempt to fill and replenish the business with capable managers. Ideally, each level of managers is replenished with capabilities greater than their predecessors; otherwise business might exceed its managerial capability.

These essentially conflicting ideals of how corporations work are too powerful to be completely resolved. They are permanent ways that may only be coped with by other ways, among which require members of the hierarchy to judge promotions, promotable, and promotability. These ways may be quite formal, such as periodic performance evaluations of managers. By the time a manager becomes an officer, reams of evaluation have been accumulated. Other, more powerful ways, involve informal representations, admonitions, and prescriptions about how to link performance to promotion. In addition, some obsequious ways do not formally condone but silently allow certain climbing practices. When combined wisely, these silent, informal, and formal ways have the potential to leverage more advancements from fewer achievements.

This triplet of different ways represents collectively how corporations work. It is up to climbers to figure out how to work them and add a few twists of their own. This requirement is not easy. Corporate ways are not uniformly represented at each level during any ascent. Masters have an extra sense about how to use their corporations at each level for personal gain. This sense has a certain blend of awareness, intuition, and practical reasoning, which is pursued by an intense sustaining ambition to see and anticipate whatever needs to be done to advance. Corporate sense is heavily weighted toward accurately seeing and knowing ways at each level that help or hurt advancements. As masters climb, they extract from their corporate sense personal rules of thumb that essentially represent their may do's and may not do's. These wits become distilled and refined as they further discover what ways work for them under what conditions at what levels.

After masters have attained and completed their tenures as chief executive officers, they possess more corporate sense than they had at lower levels during their climb. This wisdom is to be expected, which is why the attempt to extract ingredients of climbing among managers still struggling at lower levels misrepresents what climbing is all about. Climbing is like a jigsaw puzzle. Acquiring the smarts of climbing begins very slowly but increases rapidly as the end nears. Until after the last step has been completed, masters cannot fully interpret their experiences. In retirement, masters acquire a still better vision to take the long view that helps to crystallize their wits of what it takes to climb.

The rules of thumb are arranged uniquely by each master. None practices all of the rules of thumb described herein nor has the mind as orderly as the arrangement above suggests. To collect these rules of thumb requires studying dozens of masters until redundancy finally sets in. To assure that their rules have durability, the careers of masters must span several decades. You must pick and choose your rules with your wits the final arbiter.

During the five decades of this study of how managers become chiefs, management practices have changed considerably, but perhaps not as radically as in the 1990s. But climbing has not changed. The fundamentals are still in place. Ambitious people try to advance by producing exceptional achievements. Corporations continue to delegate, provide, or allow the formal, informal, and silent ways that can be used advantageously for climbing. By these ways, climbers are still trying to find and use their wits to keep the downward ways from pinning them to unwanted levels and positions. They continue to devise clever ways to catch and capitalize upon the upward ways that serve to fill and replenish the ranks. However, corporate environments do not supply the wits to climb. They are supplied by climbers based upon their evolving sense of how their corporations work and the wits to work them.

Masters estimate that as much as 90 percent of the ways used for climbing are indigenous to their corporations and ten percent represent the climbers' contribution. But that contribution may be sufficient if it is applied more wisely than by other contestants. And it need not be overwhelming. Just a little edge of wits over competitors is sufficient. The game of climbing has one similarity to football; a glancing block against a defensive player may be just enough to let the offensive runner get by. The player does not have to be destroyed. Likewise, climbers do not need the wits to destroy other contestants, just enough to let them get by unscathed. Also, players and climbers do not try to beat the game. They attempt to best other contestants. There are few maverick master climbers. One contest is enough. They do not attempt to challenge corporate ways concerning climbing and still expect to use them to win.

The mental facility for climbing between masters and those they leave behind is measured in incremental wits. These seemingly small differences make a big difference among masters. I could write a book about how masters barely made the grade and how at times many of them barely eked out advancements. Some of their highly touted may do's and may not do's were sometimes out of synchronization with reality, which almost caused them to lose harmony with their corporate ways sufficiently to consider quitting the climb in their corporations.

Masters are not super human. They may fall into a malaise when the pain of being passed over becomes greater than the pleasures of expected promotions. Although this fear of losing is episodic for masters, when things suddenly go wrong, their corporate sense is smitten. They cannot be sure any longer that they know where they are and what they are doing. Things unwanted are thought to be unpredictable, and things wanted are thought unlikely. Their desperate minds may turn inward where the inner world determines too much what is in the outer world. Masters begin to see what they want to see, believe what they want to believe, and lose touch with corporate reality.

It is most interesting to observe how masters bring themselves out of this mind. They usually use the very rules of thumb above that they violated, including getting help from trusted members of their lineups.

1
THE FAST ROUTE TO THE TOP

So you want to get ahead. How far? Are you scratching for just one good promotion? How desperate are you? Do you feel your career coming to a head? Do you need one more promotion before you will be content to settle for the gains thus far achieved? Or do you fear you have lost your touch and need a promotion to restore your self-confidence? Perhaps you have accumulated a short string of advancements, but it has become increasingly difficult to maintain. You may sense a need to change your formula. Your ambition may need to be more directly focused upon advancements or perhaps it is, but you may be dismayed by how your achievements gain few advancements.

Or perhaps you have a different ambition with a longer perspective. What happened to your dream of becoming chief or a corporate officer or a general manager of a fully integrated division or subsidiary? Maybe it is not completely dead. No one told you climbing would be easy, but you never guessed how easily it could be made more difficult. Your ambitions are simultaneously enhanced and dampened as younger people zip past as though you were standing still.

Your performance reviews are excellent. For some reason they get better the slower the climb. In any case, they do not help you understand what it takes to go all the way. You work on your performance evaluations, but your superiors seem to discount them for judging promotability. Because your personal improvement program appears to be a sideshow, you need a peep into the big tent to see the big stars of the show. The problem for you and many of your peers is that you lack examples of what it takes to achieve a progression of advancements. You suspect that what is required for a promotion bears little resemblance to what progression requires. For rearranging your ambitions, achievements, and advancements, you need a demonstration of people who go all the way. You expect to learn from examples of slow climbers as well as fast, but fast climbers would be ideal models.

In any case, the advantage of learning from managers who become chiefs at any speed is that there is no willy-nilly definition of success. Chief executive officers are chiefs. Their positions are objectively known. One may argue that some chiefs are failures. While at least one of five disappoints their boards, however, they do make the climb. In this text, chiefs go from the bottom to the top in the same corporation. If you knew the fast route, you could use the lessons for a slower route, if that be your course. Wits of fast climbers are more transferable to slow climbers than the reverse. If you believe that, you are on the right course.

The fast route to the top is to become a crucial subordinate to a promotable manager who is sponsored by a powerful superior. This triplet forms a *lineup* of formidable contestants to compete individually and jointly for opportunities for advancement. Such opportunities are usually unavailable or difficult to acquire for people outside the lineup. Spanning several levels of the hierarchy and fitted well by their individual and shared wits, the members are mutually supportive of each other's ambitions and careers. From their relationships they produce more than their share of exceptional managerial achievements and fast advancements. While masters may use several lineups on the route to the point of the summit, most use only one lineup once they get at division level management.

The Fast Route to the Top contains three ingredients, each of which any number of climbers would value. Who would not want to be held in such high regard that superiors would not think of leaving them behind at promotion time? Who would not want a future secured by being perceived as more capable at higher levels than at lower? Who would not want to be favored with the power to handpick key members of their staffs and successors without fear of reversal from above? Who would not want to be the superior in this triplet or the manager or the subordinate or the one who is favored by all three ingredients? Who, except those without ambitions to make the climb or without the skills to assist the ambitions of others or without the wits to find and exploit the easiest expression and realization of their common ambitions to climb. But for the masters, who better demonstrates that several people well coordinated by wits and skills may move up faster than each of them may separately?

Promotions are not isolated events. They mostly occur in sequences. A promotion opens up a vacancy that is filled by someone who creates another vacancy, and so on. For example, when a new chief is appointed, over half of the personnel several levels below will have changes in their positions or assignments. The candidates for promotions will not be on the sidelines waiting to be activated. At any level of the hierarchy, many contestants already have positions from which they aggressively compete for opportunities to prove themselves worthy of higher responsibility.

Managers often expect exceptional achievements to qualify them for promotions. Indeed, high performances give them an occasional push up a notch. However, as necessary as achievements are, they are insufficient for a progression of advancements such as is implicit in the fast route to the top. Masters often pass up managers with as good or better records of performance. What makes the difference? Superiors who need them at higher levels of responsibility pull up masters, and they, in turn, pull up their successors. What makes members of this triplet crucial to each other? It is not past achievements as much as the expectations of future contributions.

Think of it this way. Achievements remain with the positions in which they occur. But wits move up with the climber for use in higher positions that require new practices. Masters must learn faster than their increase of responsibilities and learn the most important rules and lessons at low cost to their careers.

When members of a triplet achieve harmony of wits, they become aligned in expectations of utilizing each other at higher levels. All that is needed is for the lead superior to have the power to sponsor at will. If extended superiors recognize this power, it is probably because superiors are highly promotable and proven crucial subordinates. The lead superior of the lineup moves up, and the manager and subordinate follow sooner or later in order of their respective sequences.

But this lineup progresses only if the superior's new responsibilities and staff require or allow for the placing in key positions the members of the lineup. More about the big *if* later. Suffice it to say that even if members of a lineup do not move up in sequence, masters have been known to reach down later and pull up previous members, including former superiors or subordinates. This bypassing of levels is also common for masters as well. Masters usually leapfrog a level or two and pull up managers who also leapfrog. Thus, members of a lineup may gain advancements far greater than their achievements.

Because this informal contrivance is not formally recognized, to the undiscerning, lineups do not exist. To the more alert managers who bank solely upon their own prowess for advancements, a lineup is a euphemism for blatant favoritism. However, astute readers of informal and silent ways of corporate life know that lineups do the work of identifying people who can manage together at higher levels. They know that combining proven wits and skills of managers in key positions among several levels expedites accomplishments, both individual and collective. Business benefits when all members of the lineup share collective accountability for their successors.

While it is smart to become aligned with smart people, masters get little formal corporate support for climbing. If anything, a pervasive practice discourages even talking about the smarts for fast climbing. However, the corporation cannot control wits. It cannot order smart minds to refrain from being clever about climbing. Shrewdness will not be concentrated strictly upon managing. Should ambitious people pretend to be dumb in order to be smart? The answer is yes.

It is okay to want to get ahead and to set career goals. Generally, ambitious people give more than they get and are easier to manage. And they may go to superiors for advice about managing more effectively. But they do not go to superiors to discuss openly the ingredients of the fast route, how to bypass levels, how to get more advancements from achievements, and how to form and join lineups. Also left unsaid is what makes a promotable manager, a crucial subordinate, or a powerful superior and how do managers get power of sponsorship. There is not even a language for climbing, let alone for mobility. Perhaps it is better that the ways of the masters remain silent. Then those who make a useful distinction between climbing and managing will continue to be rewarded for their unique wits.

There is a reason that masters of the climb have existed since the beginning of the study of *How Managers Become Chiefs,* probably much before 1949, and perhaps as long as the existence of hierarchies. It is simply smart to seek help to achieve something that cannot be done alone. If managers seek best practices for continual improvement, climbers may seek best ways to reach the point. There is always a better way, especially for climbers for whom better is faster. For that matter, few chiefs get there at any speed without the recurring advantages of being a crucial subordinate to a promotable manager who is sponsored by a powerful superior.

Knowing now something about the route of masters and this short, blunt description of what it takes, you may ask the questions about what springs forth in them that allows adjustment and adaptation to the requirements of the climb. You suspect that something less than obvious is at work in their careers.

You might be aware of the parallax phenomenon; an object may change its nature or direction if seen from two points of view. Change your perspective and the same idea or event will appear different. You probably have been trying to get ahead and achieve your dreams by use of a managerial perspective. You may have even become an outstanding manager. What you have missed by this perspective is the not-so-apparent ways associated with climbing. I say "associated" because ways may not guarantee the climb, but without them, you will not be a sure-footed climber at any speed.

2
CORPORATE SENSE

Business brings many talented people together in an environment of organized competitiveness from which a few exceptionally skilled candidates emerge for the final struggle where winner takes all. The great corporate nirvana to which the many contestants aspire with ecstasy holds forth inordinate wealth, power, and status. The quest is bound to attract people who excel at climbing. After all, what are mountains for?

Is it the nature of the corporate mountain to define the contestants by their wits and skills to scale it. From the foothills to the peak and the craggy face in between, there are climbers and there are managers. Some people have a knack for climbing; others have a special talent for managing. Unfortunately, some people have neither skill sufficiently and drop by the wayside. A few lucky ones have both of *what it takes* to ascend. Some of the latter, by compounding their skills of climbing and managing, make a torrid pace to the top that sets them apart from the pack of everyday managers.

These chiefs are the few on the slopes who know what corporations are for and what to do with them. Consequently, they make it to the top younger and faster and are by no means slouches at managing. So distinguished are their assaults upon the corporate face that they make the formidable and hazardous trip look incomparably easy, and for them the designation "master climbers" is reserved.

Masters of the climb are the benchmark for all who aspire to get ahead in business. As pace setters, they arrive early at the top using one-third less career time, passing through a dozen or so levels or bypassing some of them in a little over twenty years, avoiding many of the pitfalls and pratfalls that waste valuable time and effort. Early arrival chiefs average forty-six years of age, are ten to fifteen years ahead of the vast majority of chiefs, average twenty years younger than their predecessors at retirement, and have enough time to become chiefs a second time around. Accomplished veteran chiefs are in higher demand than rookie chiefs, especially as subjects for the continuing study of *How Managers Become Chiefs*.

However, masters are not distinguished solely by their being almost forty percent younger than forty-six and the remainder less than forty-nine years of age, but also by their quickness of transferring from employee status to managerial. Usually masters will be discovered early in their employment and will work for considerably fewer superiors than most managers who become chiefs. They will pass up and over people who are usually older, longer tenured, and more experienced and who often have longer records of performance. For this reason, masters frustrate ambitious people, excite jealousy and rage, and the apparent favoritism elicits efforts of reprisal and revenge. Stealth attacks will occur all around them, making necessary the early detection of risks and threats to their careers. They must adjust to outsiders who suddenly appear above, below, and around them and who usually possess special status and unique ideas and skills and tough competitiveness.

Speed becomes both a friend and a foe. A rapid-fire sequence of promotions allows masters to move faster than their mistakes and to gain momentum to carry them through tough times. Speed compresses experiences requiring a fast learning capability and also minimizes routine and repetitive tasks. Moving quickly from position to position, masters may not always complete their assignments or get completely on top of their jobs.

Speed also requires the ability to make instantaneous and productive relationships, especially with people who can help or hurt their careers. Fortunately, most early arrival chiefs have personalities centered on mobility that thrive on continual movement and are impatient with the old and familiar. Mobility is used as a mental vehicle that transports them across, over, and through all sorts of corporate terrain. For them, mobility was invented to keep the listless from inheriting the earth.

But speed is a tough, determined, and deceitful foe. It breaks many more careers than it makes. The analogy of driving a speeding automobile may be helpful. The speedy driver cannot read the few signs along the way, misses the correct turns, gets stuck or lost, must regain bearings and backtrack only to see slower moving cars with more confident drivers pass by. There is no clearly marked road as such, just a rough route extracted from a mental map that is continually updated because people and positions ahead are not stable, being subject to radical and rapid changes of a mobile world. The only fixed point is the mountain's apex, and the only direction is up. Until climbers can see the point and use it as their North Star, they must set interim check points, usually around division management, by which to keep their headings. Perhaps a suitable analogy is the orienteering that real mountain climbers use to navigate between two checkpoints along an unfamiliar course.

It is important to have checkpoints for another reason—to assess the value of a promotion. To climbers, it is an upward move that closes the distance between where they are and their next checkpoint. This metric prevents becoming seduced by "dry promotions," which change salary, title, and assignments but do not close the gap ahead.

However, climbers must avoid becoming trapped by mobility. The very speed of climbing may cause them to know less than they experience, to repeat mistakes whose lessons they do not take the time to learn, to become impressed by their strengths and betrayed by their weaknesses.

In many climbers' careers, by luck or circumstance, everything may fall into place to make them appear better than they actually are. Their moments of glory may be extended by second or even third chances to prove that they are as good as their results. And if they believe that, they will surely be cast aside. Many wunderkinds are destroyed by a diet of too much too soon. When arrogance combines with ambition, the potential becomes lethal. The culprit is the failure of mobility to guarantee success and the failure of success to understand itself. For this reason, most climbers who get on the fast route become roadkill sooner than later.

These facts, being some of the conditions of the fast route and characteristics of their travelers, tell very little about how masters think and about their cerebral moves that make them sure-footed scalers of their corporate mountains. The secret of the masters is that they have no secret. The depths of their psyches need not be plumbed to discover that climbing does not require breaking the barriers of the known to fashion a heretofore unknown cerebral quality. People have been climbing ever since they wanted to get out from underneath others to gain control of their lives or of others'. Still, the improbable feat of going quickly from the wide bottom to the narrow point of the corporation begs for explanation.

For you and others with ambitions of "getting there," wherever "there" is, prescriptions are often as plausible as they are fallacious. For example, it is widely assumed that what it takes to get a promotion is the same as gaining a progression of promotions or that the quality of performance determines promotions or that the skills for managing through subordinates are sufficient for breaking through the hierarchy of superiors above. Few prescriptions make a distinction between climbing and managing. For that matter, business does not either. No lexicon for the root skills of climbing, which is mobility, is as rich in substance and nuance as the language of managing. No training programs exist for learning to climb comparable to learning to manage. Nevertheless, business is perfectly happy to take advantage of youth scrambling to get to the top. "Fresh blood" is a requirement of business viability.

While "climbing the corporate ladder" is a ubiquitous and convenient metaphor, businesses do not actually supply a mechanism with convenient supports above and below. You have to build one, which, by the way, serves more as a lifeline to break your fall. You know the warning: Be kind to your subordinates, you may need them on your way down.

The aphorism that has circulated among the glib, at least since Hannibal in 100 B.C., that if you do not take charge of your career, others will, speaks little for the fact that you climb with others who take as much charge of your career as you do. It takes at least three climbers to put one of them on the fast track. If you manage your career the way you manage your job, you probably will number among the many people left behind by managers who become chiefs. The authority to invest responsibilities in subordinates to achieve expected results is not the same as power to promote ascendancy with superiors.

Seasoned managers get fed up with simple-minded methods that ignore the uncertainties of making a successful climb. The route is filled with unpredictable ambiguities, of which many are control of either managers or climbers. From the self-descriptions of masters and inferring from their mobility patterns, it becomes apparent that they use common, ordinary means available to all managers, which they organize and focus with a practical sense of good judgment and shrewd timing.

Simply put, masters know how to climb better. There is no mystery, magic, hocus, or tricks, no so-called cutting-edge practices or new this or that, at least not since 1949, when I started this continuing study of *How Managers Become Chiefs*, just the sense and sensibility about the world of business and how to use it for self-gain. This practical sense comprises astuteness of perception and judgment to relate seemingly disparate things into patterns that offer understanding and comprehension of the ways corporations actually work at the levels that masters are aiming.

Ideally, wit is perspicacity to view people, ideas, and programs in their true relations and relative importance within and without the spheres in which masters operate, given the direction and magnitude of their ambitions. In other words, masters from a mental map of their surroundings and where they are that is updated as mobility requires. From this sense of corporate ways, near and far managers will organize a perspective that gives a proper orientation and approach to climbing. This perspective is similar to the steps taken by a bowler before releasing the ball or the practice swings taken by a golfer. A perspective frequently updated and revised must give masters the effective approach to each new position and level.

Perspective is the highest facility of the mind. It serves as the general that commands into action lesser wits. Every manager has wits, but not every manager aims to climb the mountain. The ambition to climb is the grindstone that sharpens wits as no amount of managing requires.

I call this wisdom "corporate sense," which is to corporate ways what streetwise is to the disorderly, often violent, ways of urban life. Whereas corporate life is not as violent as street life, all of the qualities of street people are found among managers, such as honesty, mendacity, sincerity, manipulativeness, greed, munificence, deception, forthrightness, etcetera. Name it, and you will find it among any mass of corporate people, with both personal and business agendas. Corporate qualities appear subdued because of the discipline required to run a business. The predispositions of people to help or hurt are just as real although not always as apparent. People do not always do as they say and vice versa, and they often practice informal ways that are better left hidden and unsaid.

The higher you go, the more of what is relevant to climbing is seldom literally spoken. It takes powers of intuition to decipher what observation fails to disclose. Moving on the fast rack requires quick and ready insight without lengthy resort to rational thought. Managers must directly apprehend what is going on unmediated by notions of what should or should not be. The overarching rule of thumb of climbers is the same for managers. They must see things as they are in order to become their master. Reality sense drives their sense of the corporation and their perspective that distinguishes climbing from managing.

3
ADVANCED FUNDAMENTALS

You might call this chapter Advanced Fundamentals 201. I assume that you know the subject of the course 101. You are inundated by consultants who sell it. You read academic and popular books that extol it, attend training programs that instruct it, and are admonished by superiors who often preach better than practice it. What is it? They are contemporary prescriptions and nostrums about effective management, with all of the hype and buzzwords that leave you bewildered and frustrated because getting ahead is as illusive as ever.

You may not need any more 101 courses that patronize and instruct about reinventing yourself when you and many others around you are faced with a problem of fundamentals: Do you want to continue the stomach-churning, teeth-crunching life of a big corporation? You cannot simply be you. Everyone seems to be in a process of becoming something new or different or held in suspended ambition as a prelude to dropping out of corporate life altogether. Those who stay often commit to a charade of so-called cutting-edge practices that they believe are as blunt as a two-by-four and about as dangerous when used irresponsibly.

You note the number of people who do not have the ambition to get a promotion, even if handed to them. They reject the idea that higher is better and thereby yield the ground to those who believe that success is upwards, failure is downwards, and that staying put is loss of identity. So there you are, glued by choice or adversity to a sticky step of the corporate hierarchy.

But unlike so many, you may not have given up or become cynical as the above scenarios suggest. You are among the countless employees in the gray area, called middle management, which could be somewhere between the top and the bottom of the corporation. But you might as well be in the middle of nowhere. You even may be lost. You are tempted to get out the map or ask someone for directions, but you cannot. The only map that exists was the one in your head, which you tore up when the roads ahead became unfamiliar. You trusted your performances and line of sight to set the markers for the path ahead, but both failed when they were needed most.

People above, below, and around you move so fast here and there, often in the aimless pursuit of getting ahead or not falling behind, that you are confused by their commotion. And you are not exactly standing still. Working harder and longer, you are spinning your wheels without gaining any forward advantage. Perhaps one direction is as good as another if you are stuck in nowhere. Still, anywhere could be worse.

So you have had it. Your defeated expectations make you angry enough to climb up on your desk and shout at the top of your lungs, "Time out!" You need a breather to spell your mind of the pretentious and meaningless jabberwocky that beguiles vulnerable managers stuck between nowhere and somewhere. What you need is an advanced course for guiding your ambition that will give you a whole new perspective about what it takes to get ahead. And please, you say, no more advice from people who have never made it. You want examples of real, live people whose success unequivocally compares to your ambition, which is to go as high and as fast as possible.

Before you continue this simulated trip with masters on the fast route, I want to introduce resources at their disposal and how they use them. You may be surprised because the resources are not of the kind provided by superiors, such as offices, staffs, budgets, and job descriptions. Rather, masters' resources are what people use all of their lives and which inhere in the very nature of corporate beliefs and practices.

I am not affirming the Freudian belief that the child is parent to the adult. However, you do extend from your past what you apply to your work. You certainly do not start from scratch. But your fundamental experiences may not prepare you well for succeeding in corporate life, as indeed is the case for many people at all levels of the corporation. In spite of their prodigious efforts, they come not well-matched for either managing or climbing. If they stretch to become productive at one level of responsibility, they may not be able to change and learn at higher levels.

What is apparent in masters is the affinity of their fundamental experiences with their ambitions. They do not incur revolutions or convolutions in wits and skills. Others may have to work at radically reformulating or revising their predispositions as well as learning the specific requirements of the job. This makes more difficult the already difficult task of getting ahead. I make this point because so many climbers attempt to use ideas that are artificial and mechanical, compiled from most popular prescriptions. Their ideas are basically gimmicks that desperate minds seek to relieve them of the uncertainties of getting ahead. Their ideas usually fail because they are not material. In most cases, they have defective ways of managing that need attending to first before they consider ways to advance.

The fundamentals are most carefully practiced in lineups, which is to be expected. Climbers on the fast route climb together. Their close working relationship and their common ambition to compete successfully requires that they get the most out of each other. Because of their affinity to their corporation, the fundamentals are automatically put to work. The only time that members of a lineup may become aware of something fundamentally amiss is when they no longer are compatible. They may simply walk away from their lineup without fully understanding what went wrong. Or members may blame this mishap on something more apparent than fundamentals. Unfortunately, only a few more-discerning managers may see through what is apparent to discover what fundamental is misfiring and may also discover that one or several members have the same fundamental problem in their managerial practices. A lineup may be no more effective than the fundamentals practiced, however naturally and intuitively.

The first fundamental, *mobility*, may bring you as close as you will ever come to simulating the journey of the masters. You are born mobile and have been all your life. By mobility, I mean that you are mentally predisposed to change places, ideas, and positions with agility, flexibility, and adaptability. In this regard, your mind is well suited for the corporate world in general and for climbing in particular. An immobile mind that is rigid, slow, and incompliant stands out as a car accident on a busy interstate highway. Mobility forgives mistakes that immobility cannot.

Mobility in corporate life is akin to walking. You do not release the rear foot from the surface until the forward foot is attached. Likewise, mobility as applied to climbing has two moves, separating and attaching. How you connect to people, ideas, and positions and disconnect as you move up and the quality of these moves will determine the amount of help you receive and the severity of harm inflicted upon your career. In turn, you can also help and hurt people, intentionally or unintentionally. So you must connect to, and disconnect from, people with the right moves and for the right consequences. While there is no end to your opportunities to engage and disengage, a mobile world will test your mobility to do so. The worst fate of a climber is to hang on too long to people, ideas, and positions that have spent usefulness, or to become mentally immobilized out of fear of making foolish or stupid moves.

Masters are known by their smart moves as they arrive, perform, and depart in positions and among levels during which they support, avoid, and oppose the right people for the right reasons. Their shrewd moves are their footprints left behind as they make their ascents. (Please see Chapter 13, The Right Moves, and Chapter 6, The Mobile Manager.)

The second fundamental is *organization*. Reaping the benefits of organization is nothing new to you. You play "organization" when you play baseball, sing in a chorus, do chores at home. By working and playing together, you live in ways not possible alone. The key is to achieve unity of purpose among the members playing whatever game of organization, and if there are competing sides, to coordinate crucial efforts to win. Some players have the wits to get the most out of the others by making adjustments in players or by combining their moves into game-winning strategies.

Climbing requires organizations no more sophisticated than the games you play. There are players who want to win by accelerating their advancements. But the hierarchy is stingy with promotions. It resents people who think it can be easily made. Direct assaults are counterproductive, and artful or oblique insinuations underestimate its wily ways of corporate life. So the players look for other ways of winning.

By circumstances or contrivance, they find ways to help each other. They pool their wits with implicit expectations that their moves will be smarter than their separate efforts. People inexperienced in the ways of the masters never think that "at play" is organization. As informal as it may be practiced, organization is an ordinary idea with powerful effects upon ambitious climbers. Several people with coordinated wits and skill can achieve greater corporate sense than the sum of their individual contributions. Masters come to the corporations prepared to play organization informally, to gain with others superior benefits for climbing. In this regard, masters are not self-made.

The third fundamental concerns *hierarchy*. As you have been mobile since the beginning of life, so have you been dependent upon others. In home and school, you grow up under people with authority and power over you. While being deferential, you find freedom to exert choices and to exact special favors to relieve your dependency, and gain superior advantages. In school, you climb a ladder of grade levels, perform well enough to meet the standards of graduation from high school and college. Then, at work, you take your experiences of handling over-under relationships. The whole corporate hierarchy sits upon you, as a new employer, much as a hen sits upon eggs. Once hatched in the form of a first-level manager, you will be over and under people the remainder of your managerial career.

A hierarchy is a given. The wits to climb it is not. In many respects, corporate hierarchy is different from any that you have climbed. In the past, the predominant forces were upwards, parallel to your motivation to grow up. Relatively more students pass through the twelve grades to graduate from high school than new employees pass through twelve or so levels to become chiefs.

However, whether relatively flat or tall, corporate hierarchies exert a gravitylike pull toward the lowest levels of management, where most of the work is done and where business tries to keep people down and closest to their proven skills. The asymmetrical nature of hierarchy means that the higher you go, the less likely you will go higher and the more likely that people will have the experiences to fend off aggressive climbers from below. The hierarchy destroys more ascents than it makes, which is why few people acquire and maintain promotability.

But there are countervailing forces to pull you up, the foremost of which is that superiors need help to enhance their own climbs.

Masters seek subordinates with moves smart enough to help them avoid the many snares and traps that ruin their future value. Masters do not waste time investing in subordinates just to have them available as replacements. The hierarchy requires that people learn and grow as fast as increases in responsibility, that they learn without being taught and provide an independent sense of wit, and that they know how to assist others on the fast route. (Please see Chapter 8, Getting into the Lineup, and Chapter 9, The Power of Lineups.)

You may get an occasional push up by the sheer force of past performances, but a steady progression is the result of being pulled up because of your superior's expectations of your future contributions. In other words, your objective is not to control your career but to get control of the hierarchy of which you are a member at any given time.

Whether pushed or pulled up, masters excel at *relationships*. Once again, you will use something that has been with you from birth. As an infant, you signal when you are hungry and learn other ways to access the resources of nurturing and authoritative people as you grow up. Relationships are a universal attribute of all organized living. When used wisely in business, relationships gain quick and easy access to information, knowledge, and expertise. It takes skill to glide effortlessly in and out of productive relationships with little cost of time and leave a reservoir of good will to be tapped in the future.

The disadvantage of people with poor relationship skills is that they fail to multiply their effectiveness through the wisdom of others. They must rely too much upon themselves, which is the hard way to manage and to climb. For example, performance is not a fact but a judgment, as is promotable, and the link between performance and promotability. You climb by winning the game of judgments. With progression, you will meet many different superiors with whom you must develop a relationship of mutual respect and trust. (Please see Chapter 16, Relationship Sense.)

Trustworthiness is what wins favorable judgments about performance and promotability. Your superiors are confident that you will remain predictably wise in all essential matters, that your affinity to them is not artificial, and you will put their careers ahead of yours in order to make the most of opportunities for advancement. No one gets very high in the hierarchy who is not trusted by somebody already there. Performance counts, but relationships determine the credit given to promotability.

If climbing seems to have a *power* motif, be assured that it does. This fifth fundamental requires that you take your blinders off and see and understand people for what they are, including their motives, words, and deeds. Power is universal to all human affairs. Everyone has some power and many want more of it. Power is to the human world what gravity is to the physical. Both may be used for good or evil. Power is the key to productive relationships. It exerts a check from below on hierarchies above. Power is both cause and effect of smart moves to gain help and avoid harm. Without power, you cannot climb.

Smart climbers make a useful distinction between authority and power. Authority is delegated from superiors through the chain of command. Power is personally earned and owned. You cannot transfer or share it. You cannot empower people, but you may distribute authority wider and deeper to grant more people the freedom to make discretionary judgments. This act may be properly called "authorization."

Power is what power does. The consequences are clearer than the motives behind them. Euphemisms for power abound such as "getting people to buy into a program." But the function of power is to get people to do what you want them to do when you have no authority over them or choose not to use it. While you have no authority over your superiors, you must gain the power to command their attention, respect, and trust, to control and check their judgments about performance and promotability and to become too valuable to be left behind when they move up.

Because of extensive moralizing about power, people who have it must be careful not to reveal it. But their power to help or hurt, however illusive and often obsequious, must be accurately sensed, or you will believe that you have more support than you really have and less opposition. At crunch time, your presumed support fades, and you are left holding the bag. You can never have too much power, but you may appear too powerful. (Please see Chapter 17, The Powerful Superior.)

Few things can help your career more than connecting to powerful people or hurt your career by offending, ignoring, or discounting them. The effects of such negligence are seldom fully comprehended until it is too late. After your denouement, you may play the victim and blame those "others," when in fact, you have only your blindness to blame. You may even cast the struggle in terms of a morality play between the forces of good and evil wherein you always end up the good one, of course. Nothing casts doubt upon your promotability more than a pattern of foolish or stupid uses of power. You are dangerous to superiors and subordinates who depend upon you to stay above the fracases or to protect them when they are vulnerable and when authority is not useful or sufficient.

These fundamentals, mobility, organization, hierarchy, relationships, and power, are unavoidably integral to almost every move you make. They are so integral to lineups that members take them for granted until things go wrong.

Perhaps through no fault of their own, people may not be well prepared for lineups. They may find difficulty subordinating themselves to the interests of an informal organization or are either too deferential upwards or dominating downwards with the members, or both. They cannot easily connect with and disconnect from people to optimize and extend their wits and cannot distinguish between the need to use authority or power, and thus, they misuse or abuse either or both.

Or perhaps they make getting ahead incomparably difficult because they do not know enough to see and use these fundamentals. Knowledge is a great friend to those who need to make major adjustments and adaptations in these fundamentals. It is surprising how the ambition to get ahead allows people to pick up on these fundamentals and continue to learn and refine them as they gain experience and promotions.

In this regard, I must say that managers who become chiefs are not always conscious of the way these fundamentals play out in their ascents. Of course, one reason is that it is difficult to act and observe themselves at the same time. But it is also true that they simply and intuitively do what their past experiences predispose them to do, only they employ them better than most climbers.

In auditing the positions through which chiefs pass and the experience they pick up along the route, chiefs talk about these fundamentals without identifying them with the same words that I use. In some cases, had they been more aware and focused upon the fundamentals, they could have made the route to the top less arduous and lengthy. While master climbers are not perfect specimens of the wise use of fundamentals at work, it is apparent that because of them, they are well matched to corporate life and to lineups in particular. If such a thing as natural climbers exists, masters are the nearest approximation.

With your fundamentals in place and ready to be used, modified, or reformulated, the question becomes how do masters use them to make fast and sure their climbs. And how may their wise use of fundamentals help you to get ahead. No matter what level you find yourself, masters have been there too. The question is what did they do to get from wherever you are to the final point of their ascents?

At worst, the masters may help you realize what others may only suspect; that you are fundamentally ill-matched for the corporate life, let alone the climb. However, since childhood you have had to learn to adapt and adjust to many strange environments. So do not discount the power of mobility. When you turn this page and go to the next, you are separating and attaching, using the barest moves of mobility. It is ironic that this very fundamental skill is so little understood and seldom practiced wisely. And just because masters take the fast route, it does not mean you cannot use the mobility on a slower route. Remember, even a stone has a future, it just takes longer. While your career is not as dormant as a rock, you may extend the future and govern your speed to accommodate the pace that your ambitions prescribe or allow. What it takes you to go anywhere fast or slow requires that you first acknowledge the fundamentals inherent in the climb. Otherwise, stick with the 101 course about which you are all too familiar.

4

THE SUPERIORITY OF ORDINARY BEHAVIOR

Suppose you had gone from the bottom to the top of a large industrial corporation, accumulating experiences too numerous and diverse to mention, let alone remember, and I ask you, as I have many chiefs, what does it take? I am sure you would agree it is a daunting task for managers to explain how they become chiefs. Climbing is a complicated feat that extends over several decades involving a progression of sequential steps, none of which explains how managers become chiefs. It is the whole effort that lifts them from the base to the point.

However, chiefs are happy to oblige, because usually they are eager to push a convenient perspective about what it takes to succeed. For them, management is the central force for running a business. Their heroes of the economic system are the eminent exemplars of the practices of management. While describing their notable achievements against the prevailing circumstances, they will inevitably ground their successes in one or a few practices by which they become known experts. The whole gambit of management practices will be covered several times if enough chiefs are included in the *mobility study*.

Chiefs may view themselves to be great strategic planners, creative organizers, adept controllers, shrewd coordinators, or all of these in one great skill. Not a few will express their ability to communicate, lead, motivate, or whatever. In addition, they usually mention the necessary qualities of personality and character. Whether humble or arrogant, chiefs will usually conclude a rational, practical justification for the power of their practices and personalities to effectuate their ascents.

Collectively their representations of personal qualities are diverse enough that no one should refuse to make the climb because of this quality or that practice. After many decades of studying how managers become chiefs, the net conclusion is that any set of personal qualities may prove to be a winning combination. Their diverse explanations may well be called "theory of everything and everybody." Almost anyone who displays any set of personal qualities effectively may succeed, or so the chiefs collectively would have us believe. However, the idea of mobility sharpens their focus precisely upon their moves. From this phase of their interview, the truth comes forth: It is smart moves that appeal most to their superiors.

Smart moves attract sponsorship and have the power to nullify the most obnoxious or admirable personal qualities. Masters seldom win personality contests. But without smart moves, their personal qualities loom larger than otherwise.

Maze bright managers treat as the death knell the ascription; "You've got the right personality to go to the top." The superior who may say that is either dumb about what it takes to climb, desperate to have lackeys, or trying to mollify a frustrated climber. Who can possibly be so wise as to know what personal qualities will sustain a climber over a twenty-plus years' trip to the top? Personal qualities are more apt to get you a promotion than help to sustain a progression of moves to the top.

The more enduring power of masters to climb is their smart use of mobility, but they may not be aware of this fact. For example, masters may say that they want initiative in their successors. However, initiative hides as much as it reveals. So when they are asked to give examples, they invariably describe some sort of moves whose consequences inured to their benefit as superiors. Initiative in the service of dumb moves is incompetence, which, of course, masters do not appreciate. Other words that also obfuscate the real world of climbing include integrity, resourcefulness, and creativity, all of which are meaningless without descriptive behavior. Even the term "smart moves" must be carefully described, or it will also become a convenient catchall of useless ideas that disguise the real world of climbing.

Of course, there would be less misrepresentation and obfuscation of what it takes to go to the top if chiefs and managers were trained from the start in the proper use of the idea of mobility. Until then, they are dependent upon words and ideas that have more usefulness for managing than climbing.

Furthermore, mobility, when aptly used, would be helpful to understanding managing. For example, mobility involves moves and movements. Managers who become chiefs mobilize the resources and actions of others in what seem very complicated and protracted efforts of the magnitude that appear to require extraordinary wits that presumably can only come from lengthy experience in big business. They move people into key positions to develop competitive strategies, revise whole sets of work practices, or rebuild weak divisions and businesses.

While they report these kinds of movements to me in the Mobility Study, I always wonder what is the first move they make in their extended responsibilities. They have to begin somewhere, but to find that first step in a complicated management maneuver is like looking for a needle in a haystack. However, first moves indeed exist and can be eventually identified along with subsequent moves upon which management achievements depend.

The problem is that "results driven" corporate ways that allow wide amounts of discretion for managing tend to eclipse their moves. It only appears that managers become successful because of their results, when, in fact, it is their moves. Achievements are merely the symptom of their actual success, which is the wise use of mobility. The next time you hear about someone turning around a business, division, or department, ask what were the few key moves that made the feat possible.

However, the practice of smart moves is not a codified expression of corporate ways. Seldom are you told or instructed that huge programs are successful because of a few, well-timed moves. The incongruity is due to a superstructure of management theories and practices that have evolved over the years with neat variations and exotic appendages but without consideration for the basic elements of human behavior. While their many management achievements are insightful, one cannot understand what it takes managers to become chiefs without resorting also to an anatomy of everyday behavior. I know this finding will not flatter some chiefs, among whom are a few Grand Pooh-bahs and High Everybody who believe that they perform complex, weighty, systemic activities far more intelligent than anything that could be contemplated by the hoi polloi. However, I discovered that the only thing remarkable about their weighty actions is their conventionality.

This report does not decry the importance of clever strategies and ubiquitous practices of management or that no one may ascend without managed results, or that both practices and personal qualities are as diverse among chiefs as among first-level managers. But here is the rub. Try using any of the highly touted practices without performing ordinary moves. Without mobility, managing is hardly more than a compendium of intellectual prescriptions. Take planning, for example. It is merely a grand idea until someone mobilizes people into action for the purpose intended. Experienced managers know this, but somehow, once they occupy the corner office, they lose sight of the ordinariness of what they actually do.

It is elementary behavior that carries forth the practices of management. It is ordinary moves that culminate in exceptional performances. It is the rudiments of mobility that show agility, flexibility, and adaptability. Wits are not something special and preserved in a container to be opened and used when unusual circumstances require. Smartness is expressed in everyday behavior or it is not expressed at all. So when managers decide to do something big, what are their key moves?

Masters are even more illusive and obscure about their climbs than about their managing. It would appear that they got their promotions because of efficient management practices and valuable performances. Indeed, this is correct, but only partly true. It turns out that the moves they make to ascend are as elementary as those they make to manage. How masters become discovered as worthy of higher responsibilities is an art in itself. They certainly do not sit on their fine accomplishments and wait for superiors to discover that they are good stock for the upper reaches of their corporations.

In fact, masters are not discovered by their immediate superiors as much as by extended superiors. With the latter, it is not results that count, because achievements stay with the position wherein they are made. What travels with masters is the smartness by which their moves are contrived and executed. Extended superiors have the confidence that masters have the wits and maturity to apply smart moves to greater responsibilities and the quickness to learn new or better moves when necessary. It is smart moves that make difficult responsibilities less difficult, that make masters light under foot and easy for superiors to promote.

Because elementary mobility is variously applied to both climbing and managing, it is the common skill that demonstrates the bulk of what it takes masters to climb. Throughout the text, elementary moves will be described that increase masters' promotability greater than their achievements.

Now apply this insight to your own everyday behavior. Say you are planning to go on vacation. Are there not certain activities that you could lift from other endeavors and insert into your preparation and enjoyment of your vacation? If at the office you are going to hold a committee meeting, are there not whole sets of activities that are similar to your vacation activities?

I am not talking about incidental things. I mean moves so important that the outcome of your vacation or committee meeting will depend on them. You see, you do not always consciously know what you are doing. By habit you favor certain moves and insert them into this plan or program as though they were universals to be used as needed. Guess what. They are! You are seldom as good as your results unless you are as smart as your moves.

5
THE FORMULA

Little value is derived from making simple things complex or spinning profound explanations that make little practical sense. This truism holds especially for managers conquering the improbable odds of reaching the point of their corporations. Chiefs apply a few powerful ideas packed into three commonly used words. I labeled this mixture a "formula" to express a fundamental method integral to both managing and climbing. This formula is most demonstrable in the ascents of masters.

The formula is simple. It is derived from a common expression of people wanting to earn a living by working for others and doing their tasks well enough to gain higher paying jobs. The words ambition, achievement, advancement may dress up this pursuit, but the formula works the same for its true believers whether they are freshly minted college graduates or chief executive officers. Ambition drives achievements, and achievements drive advancements. By whatever means this tripod of A's may be used, people attempt to build their careers.

Ambition is what drives people to work harder than their peers, to achieve more and improve themselves to become better than their jobs. Ambition means predisposition to over-earn one's keep. The surplus is the employee's contribution to the business. Those who achieve more and better results than the cost of their keep may be singled out and rewarded. Nothing is promised, not even opportunities to do things better or to do better things, just a job, responsibility, and an unspoken ubiquitous formula for success.

The stabilizing leg of the triplet of A's is achievement. This means that while ambition may focus upon both, or either, achievement and advancement, achievement is the qualifying condition. Ambition, openly directed by advancement without proper regard for achievement, risks the interpretation of greed. The formula expects that no one use others strictly for selfish ends. Such practices dilute and detract from business effectiveness.

Because all things must be cleared by achievement, the formula keeps ambition from becoming uncontrollable rivalry and advancement from becoming a demoralizing favoritism. Performance-based rewards are the ideal prescription for engaging self interests in the service of business interests. Promotions that ignore or bypass achievements make a mockery of the primacy of the good of the business. This sham is what the formula hopes to avoid.

Few chiefs do not decry the practice of rewarding seniority, loyalty, and personality. In the 1950s* to the 1990s it is perform, perform, perform. The words today are about best practices and continuous improvement, but they carry no more value to believers than the sloganeering of previous decades about "Nothing succeeds like success" and "hard work will get you ahead." Whether the word performance is used for achievement or promotion for advancement and drive for ambition, the formula by any comparable words has the same effect. It organizes and justifies the efforts of believers to serve both business and their self interests.

Masters in particular do their goodly share of espousing superior achievements as a way of life and the only way to get ahead in business. They either command that subordinates excel or strongly expect it. In either case, masters cannot surmount the rigors of corporate life by suffering subordinates who do not exceed their expectations. Without a fervent ambition to achieve and advance, managers will not make the grade with masters. In fact to many masters, the only achievement that counts is advancement, and the only ambition is for the climb. Masters do not want key players to let up on achievements because of sated ambitions to get ahead.

---

*The book by William H. Whyte, *Organization Man*, 1951, presented a false reading of corporate life for climbers. Whyte borrowed Max Weber's analysis of bureaucracy and imposed it upon big business. This was a mistake. During the post-WWII years, big businesses grew so fast that they had a shortage of managers, during which time the largest batch of early arrival chiefs occurred. Also, veterans and MBAs began to use more than one corporation by which to ascend. They were loyal to their careers and hardly the bureaucrats or "organization" people Whyte falsely described them. Whyte described this bureaucratic theme in the presence of Perrin Stryker, also a member of *Fortune* magazine, and me. Stryker wrote the Foreword to my book, *Anatomy of Leadership: Princes, Heroes, and Supermen.*

When they are needed at higher levels, masters expect them to come running and not to temporize because they have never had it so good.

However, the formula of ambition, achievement, and advancement does not have universal appeal with the same intensity and lasting staying power as found in masters. There are many people whose ambition is to use the formula for gaining a living and becoming independent. Still, they must achieve in order to maintain tenure, which requires a certain amount of ambition, even if they are not driven by advancement. Then there are people who want advancement but do not have the ambition to produce exceptional achievements. They hope to succeed on the cheap.

While the formula seems fair and sounds logical, it is also deceptive because of its ambiguity. The triplet of A's rests upon an unstable, shifting premise. It is formally called the asymmetrical function of supply and demand. Failed climbers know this condition, that the higher they go, the less likely they will go higher. The acute angle of the slope and the hierarchy leading to the point requires fewer managers at each level above than below. But the supply of ambitious contestants for each level is greater than the demand. Even with business growth, the asymmetrical effects will prevail although less noticeable. The formula of A's in some respects works all too well. Expectations of advancement increase greater than achievements. If supply and demand are not brought into line, much talent will become frustrated and leave or stay and make it difficult for others to advance. Fierce power struggles may ensue when supply and demand are woefully unbalanced. To control lengthy queuing up for promotions, standards of advancement must be set. Presumably, superiors will use these standards to select out the few who are sufficient to supply the demand for higher level managers.

The problem is that during cycles of growth and shrinkage, business changes are required in management practices and expected results. Now who meets the standard for advancement—the manager who uses new practices to achieve expected results or the manager who surpasses expected results with established practices or the manager who is both better at practices and better at results? In each decade of the study, few chiefs do not support the standard that managers are expected to improve in one way or the other and preferably both ways. They expect this standard, when properly upheld, will control the supply of managers available for promotions, and because of this standard, managers will show continuous improvement in their skills and results in order to move to higher levels of responsibility. This faith continued to inhere in the contemporary version of the formula.

In effect, who sets the standard of achievement sets the standard of advancement and influences the form and magnitude of ambition.

This practice exposes the ambiguity in the formula. Performance is not a fact but a judgment. Did the events representing the results actually occur? How much value should be assigned to them? How much credit should be applied toward promotions? Do the increased responsibilities represent true promotions? In other words, who is a high performing manager and who is promotable and what is the linkage?

These judgments place much discretion in the hands of managers. They do not want to lose control of the definition of performance because if they do, they are afraid that they will lose effective control of their subordinate staffs. Nor do managers want their judgments about the subordinates' performance to be without credibility with their superiors. By these judgments, managers gain the discretion to make assignments and promotions at will, which is key to their achieving and advancing. Other checks of sorts are placed upon managers who are careless or self-serving about their judgments, but none is sufficient to completely control the struggle for winning favorable judgments, nor should it be.

The wise use of authority to define and evaluate performance of subordinate staffs and the power to gain from superiors' support for these judgments may work to the advantage of everybody. Ideally, the superiors get the performance they want from managers who get the performance they want from subordinates. The subordinates hope that their managers' judgments carry weight with superiors to enhance the subordinates; promotability, which, of course, is also a matter of judgment.

However, in practice, the judgmental link between performance and promotability makes it difficult to choose what kind and amount of achievement is necessary for gaining what amount of advancement. For this reason, most managers may just do what they are assigned and do it as well as they can and estimate the value to the business or to superiors and hope that as much credit as possible goes to them for securing their tenure or gaining promotions. Still, it helps to know what links performance to promotions. After all, people may not want their ambitions to drive them blindly into the future. Besides, many people gain their identities from their achievements. They reinforce self-worth. To mangle Descartes's syllogism, the logic for many people is, "I perform; therefore I am."

The satisfaction to stand well with associates because of admiration and respect for achievements is second only to self-confidence to continue valuable performances into the future. Continuous improvement is as important to current notions of performance as "don't change what isn't broken" was to reliable performance of the past. While climbers gain their identity from their advancements, judgments about their performances and promotability are taken seriously by all. Climbers and managers live and die by judgments.

Few climbers have not been disadvantaged by careless judgments about the link between performance and promotability. On the other hand, anything as important to business and careers should be judgmental. Business changes too fast to judge by the mechanics of quantifiable results, which is why managers both love and hate numbers. They know the importance of financial numbers, and with certain responsibilities, they manage by the numbers. In fact, they try to make the objectives and results expected as quantifiable as possible. "If you can't measure results, they don't exist" or "what you measure, you get, and what you don't, you hope for," are notions that still have credibility for many managers.

However, it is a mistake to believe the numbers are objective; just because numbers may be assigned to performance, it does not make them more valuable and creditable. Managers finagle them as well as superiors, but with subordinates, they retain the right to judge the value of quantifiable or qualitative results and how much credit should be given to whom. If managers cannot do that reasonably well, their authority to pass out assignments arbitrarily should be restricted.

During the course of their climbs, masters must adapt to a number of differing perspectives about the link between performance and promotability. Superiors usually have an implicit or explicit overarching expectation that serves as an informal operating rule to set the terms of their relationship with their managers. Specific performances are evaluated within the perspective cast by this operating rule.

For example, some superiors are easily threatened by performances that exceed their expectations, even though they praise high performances vociferously. Other superiors view exceptional performances as the norm. The more managers deliver, the more their superiors expect. Or superiors operate on the rule that collective performance is more valuable than individual, which often means managers will get little credit either way. Superiors may preach the importance of performance but actually value personal qualities more highly. They may tolerate personal qualities manifest in achievements but be opposed to the same qualities for promotions. Such is the maze of operating rules through which masters climb.

Climbers hear superiors use the words quite often, "I assumed that you have a fine record of performance. What I want is someone with the personal qualities that will assure a good fit with other members of my group," or "qualities that I want to represent what our business stands for" or "qualities that I (the superior) wish to represent me." In other words, personal qualities may count after or before requisite performances are ascertained. Each superior has a set of values based upon some combination of personality and character. Upon these values, superiors may operate and by which they often judge promotable people. These values are seldom spoken except when managers are being dressed down or encouraged to aspire upwards.

So when you hear the words, "I've got the right job for you," hearken to just what they may actually mean. Is the admonition sincere and representative of an authentic interest in your future or contrived to tap and direct your ambitions? Does *right* mean something to which you have a just claim or a perfect fit for your skills or a chance to prove yourself better than your record of achievements or a combination of personal qualities expected of promotable managers? Regardless of which of these conditions pertains, chances are the latter meaning is involved in all uses of the words. Many superiors cannot entirely avoid looking for themselves in managers important to them and thus secure a personal basis for trusting them in key assignments, or for finding people whose personal qualities will complement their own or fill in their voids.

Thus, personal values are not to be ignored. Superiors may wear them as epaulets to distinguish themselves from others or their values may actually be silent and integral to their relationship. Whichever may be the case, superiors must be carefully read and their values realistically assessed and, if possible, accommodated. If not representative of your past behavior, you should be prepared to learn and use them. There is nothing wrong in finding the resourcefulness to change. That is why by nature you are given mobility. What is hazardous is to wear these values as silhouettes rather than real substance that they frame. Charades are common, and masters are not without this blemish. But, generally, falsity in the pursuit of success may be noticed by both superiors and subordinates. While it is not always easy to be yourself, yourself may be more than what you assume. Your personal representation need not supplement your superiors but it should at least complement.

But masters do what they do with all of their superiors. They read carefully their superiors' operating rules and values, and meet and help them on their level in order to eventually get sufficient control of them. Because they have to practice these wits and skills, they expect their subordinates to do the same with them. How well each deciphers, accepts, or complies helps to determine the quality of their relationships.

Climbing requires ascending through a hierarchy of differing views of performance and promotable that may be more apparent than real. Typically, one half of the bosses through which masters climb to the top do not mean what they say or say what they mean about performance and promotable. They may not necessarily practice trickery. They demand performance but do not want performance to dictate their crucial subordinates and their most promotable.

As a means to retain flexibility about the link between performance and promotable, superiors may use annual performance evaluations and more frequent reviews. It is their way of controlling or limiting managers' expectations of the future while they still hold out the bait for higher performance. Even the sundry items of performance evaluation that do not bear directly on recent performances are used mostly to keep the issue of promotability under their control. This is particularly true of superiors who cannot assure their own advancement, let alone that of others.

Still, the only evaluations of performance that count are in the minds of bosses, and these private judgments may not square with their written evaluations or public expressions. Needless to say, climbers require considerable wit to sense and to respond to these differing views and issues of performance and promotable and to know how to handle bosses who are easily threatened or believe personality counts more than results. By means of their relationship skills, masters attempt to avoid two pitfalls—make performance an issue and sacrifice their own performances and personalities.

Masters work for some of the most demanding superiors and invariably develop a relationship whereby they gain opportunities to prove themselves. Of course, they are careful not to take advantage of their acquired power. Still, they may not avoid entirely being viewed by others as the boss's fair-haired subordinate. Because the boss places a high value upon their special relationship, masters often become more promotable than the others, which is why they often advance past peers who have achievements as good as or greater than theirs.

The easiest superiors to maneuver are those who insist upon performance as necessary and certain personal qualities as desirable for promotability. They are vulnerable to managers with good relationship skills. As master climbers say, "relationship skills can make palatable even our most obnoxious qualities." To become a high performer and promotable does not require that you master your responsibilities as much as master the minds of superiors. Results count, but relationships determine their value and credits toward promotability. This is not to gainsay the temptation of superiors to be disingenuous and to dissemble. If judgment is the solemn duty of superiors, it is also the refuge of rascals. An authoritative judgment is still an opinion, however judiciously derived or cleverly disguised. What passes as best for business leaves much room for creative expressions of selfish interest. Such is the reality that masters face on their way to the top.

However, the formula is not expected to solve the problems of people working together or to make them virtuous. The formula is no respecter of motives, good or bad. Masters are no more or less apt to take license with the formula than other chiefs or the managers left behind during their ascents. But masters live in a goldfish bowl. Their fast ascents make people more suspicious than usual of their being too ambitious, of stealing credit for others' achievements, and of manipulating superiors to gain undeserved advancements. The formula may become used to indict masters.

Passing rapidly through a massive hierarchy means passing over more superiors than usual, displacing some of them and frustrating and antagonizing many of them. If masters had to depend for their constituency upon support from below, they would rapidly move downwards rather than upward. It is not by coincidence that masters are so intensely upwards focused. They are pulled up by a few superiors more than pushed up by many subordinates.

It is a fact that the pressure to retain high performers at the lowest levels may dilute or destroy ambition to climb. In every decade of this mobility study, chiefs have complained about subordinates who will accept promotions but will not work to achieve them. For these people, using the corporation to gain a living and become self-dependent is one thing; selling their souls for an ounce of advancement is another. Several times during the mobility study, my clients and I noted as many as one of five managers turn down promotions except on their own terms, and almost as many will not accede to any promotions at all. This immobility is no less real today than in past decades. For them the formula of the A's has little operative value.

In stark contrast, the formula has the power to make other people addictive to climbing. The people most susceptible have the insatiable ambition to get out from under bosses and to run their own show, which usually means to go all the way to the top. Second, they have mobility-centered personalities whose every essence thrives upon movement, and third, they experience several fast promotions, usually early in their careers. The habit takes hold because of the following sequence.

- Achievements increase expectation for increased responsibility, which then increases expectation of advancement.
- Advancements increase expectation of increased responsibility, which then increases expectation of advancements.
- Advancements increase expectation of advancement.
- Advancements become the overriding expectation.
- Thus the habit of climbing becomes set.
- The addicted climber is born.

I do not know how many masters are obsessed with the formula for climbing. The strongest addicts keep their habit well hidden, even from their confidential advisor. If people addicted to the climb cannot continue their ascents, they will use another corporation, even two or three until they finally get there. Nowhere in the formula does it say that one has to seek advancement in a single corporation. The masters herein described use one corporation, but that is largely because they needed only one to make a successful claim for the top job. Many people with similar ambitions simply pick up their career and place their fate in the hands of other corporations.

When I first discovered these addicts of the climb in the 1960s, they called their intercorporation mobility "professionalism." They viewed themselves as professional people who sought the right environment in which to ply their trade, much as physicians and professors do. While many had ambitions simply to make a better living or to better enjoy the practice of management, among them were those who would do anything to become chiefs and usually did. Managers addicted to the fast climb do not misuse the formula; they simply become exceptional expressions of it. Masters may not be climbing junkies, but they are driven by something far stronger and more insatiable than the ambition to become exceptional managers.

6
THE MOBILE MANAGER

I believe that in each climber, a butterfly lives. Fated to crawl the earth, they suddenly sprout wings to become reborn as the mobile creatures of the sky. Butterflies can turn on a dime, change the pitch of their wings to zoom vertically, stop, change course to flutter horizontally, and eventually descend upon a leaf or petal in search of instant gratification. Who would not like to defy the gravitational pull that keeps people down where most of the work is done and sprout wings to ascend to the higher reaches of corporate life where much wealth, power, and fame reside?

Were butterflies to transform into managers and let loose in big corporations, their mobility would not be the least bit encumbered. They have the first ingredient of what it takes. If you do not have the wits and skills of mobility, then direct your ambitions elsewhere. A successful climber you will not make.

If this advice seems too arbitrary, then follow this feature of the masters. They are optimally matched for mobility with their corporate ways. Climbing is mobility, and fast climbing is mobility in high gear. Mobility is not something masters impose upon business. The corporation is mobility institutionalized as a way of life. Youth enters the bottom rank; their elders emerge from the apex and at all levels in between. People move in, out, and around in every direction and speed, passing over or dropping down, pushing or pulling here or there, a variable household of struggling people bound together by their common need for corporate succor.

While their movements may be organized or spontaneous and sometimes chaotic, people are always somewhere, coming from somewhere, going somewhere. All of them must exist under the inexorable fact of mobility; that what starts will eventually end, anything gained will be surpassed, offset, or reversed. People may delay or rush the inevitable by altering, modifying, or transforming the novel and the familiar, but they can never run out of circumstances in which to engage or disengage. People cannot do nothing.

Mobility is not an option. Something about you is always in motion, your mind, your body, and usually both. Managers may move smartly or unwisely with the inevitable, unending ebb and flow of people, ideas, and positions. They may divide time into artificial horizons such as fiscal years, but consequences abide by no such boundaries. Things just keep moving on, often carrying managers and their staffs kicking and screaming into a future not wanted or predicted. Managers may repair to their office to sulk in quiet about their tepid or stupid moves, but even so, they are still mobile, much akin to passengers sunning in deck chairs of a cruise ship. Both people and the ship are going somewhere. Defying the principle that one cannot be in two places at once, their minds may be in a business division miles away while their bodies are prone on deck absorbing the soothing rays of the tropical sun.

The most mobile of managers have the better chance of moving with and capturing the power inherent in corporate ways. These managers are movable and easily moved, changeable in appearance, mind, and position with agile, flexible, and adaptable mentalities all geared up to become useful and comfortable in a fast-paced world.

As climbers, they are physically and mentally predisposed to arrive into higher positions and assignments, perform expeditiously, and make ready to depart for the next round of higher opportunities by which to prove themselves. This mobile triad of arriving, performing, and departing among managerial assignments on one level is used to depart for and arrive at higher levels of responsibility. Ideally, mobile managers break cleanly from lower positions and connect swiftly to higher positions with smooth transitions that leave few unintended consequences for themselves and their successors. At all times they are in the mode of engaging and disengaging as they continually acquire different people, ideas, and positions and pick, choose, and separate out the useful from the useless.

You may enter the minds of mobile managers by asking them what ideas did they leave behind in the previous job and what they did bring forward to the present job, and of that, what did they eventually drop or keep? In addition, what new ideas did they embrace, and how long did the new stuff continue to be used? The skills, ideas, and experiences that they separate from or attach to in the course of entering and leaving positions and levels of different or greater responsibility are what connect climbing and managing together.

Climbers must also be smart about whom they leave behind or take with them with each promotion. What personnel awaiting their arrival should be keyed upon and who might be dispensable. Climbers may get the mix of talent sorted out eventually, the sooner the better, but rigid, inflexible, and tentative minds are not the stuff wanted by mobile managers or useful to their superiors.

The skillful, ambidextrous use of mobility for both achieving and advancing is what makes mobile managers attractive to members of a lineup. Mobile managers attract mobile minds because of their common wits to find expeditious and efficient moves to make difficult tasks less difficult. One cannot be ponderous and heavy-footed and expect to keep pace with the swift-footed. Elephants may eventually get the job done, but generally lineups are reserved for jaguars. (Please see Chapter 20, Conclusion: Efforts vs. Wits.)

In short, ideas rule, whether represented by people, positions, or corporate practices or policies. Ride a good idea, know when to dismount before it dies of overuse. Avoid attachments that slow you down. Separate from ideas that invite rigidity. Stay light, loose, and limber and on the ready. Career time sets the pace, promotability gives the edge, and the lineup offers the best chance to gain and maintain upward progression.

Mobility is also something interpersonal. Any lineup of three people who find agility, flexibility, and adaptability personally difficult will not be able to take advantage of the power of mobility. In a lineup, managers must react to moves made by subordinates and superiors, pivoting upward one moment and downward the next. They occupy the swivel seat that demonstrates how loose they must be to make a lineup work. It is the manager who makes the lineup work and must teach the subordinate by example, the initiative and reactions appropriate to their relationship. If the manager is mentally and physically lethargic, rigid, and clumsy on the uptake, the subordinate has little reason to demonstrate mobility. That is why the idea of the *mobile manager* is proper for the member in the middle of a lineup. No one is more mobile. If the manager exerts a drag upon the superior's need to move expeditiously and effectively, the lineup will eventually expel or bypass the manager.

Because lineups are informal groups that help members share their wits to make it less difficult for each member to manage and to climb, members must put aside temporarily their individual problems to attend to a specific problem at hand. Call it mental separating and attaching or whatever, the key question is, do you have the capacity to get involved in another member's problem while you are deeply involved in your own?

Suppose you are the mobile manager in the swivel chair. Your superior or subordinate comes to you with a breaking problem that needs to be nipped in the bud. But you are so preoccupied with your own problems that you can offer little help. You can't be this immobile if you want your superior and subordinate to depend upon you for help, neither can you expect to get help from them. As busy as you are, you must make time for members above and below, or the lineup will fizzle out. This means that you must have time under control, or you will be out of patience to help others. Also, you need self-confidence that you can break off from what you are doing and not feel anxious or used. If there is one thing that climbers hate, it is a faker, one who pretends to be listening and helping, who lacks the courage or manners to simply say, "Give me a few minutes to clear my head and give you my fullest attention," or something to that effect. The moment they catch someone faking, members of a lineup wonder what other forms of dishonesty the faker practices. Masters seldom break a promise or connection that represents a commitment. They obey the implicit rule of the lineup; always be there. To get help, you must give help. At times, subordination of your interests is expected. Sitting in the swivel seat, you practice close-quarter mobility. You are always prepared to change your pitch. You light here or there as expected of graceful butterflies.

The ambitions of masters generally kick into high gear when they discover, usually intuitively, that mobility is their plentiful skill. Early in their managerial careers, they learn the ease of being mobile. Their personalities typically are centered upon movement. They are not content unless they are always on the move. Easily bored and impatient with the slow and familiar, fiercely focused upon novelty and challenge, masters are easily receptive or converted to the mode required of climbers, and well they should be.

Time and experience compression does not make the difficult journey less difficult. The skills of mobility are what make the fast route relatively easy for them.

If you do not intrinsically enjoy focusing your moves upon both ambitions of climbing and managing, you are going to become exhausted. Battling the odds of becoming both an exceptional manager and a fast climber is no place for those who cannot move wisely and responsively back and forth and in between these two ambitions in order to serve them equally well. Typically, less mobile managers end up focusing upon managing more than climbing, which may be why they are better managers than climbers.

But, alas, the butterfly in each climber provides a profound weakness. Its wings flutter more than lift. Butterflies are too weak to support a lift to the light mountainous air. The butterfly dreams of taking flight and soaring to the top become a peripheral flutter of moves and movements that have mostly horizontal thrust. It is doomed to skim the treetops or hug the earth from which it comes. Butterfly-type managers move from assignments to projects to group tasks with little continuity and predictability. For them, nothing seems set. Entire programs glide in and out of focus, creating gulfs and fissures among people who had been standing side by side.

Change is so fast that the structure that defines positions and responsibilities is unstable. Tipping points unpredictably alter the balance of life into flux, access to people becomes obscured, relationships are disturbed or terminated, the path ahead becomes obfuscated. Much time is lost or squandered playing it safe, lying low, or pretending to be reinventing themselves. Then suddenly the air becomes clear, vision returns to normal, and managers begin to play catch-up. Inevitably, some managers come up on the short end and others whiz by with newly carved futures. From the outside sally forth new managers whose superiors treat them as cuckoo chicks who hatched in the nest of another species and get fed better by their foster parents than the latter's natural offspring. Seeing the success of outsiders, insiders seek greener pastures elsewhere. With some coming in and others going out, the net advantage to those who stay may often be nil.

Mobility does not guarantee a lift to the higher reaches of the corporate mountain. It is a mental preparedness to utilize additional resources for gaining vertical thrust, including the lift afforded by lineups. Mobility without power is motion without movement. But without mobility, you will have no need for power. Your very survival will be at stake. You simply cannot ignore mobility. It is the most telling feature of corporate life and the necessary, although insufficient, quality of successful climbing. As the most natural characteristic of all living beings, it is ironic that mobility is least understood and willfully used and too often serves as a metaphor for getting ahead rather than the substance of it.

The corporation offers no language for mobility. Its words are not framed with the precise meanings and nuances as the language of management. It is much as though management language carries all the necessary wisdom for succeeding in business. If you believe this, you are limited to the life of a butterfly.

7
THE INVISIBLE CLIMBER

A painter is asked by the owner of a two-story building to paint it. The painter declines because of a handicap that precludes climbing a ladder. A second painter accepts the offer but charges twice the hourly rate of the first painter. The second painter explains "Climbing a ladder takes skill." Humor aside, the painter speaks the truth of course, but because "results count," little attention is paid to the ladder or the climbing or the skill to reach the peak of the building. The owner, knowing the painter reached the top, assumes away the skill required to get there.

Business pays for painting the building, and if the results justify the costs, the painter may get a bigger, higher building to paint. Many managers are as the first painter. They have a handicap for climbing, just as others may have an impediment for managing. But to reach the corporate peak, managers have to be skillful both ways, even though managing (painting) is the only formally acknowledged corporate skill.

As in the case of the painter, business assumes away the facts of climbing. When did your corporation hand out rewards for the best or fastest climbers? If "fresh blood" to nourish tired levels of managers is so valuable to business, why are the feats of getting there so officially ignored? Awards and rewards of every stripe are available to successful managing. As you know, pay raises belong to the new position, not to the climbing.

However, the incentives for managing attract ambitious climbers in sufficient number. For what other reason is the supply of contestants greater than the demand, and why do outsiders compete successfully with insiders in over thirty percent of the positions at division or subsidiary levels and higher if it were not for the incentives to gain higher levels of managerial responsibility? Managing (painting) pays well enough; no need to also reward climbing.

There is another reason why climbing is not a formally recognized enterprise. Climbers do not build businesses. Climbing per se does not directly benefit the bottom line. Using the analogy of the two-story building, the painter may climb up and down the ladder all day and still the building needs to be painted. Have you heard of a ladder-climbing contest, of rewards for the fastest climber or the fastest ladder or the equivalents of such among the ways of corporations? I do not mean to be facetious, but think, why are masters given credit for their achievements and often disparaged for their fast climbs?

Of course, corporations make attempts to identify high potential managers by various means, including tests, performance evaluations, and periodic interviews. So-called paths for getting ahead may be configured that oftentimes invite more excitement among managers than true promotions. Using the mobility patterns of managers who become chiefs, I helped clients initiate these career path programs many times in the 1960s and 1970s. In fact, when my clients and I compared the progress of managers before and after they were both identified as high potentials and given prescribed career paths, we did not see faster advancement for the next five to ten years. The halo of career-pathing lasted about as long as it took a younger, more astute climber to pass up the so-called career-advantaged high potentials.

Seldom are career prescriptions used by managers with a clear sense of how their corporations work and how to work them and who have the wits to see the faster routes ahead. Master climbers seldom attribute substantial assistance from these programs. More often than not, master are career path-busters for whom there is seldom praise offered for their climbing ingenuity. In almost all cases, their speedy progression is attributed to their managerial skills, leaving the net effect that climbing is not an officially recognized enterprise. In other words, finding and using fast routes is not officially rewarded compared to finding and using the best practices for achieving managed results.

Managed achievements must pass inspection of their contributions to business. They must be weighed, valued, and credited to those responsible for them. Where necessary, managers are held accountable for their malperformances, which could limit their climbs. But when did you ever hear of a climber penalized for climbing too high or too fast or too slow? While there is no public reward for skillful climbing, there is no official penalty either.

Your reward for climbing is inherent in the climbing. First is the achievement reward. You continually face new, more challenging responsibilities to prove your capability to get things done through others. You will extend your wits and skills through more levels of employees, thus giving you more substantial involvement in running the business. You will gain increasing amounts of discretionary judgment. The authority delegated to you will be wider with more freedom to assert your will. With greater level comes the power to sponsor. You may hand-pick your members of your staff, replace, demote, and terminate them as your responsibilities require. Your judgment in these matters will be less subject to challenge the higher you climb. Innovative and imaginative practices are not only permitted, but expected. In most cases, you will be dealing with more sophisticated, mature, and wise people above and below you. They require less face time for instructing, and coaching. People catch on to the ways of the corporation without having to be told. Your sources for reward are more powerful and available, making motivating and controlling easier. The higher you go, the more you will be involved in key decisions by virtue of your position and responsibilities. They allow quicker access to superiors and their peers.

Second is the reward of advancements. You not only get closer to fulfilling your ambitions, but the higher you climb, the easier to see ahead and plot your next moves. You will have fewer competitors because of fewer people at each level. You will face fewer outsiders brought in to infuse the business with fresh expertise and, of course, the perks, status, financial rewards increase disproportionately to your achievements. You are paid more to do less, because members of your hierarchy below are paid less to do more.

In contrast to these informal ways affecting climbers are the risks, many of which are silent. Masters recognize them as ways that rule climbing without specifically determining who gets to the top. For example, the asymmetrical nature of the hierarchy dictates that the higher one rises, the less likely one will go higher. The higher one goes, the stronger will be the drive among people to preserve their gains. With few exceptions, people will fight harder with more experience to fend off climbers from below. Even though peer contestants will be fewer, the competition will be more intense, owing to the fewer positions above. The higher you go, the stronger and more adroit must be your skill to defend your reputation for being promotable.

You must expect unpredictable difficulty at higher levels. The level above may be twice the difficulty of the level below. The delegation of authority is usually unevenly divided up, with some getting heavier workloads than others get. Your risk of being displaced is greater. When you show the slightest weakness, others will step forward and nominate themselves for some of your workload. Of course, this is always done in the interests of business. Opportunities to prove yourself are more visible, but the risks are greater. When you fail, people several levels below you will carry the brunt of your mistakes. Thus the impact upon business will be greater than at lower levels.

With fewer levels and people key to the chief's need, the more positions and levels expand and contract without regularity and predictability. Chiefs need maximum flexibility with their staffs to meet the exigencies of business competition. When levels and people contract, the queues of available people will grow longer and, like an accordion, shrink with expansive moves by the chief. At lower levels, such accordion-like queuing may be just as common, but at higher levels, the stakes are higher. This is true because the higher you go, the more you have invested in your career. Also, the closer you get to the top, the stronger the ambition becomes to get there and the better the chances. After all, there are more levels below and fewer above.

What few people tell you is that if you are in the wrong lineup, you do not have a chance no matter how close you are to the top. For that matter, no one even talks to you about a lineup. It exists but should not be seen. Anything that casts doubt on the veracity of the notion that performance counts is discouraged. Masters do their goodly share of espousing the direct link between performances and promotions. So accustomed are they to speaking this way of succeeding that they come to believe it. I have found no interview or counseling technique that allows easy penetration of their minds to gain the unvarnished truth about their fast climbs. It is interesting to note that chiefs who arrive at the top late in their careers are more apt to talk openly about all these risks and obstacles found in their path. Late-arrival chiefs are also more open about lineups, particularly those in which they had their momentum arrested. It should be obvious that climbing is an allowed motive and skill but not an officially recognized or sanctioned away of corporate life.

Still you must not treat climbing as a second-class effort, or you put your future at risk. You have no choice but to take climbing seriously if only to gain a fallback position at a high enough level to meet your minimum standard of success. Masters seek the ideal when there is no other way with a comparable payoff for trying to go all or part of the way.

The ideal includes using lineups. To the naïve, these contrivances appear to be a them-who-has-gets game. To be invited into a lineup, you must be promotable. If you are promotable, why do you need a lineup? Is it simply to get more of the same or a stronger guarantee of upward advancement? The answer is yes. It is called getting and keeping an edge on competition.

Furthermore, the probability of getting hitched to a lineup may seem to many people far-fetched. They fail to understand that the probability of becoming a member of a lineup is less far-fetched than the odds of going from the bottom to the top or to any of the higher reaches of the corporation.

The odds are not made appreciably more favorable by blasting away at the barricades with your presumed exceptional achievements. Superiors do not have to give way to you just because you think you merit promotion. You may finesse, insinuate, ingratiate, snooker, inflect, convert, proselyte, and romance, or whatever you may be predisposed to do, but you cannot extract from others what is not in their perceived interests to give. You may insist that your achievements be recognized by promotion, but remember, this is a form of intimidation. Coercion of any type may work once, but it is not a long-term career strategy. The function of a lineup is to serve as a proxy for the interests of the members. The lineup stands in and replaces the need for its members to be personally aggressive about promotion.

Because the informal organization of a lineup exists with the formal, the two organizations overlap and are so intertwined that where one leaves off and the other begins is not divisible. All that is directly visible is the formal hierarchy that officially identifies who is superior, manager, and subordinate. For this reason, the members know that the efficient use of lineups for achieving and advancing cannot be isolated as to praise and reward for the members for climbing. Furthermore, business would appear foolish if it did. How can business formally recognize something that exists only informally? In other words, to use once again the analogy of the painter, why acknowledge the ladder and the climbing of it, when the owner needs to pay only for the finished results.

Many corporate ways are powerful because they are oblique. Were they directly aimed and expressed, other ways would be found by managers with a keen sense of how to work their corporations. Whatever way is found to advance faster, it too must be responsive to the needs of managing. All forms of power, including lineups, cannot for long exist without supporting the business. The higher you go, the more numerous are the people below to see your contributions or the lack of them. They will make judgments about your business contribution that even the chief may not be able to explain away.

If a new chief places in key positions members of a lineup who do not perform so as to gain the benefits of formal organization among the several levels of the hierarchy, more people will know of their malperformance than just the chief. No lineup can be justified because it serves solely the interests of the members. However, it will not be the idea of a lineup that is criticized, but the lack of judgment of the chief. When members fail, the chief will be accused of favoritism. When they succeed, the chief will be praised because of the members' achievements. One way or the other, results seem to count.

If your lineup fails to achieve its intended purpose, you have as good or better chance to get a promotion because of your singular achievements made possible by the sharing of wits and skills of the members. You do not have much to lose. But if you win further promotions, the lineup will not be credited, at least formally. Nor may you openly speak of the value added by the lineup to your achievements and advancements. You may credit specific individuals as an attempt to show gratefulness, honest or contrived. But as far as you and they are concerned, the lineup does not exist. Its power may never be seen or heard and remains one of the less audible and less visible ways of corporate life.

As I said, at the top, few notice the mechanism whereby painters reach the pinnacle of the building. The ladder and the climbing of it are assumed away because the results are what the owner sees and pays for.

8
GETTING INTO THE LINEUP

The power of a lineup to offer its members exceptional advantages is most demonstrable in master climbers. They will be exposed to two lineups on average. However, a third of them will get picked up by a lineup at division levels or below, and then use this lineup all the way to the top. Usually the lead member of the lineup will have the power to sponsor at will the promotion of a lower member. Without this power, a lineup is incomplete but still may outwit any other collection of people for exploring opportunities for advancement.

It has been stated that to get into a lineup, you have to be promotable. This idea is not the same as being eligible for a promotion. Promotable means that you are judged worthy of higher responsibilities. You may or may not be eligible for promotion at the moment of gaining access to a lineup. But the lead member judges you to be capable of going to higher levels. In turn, this lead member of the lineup may be judged by extended superiors to be promotable. Anticipating a promotion, the lead member notices how you may be vital at higher levels and prepares you for membership in a lineup to expedite your preparation and development.

No one gets to the top without sponsorship and trustworthiness. Business is no more rational than it needs to be. It is unreasonable to expect people to float to the top just by the sheer force and magnitude of their mangerial achievements. Judgments about promotions are formed within the power of relationships. Relationships predict promotability better than performances, and relationship cannot be forbidden, since no one can create much value without them. No business necessity is strong enough to compel people to accept each other without regard for their motives, apparent or hidden. Few managers get to the top who have not been at some time undercut by their superiors, subordinates, or peers. The route to the top is strewn with managers sidelined by those trusted the most.

Many mistakes will be made due to the eminently human condition of business. Some people will advance who should not. Some people should not be trusted with the careers of others. Nevertheless, much value accrues to business because people seek each other's assistance and are smart about placing their trust. Masters use lineups partly because it is the smart way to test and gain trustworthiness and partly to find refuge from the irrational practices that do more than hurt climbers than help them.

These being the essential conditions and reasons for the formation of lineups, the question is, how does one get invited into a lineup? Many subordinates vie to be swept up by the momentum of promotable managers but lack the adroitness necessary to avoid the demeaning appearance of currying favor. They wish to "hitch their wagon to a rising star," but few know how to get this by-invitation-only connection.

Insinuate is the correct move. You don't walk or talk your way into a lineup, either as the crucial subordinate, the promotable manager, or the sponsor superior. To gain membership, your value to the lineup is first gradually expressed in smart probes, subtle, indirect, or covert moves with artful or oblique variations. You allay suspicions about appearing transparently eager to render assistance out of the ordinary. If you fail, the attempt makes a potential relationship vulgar and profanely indecent.

For example, if you were raised on a chicken farm you may have watched chicks break out of the eggshell. They accumulate enough internal body mass and pressure upon the inside wall of the shell that with just a little peck of the beak, the shell explodes. This is called "pipping." For managers, the trick is to accumulate weighty accomplishments and corresponding respect, such that just a little pip and the required mutually trusting and supportive relationship begins to form with a superior. It has been my experience that most climbers do not know how to pip. They attempt to penetrate prematurely a manager's sense of protection and privacy rather than wait to use timely and propitious moves. (Please see Chapter 14: Basic Moves: Away, With, Against [AWA].)

By natural proclivity, managers often believe that subordinates can best serve them by doing excellent work and sharing their skills with and upgrading the efforts of peers and subordinates. Managers do not usually want to cross the barrier of professionalism that separates superiors from subordinates. Furthermore, managers are not using their whole waking day to look for lineups. They are working, doing their jobs. They may meet someone and then, click, a connection is made. As it grows stronger, the line between them becomes blurred and then crossed. Neither one may have expected this to happen nor have secretly wanted it. In any case, the connection is not made overtly or apparently.

Any relationship that appears to give someone an unfair advantage must be kept quiet. Any overt display of such a relationship is like flaunting one's advantage in front of less fortunate people. This covetousness does not imply that lineups are unfair. Lineups do things for business not possible by soloists, which is why lineups have lasted all these years, probably ever since managers wanted to be able to select their key people if they were to be held personally accountable for results.

Fortunately, because lineups do not pip at once, they are not apparent to most people. In fact, a couplet usually forms first, which comes from manager and subordinate discovering that meshing of their skills, wits, and personalities is both advantageous and easy. Once they achieve comity and comfortability, the couplet may go to the second level of the relationship, which is to exchange the specific wherewithal to make it easy for them to pursue their individual responsibilities and careers. This stage is marked by a mutual regard for their ambitions and the need to form strategies for using each other to further their careers. They compare experiences, interpret important events, and draw upon each other's connections above and below to understand what is happening around them. They will report their own managerial problems in detail without the usual formality and reluctance between superior and subordinates. Now the usual things that distinguish bosses from underlings may partially give way to their taking turns playing adviser and advisee.

The pair may advance to the third stage in their relationship, which is a period of stability and endurability. They come to expect each other to be available when needed, to anticipate each other's needs, and will make efforts to keep their relationship useful and necessary. They may not connect with each other as often or as spontaneously, but rather, they will accumulate an agenda of items before their meetings.

However, most twosomes do not get to the third stage of extended continuity and interdependency, and fall back to ordinary relationships. Pairs of sorts come and go. For a variety of reasons, people get close for a while and then cool off, one of which is that people usually have limited time to establish and maintain closer ties than normal. They are busy doing things that interrupt for a protracted time their formative relationships. They may reconnect later at the same or higher levels, but even then, it may not be convenient or propitious for either of them.

A second reason is that members may be immature. They are not ready for the implicit responsibilities of making a lineup work. For one thing, members may brag to outsiders about their special connection or seek special privileges not proper to the relationship expected, or may not have organized wits. Their smarts soon wear thin, become repetitiously displayed and parlayed and wear upon the patience of others.

Then, too, some members are not capable of handling themselves wisely in informal, unstructured relationships. They feel most comfortable where there are clear lines of authority and responsibility and well-defined goals and plans. A lineup has sessions that approximate bull sessions with authority differentials collapsed, and members simply share openly their concerns and exchange their experiences and wisdom. People who thrive on structure minimize the advantages of a lineup, which for these reasons may be eventually dissolved.

A third reason that a couplet will reverse its formative relationship is that one of them attempts to maintain a strong presence in all affairs of the other member. The ways of discretionary judgment should allow the members as much slack as possible. But some managers suffocate subordinates. If you modulate your relationship by regulating the frequency and intensity of your contacts and sessions with the boss to get your work done and still be a respectful subordinate, you can be both close and distant.

As far as masters are aware, controlling the frequency and intensity of their relations with the boss is a set of the moves all managers must know how to do intuitively and automatically. In other words, they know when to hang around or stay away without having to be told. However, modulated moves in and of themselves do not make subordinates crucial to their managers. A twosome should have a stable and endurable relationship before they join at the hip. Otherwise there is too much chance of becoming disconnected and then feel that one has been used or abandoned or that one of them or both did something wrong.

Awareness of mutual dependency is the fourth stage. Usually there is some significant event or experience that drives or pulls them closer together. They may desperately need to be collectively smarter than either one of them. This insight most likely happens at the point or shortly thereafter of a promotion of the manager or a major opportunity for one or both to prove better than their present positions. Or it may be the requirement of greatly enlarged responsibilities, which is common for fast climbers, that the subordinate be given a key role.

Also, they may be pulled together by a fear of failing in a promotion. If not a promotion to a position, then it is after arrival in a critical and difficult assignment or opportunity that they may find their need for each other. Or somewhere into the performance stage, unanticipated difficulties may cause a subordinate to step forward to assume personal responsibility in whatever way necessary and possible. Besides rallying the "troops," this subordinate may help the manager to determine that a key move is necessary and help devise the move and implement it in order to augment a weak plan or intervene in a failing program. If the manager and subordinate demonstrate that together they can accomplish more with less difficulty over a sustained period of time, then this fifth stage is set for the coupling to achieve proven trust and respect. Their lineup has proved endurable.

Plans are never perfect, and managers always need help in correcting them. Masters claim that plans are schemes awaiting failure. When the chips are down, they will see who is prepared to move quickly and smartly. Masters often find their key subordinates in the flux of disorder or chaos, which is common today.

When a couplet gets to the fifth stage of proven endurability, whatever they did to get there becomes a baseline from which they make any further moves. Whatever combination and degree of moving into the boss's world and out and staying away must conform to the baseline. Masters do not ruin a productive and comfortable relationship by exploiting it or taking it for granted. They never cross the baseline except under one condition, an unusual circumstance that makes crossing the baseline imperative. When the situation is resolved, they go back to the baseline. This may be difficult to do because the two of them have been working closely together. But this recent increase of proximity should not deter them from returning to their base line. When masters say they like subordinates who are light under foot, it is their making these smart moves that they have in mind.

Meanwhile, the manager must not be preoccupied solely with these downward relationships. The manager must serve the superior as ideal subordination requires, becoming indispensable to the superior's accomplishments. Anything that helps the manager, helps the superior, which is where the subordinate comes in. If the subordinate is viewed as crucial to the manager, the superior may want to exploit the combined advantages by an informal understanding of their combined future worth.

Once they see how each of them could be invaluable to the other in a future opportunity or promotion, they make sure that such a relationship is not terminated. They are at the sixth and last stage. They treat each other as though they will always depend upon each other. The lineup, secure in its sixth stage, continues to exchange confidences, compare their corporate senses, alert each other to adversaries and enemies, connive to protect their flanks and rears, and exchange wits about how to deal with difficult assignments, opportunities, and obstreperous people above and below them.

But nothing is guaranteed. Always the question at the sixth stage concerns whether the members will continue to work together at present and higher levels or will they become incompatible when the chips are down. When their careers hang in the balance, will they turn inwards for solutions and fail to become collectively smarter than their individual wits? It is in moments of crises that masters come to know with whom they are working, upon whom they can steadfastly depend, or who will ditch them in moments of need and look out strictly for themselves. Successfully mounting a crisis may reinforce the value of a lineup at the sixth stage and membership of it. The members will sacrifice many things before they will abandon the lineup. One member may receive a multilevel promotion and reach back later and bring up the other members. Such is the power of the sixth stage.

So pause and ask, where is the bent of your mind? Can you grow as smart as other members grow smart? Can you keep up? At what point will your responsibilities exceed your wits and you become the weak mind of the lineup? When in desperation will you begin to pretend, to issue forth ill thought-out intellectual fabrications to impress? How soon will you read the signs that your free ride is about over? Can you hide for long your loss of self-confidence that is required for credibility? In a crisis do you have in reserve a fresh perspective that can bring members away from the trees to see the forest? In other words, can you become and remain a long-term contributor over several levels and positions? These questions get at some of the reasons that formative lineups become unstable or why they exclude members and perhaps why you will never get invited into one.

But if you do, you have a vehicle that has the capability at least for the near term of taking you where you want to go faster and easier. You may need several lineups in your progression to the top. If you display the smarts to get in one and maintain membership status, you probably have the smarts to work future lineups. So ask the question, "What is your most valuable asset from your superior's perspective?" You might want to check your answer with Chapter 12, The Promotable Manager.

9
THE POWER OF LINEUPS

The function of management is to ensure that everything does not happen at once. Sometimes it does, or so it seems. You go to work expecting to have the necessary stability to follow through and complete your assignments. You may be matrixed with several superiors because of overlapping assignments, but you know or should sense who has the final judgment about your performance and promotability. Superiors are supposed to make it as easy as possible for you to do difficult assignments, while other corporate ways make it difficult for you to climb. While you may have sufficient control of yourself for managing, you never have enough control for climbing. Still, you may pride yourself for bifocal vision to discern events and movements both near and far. You feel confident of your wits to read the corporate tea leaves and see ahead enough to be forewarned and prepared for most eventualities. In this regard, you feel in sufficient control of your career, at least for the time being.

Then, out of nowhere, turbulence strikes, much as wind shear, unexpectedly and sends a plane plummeting until the pilot regains control. Everything becomes topsy-turvy. You are no longer standing side by side or above and below people upon whom you depend. You are not alone. The whole hierarchy seems to be reeling from a devastating blow delivered at the point of the hierarchy.

This condition is the changing of the chiefs. You now feel the effects of the primal rule of corporate life. You may experience this stomach-churning teeth-gnashing, mind-blowing rule for the first time or third. It makes no difference. The stability that your confidence requires may eventually return but perhaps not before you have been painfully repositioned.

The changing of the guard at the top involves more than the guards that change with the chief. All personnel serve at the behest and pleasure of the CEO. This is the *primal rule* of the hierarchy.

No one in authority is more obliged or competent to change at will the hierarchical positions and people than the chief. The earliest moves of the new chief aim to get control of the hierarchy, to present the new business and strategic plans, to restructure and refurbish the hierarchy to support the business plan, and to require the COO to dress up the lines of command by moving people and positions around at lower levels for achieving operating responsibilities and efficiencies.

An insider chief will change on average a third of the officers by replacing or terminating or dramatically altering their duties or positions. An outsider chief will likewise affect eventually about two-thirds of the officers. Whether new or old, the moves of the COO to achieve operating efficiencies may reach the lowest levels of the organization. Primal screams may be heard down the hierarchy as superiors change some of their managers, who, in turn change some of their subordinates while some people transfer to new positions or levels inside or outside the corporation. The primal rule serves to provide new opportunities for its beneficiaries and risks to its victims.

The awareness to anticipate and comprehend the new opportunities and risks for promotability and the mobile skills of agility, adaptability, and flexibility to seize and exploit them are not as widely distributed as the changes wrought by the primal rule. This usually leaves many managers ill prepared for the disorder. Less than one-tenth of direct reports from division managers to the chief operating officer will be left untouched in some way. And these *untouchables* usually are managers well fitted and comfortable with their positions and are too valuable to mess around with. Besides, they usually pose no threat to their superiors.

If your record of performance mildly but tolerably threatens your boss during ordinary times, the implementation of the primal rule may escalate the threat without your shaking one fist. As a general rule, the disorder created by refocusing, restructuring, or restaffing the business offers a convenient cover for superiors to get rid of pesky, high performers who threaten to show them up or pass them up or who are just plainly unwanted. Fast climbers are not paragons of virtue. They are just as apt to use restructuring to get rid of people they don't want. Masters do it. While people are being moved here and let go there, it is tempting to separate out those with whom they have difficult, irreconcilable relationships. Masters consider this fair because they incur the same risks as well.

Fortunately, such an environment represents the preferred conditions of mobile managers. They have the skills in place to exploit lifts during the height of the execution of the primal rule. However, while new and big things happen to the beneficiaries of such rearrangements, they can never afford to be without the benefits of lineups. So while the primal rule destroys, it also creates.

The implicit, unspoken reason for lineups is that the benefits of formal organization cannot be achieved at any given level without them. It takes at least three levels whose members must be coordinated and controlled for maximum results. For example, when the primal rule is invoked, the CEO uses the chain of command to change it. This new hierarchical order of people and positions is expected to reap the benefits of the formal organization. But as experienced managers know, a lot of slippage occurs between what the CEO wants and what is actually done at lower levels. The new chief may lose control of the business because of persistent unintended consequences. If strategic plans approved by the board of directors fail to be effectively implemented, the chief may resign or be terminated and another chief elected who is expected to do the board's bidding better. Then another variant of the primal rule may be launched.

In spite of using the primal rule to stack their lineup in favor of success, about one out of five new chiefs will serve three years or less. There are several reasons, among which is their failure to gain sufficient benefits of organization due to loss of coordination and control. For example, hierarchies were shortened in the 1980s and 1990s because the bottom of the business was not coordinated with the top. Middle management was perceived as a major culprit. Managers blocked and interfered with the efficient distribution of authority and work and were eliminated in wholesale numbers.

However, the problems were not simply at mid-hierarchy but also at the bottom and foremostly at the top. CEOs were removed in massive numbers. While chiefs cannot directly control the whole hierarchy, they must control at least two levels below them. The rule of thumb is that if there is slippage in the effectiveness of organizations, it will most apt be among members of three levels who are most visibly and directly related to each other by authority and work.

For this reason, new chiefs usually remove or reposition people at the levels immediately below them. If chiefs cannot control these levels, they cannot expect to control the remaining hierarchy.

Do not confuse control with mode of managing. The proof of control is the congruence between what you set out to do and what is accomplished. With congruence, you are in control. Of course, your mode of managing, whether arbitrary or permissive, partly contributes to the outcome, but if little congruence occurs between expectations and results, you are managing out of control, regardless of the mode used. Superiors may foster forms of creative expression among managers and their subordinates, allowing wide degrees of discretionary authority about how to achieve their goals. Such relaxed authority may be proper as long as the results conform to the expectations of the chain of command. But when they do not, the misuse of authority may be the offense, and the first to be held accountable will be the superior. The mode used never justifies loss of control.

Loss of control may be illustrated by a series of connected sprockets with the larger wheel transmitting motion to the second smaller sprocket enmeshed with a still smaller third sprocket. If the big wheel turns just a little bit, the smallest sprocket goes a hundred miles an hour. This illustration, while somewhat humorous, simply refers to overreaction to authority. That such occurs is indeed commonly known. Overreaction may actually diminish the potential for control. No doubt this fate awaits many plans and programs. Masters often stay awake nights wondering who is going to read more into their orders than intended. They know that loss of sufficient control occurs because of the best intentions of hard-working people. Also, they fear the laggards who practice malicious compliance, which is to go ahead with a plan or program when they know it will fail and reflect badly upon the boss. The authority and power of chain of command to make or break managers is precisely why lineups are needed. By sharing wits, the members know more precisely what is a proper execution of orders at the various levels they represent. Lineups are powerful tools for assuring control and coordination among levels of the hierarchy without apparent use of authority.

Assume that you are the manager sitting in the swivel chair, prepared to turn upwards toward your superior(s) and downwards toward your subordinate(s), as circumstances require. You are one of the three levels that will be the most crucial to your superior's effectiveness, if you include the superior's effort. However, your superior is also a subordinate of an extended superior, who in turn is a manager to a superior, and so on to the point of the hierarchy. And your subordinate may be a superior to a manager with extended subordinates and so forth down to the base of the hierarchy. From the corporate point to the base, interlocking and overlapping triplets may extend, connecting the myriad of people and positions into a unified and coordinated structure, at least such is the organizational ideal. As the manager, you feel the impact of this interconnectedness when your superior informs you of changes required by extended superiors and when you must rely upon the judgments of your subordinate staff to produce the necessary results.

You will have the same concerns and fears as your superior, namely that slippage will most likely occur among the first and second levels below and, at the very least, that you will hold them accountable for the discrepancy that occurs below them. The minimum requirement is that you have the right subordinates in place invested with the right amount of authority and work responsibility, and because much is at stake, you must be certain that the second level below you is also properly staffed.

Of course, proper communication is vital. To that effect, you extend your presence and relationships to two levels or more of subordinates for them to understand accurately what you intend, with little guessing on their part. While your personal exposure to lower levels is vital to gaining and maintaining control, your desire also to select the key staff at each level may make you appear to want more control than necessary. Novice managers accept this practice of apparent overcontrol as proper because it helps them to have initial success. But with more experience and self-confidence, they may want to select their own staff members with a minimum of deference to higher authority. To earn this power, they must prove to be as smart as their superiors for picking and using winners.

This skill is not commonly distributed among managers. Managers may be capable of using inherited subordinates efficiently, but to personally hand-pick them requires a different skill altogether, especially in regard to finding and selecting replacements. But seasoned managers want that power, because if they are going to be accountable for their results, they want to select and pass out assignments to the staff upon whom expected results depend. Superiors understand this need, as do all ambitious managers. The freedom to select subordinates gives the manager more apparent authority over subordinates. The latter will anticipate what the manager expects of them rather than second guess the manager's superior.

Now as the manager, you will be put to the test for your superior to see the veracity of your self-choices. Without prompting, do you wisely recommend subordinates for key assignments and positions? Do you avoid placing too much authority and responsibility in others unfit for major assignments, and whom do you abandon or terminate altogether for the sake of efficiency? In other words, do you move smartly and timely *away* from, *with* and *against* (AWA) the right people so as to develop a mix of talent that will achieve the benefits of organization. (Please see Chapter 13, The Right Moves.)

Suppose the exceptional performance of your staff justifies these moves. Then you win two important judgments. You are perceived as good at organization and good at staffing. Next, you have another favorable judgment to win from your superior. Can you find and develop a replacement? The superior has gained credit toward promotability because of your achievements, as perhaps you have also? The superior does not want any appreciable erosion of your accomplishments after you vacate your position. When you depart, will your successor's arrival have a seamless transition that allows getting quickly to the performance phase so that there is a minimum of disconnectedness between your regime and your successor's? And will your successor's departure be as smart as yours? All of these questions will be answered by your superior in the form of favorable or unfavorable judgments.

The rule of thumb is not to leave any vital position unprotected. Unproductive positions may be taken away because of slippage in the benefits of organization. They are simply a waste. You may even recommend to your superior such restructuring. Meanwhile, it is smart to maintain the status and integrity of vital positions under your control by shielding them from inadequate occupants. Masters do not like to lose key positions one or two levels below them due to the incompetence of their occupants. In fact, they will often sacrifice the occupant to save the position.

Successors usually, but not always, come from positions that are vital to the benefits of organization. Generally, you do not expect to get your successor from a weak or secondary position or expect a record of high performance in a nonvital position to impress your superior. So you make sure to move your most likely successor into a crucial position or into a weak position upgraded by exposed assignments. This game of winning judgments is done by increasing the value of your position and never to sully it by controversial performance or by allowing it to define your promotability. You must always be judged to be better than your position, especially if, initially, your position is weak.

The next questions are: Does your superior have confidence that the wits of your prospective successor are derived from positions crucial to your effectiveness? Will your successor remain crucial at higher levels or will your successor cause slippage in your superior's control at your head or the one below you? Suppose the answers to these judgmental questions favor your promotability and that of your subordinate. Still, an alignment of this sort is not fully developed even though much has been gained by each member.

This basic unit of superior, manager, and subordinate must prove its durability. A competing lineup may emerge. The superior has more than one manager, perhaps as many as a dozen or as few as two or three, each with subordinate staffs. These managers are not sitting there twiddling their thumbs. Each may be competing for the favor of the common superior, for discretionary authority to assign work, and for power to check the superior's authority when it is necessary and self-advantageous. While the most ambitious to climb will seek favored status, others will also seek it simply because they wish to do well in their jobs and avoid fighting for survival. For whatever reasons, few managers do not have the urge to secure a firm footing with their common superior and hopefully gain an advantage over their peers.

It is a fact of corporate ways that people in a survival mode will fight to gain favorable advantage with superiors as strongly as with promotable managers. Contestants regardless of status have uneven skills for the struggle. Some become pliable supplicants and others become crude belligerents. "Glad handers" may not be welcomed either. Masters view them as the emotional equivalent of dunces with touchy-feely gestures that betray the lack of emotional maturity.

THE POWER OF LINEUPS 69

When the chief invokes the primal rule, some lineups win and others lose. Sometimes existing lineups are broken up just because one of the members is more valuable to superiors than the others. Masters may bypass the lead superior and then later pluck subordinates for quick elevation to them. It is not uncommon for masters to have two lineups working for them. The primal rule may want promotions for the less favored lineup than the preferred. Also, the vast changes ensuing from the primal rule may cause members to ditch their lineup and to form new ones.

For example, take the case of the new corporate chief finance officer who comes in from the outside with the new chief executive officer, creating a mammoth earthquake. Sales drive the business, and as division sales vice-president, you occupy this strategic function. The division general manager occupied your position before you, and with the operations vice-president, you three members formally drive the business. But actually, the GM's lineup does not conform to this formal structure. The division financial officer reports to the GM with a dotted line to the corporate CFO position. This division CFO is better technically as a controller than as a financial strategist. The controller is better as a CFO and represents the third member of the GM's informal lineup. Even though the controller is one level below the vice-president for operations, the controller shares power with you and the GM to set and check informally the strategies and moves of the division. Hence, for all practical purposes, the operating vice-president is outside the lineup but is used by it for purposes of climbing. The GM and you believe that the controller could someday run the division.

The hierarchy above the GM has been devastated, but your lineup is fortunate to still be connected to a powerful, surviving, extended superior two levels above who has been the GM's sponsor. Your lineup senses that numbers are going to run the corporation and sees a chance to get in on the right side of the issue. The GM sends word through the sponsor two levels above to replace the division CFO with the controller. After making several private representations to this effect, the new corporate CFO agrees to the move. In effect the controller, acting informally as the CFO, formally displaces the division CFO. Now the new division CFO is formally your peer, but informally remains subordinate to you in your lineup. The reading of the silent intentions of the GM is that you are the successor apparent. The new division CFO anticipates this, which is why the two of you work closely together. Both know which way is up. The new division CFO also senses that for some time the GM and you have been preparing and positioning the new division CFO for the division manager's job. With you as the GM's successor and hopefully the new division CFO as your eventual successor, the lineup makes plans to be ready to move up.

Eventually the corporate CFO discovers the improvement in the numbers of the division and recommends that the CFO move the GM up to corporate vice-president responsible for three additional key divisions. In effect, the GM displaces the extended superior directly above. Now the former GM is a direct report to the sponsor-superior, the same superior that the GM used as a conduit to relay the message to promote the controller to division CFO. By the way, this sponsor was the first boss that the GM worked for fresh out of college. The GM after serving briefly as a non-manager was promoted by the sponsor to first level manager. This sponsor has always held positions two levels above the new corporate vice-president until recently.

Thus far, as a consequence of the primal rule, at least two people have been displaced, but the lineup's maneuver is not complete. The division operations manager becomes strictly a manufacturing vice-president and the division CFO assumes responsibility for all other staff services plus accounting and finance. This downgrading of the operations vice-president is as much a consequence of the primal rule as displacement of the division CFO and promotion of the controller. Notice how the new CEO and corporate CFO are in a position to get control of several key divisions. This feat was their intention.

Lineups do not conform to the formal hierarchy. The new corporate vice-president has become the point officer for the corporate CFO, and together they have far more power with the CEO than their formal status merits. Now as the GM, you are in the swing seat facing both the corporate vice-president and division vice-president of finance. But it is entirely possible that you or the vice-president of finance could become the lead member. In other words, the lead member of a lineup may not be necessarily the hierarchical superior.

In this case, the superior recognizes that the manager has a far better chance of moving up, and the other members give support and advice needed to properly and favorably expose the manager to extended superiors. (Please see Chapter 11, Bypassing Levels.) Other times, the superior may formally serve as the subordinate to the other members. While the members of the lineup treat each other as equals, they usually understand the order of succession. In lineups that are still forming, the order of successions may not be clear. Still, the objective remains the same, to find and develop the strongest lineup of promotable managers as possible even if it means getting only one member on the fast track first.

All lineups do not serve this objective equally well. Lineups are no respecter of the quality of people forming and using them. Superiors may form them with weak managers and subordinates who are far too deferential to stand up and check the authority and presumed wisdom of the lead and other members. In this case, the lineup is no smarter than the wits of the lead member. However, the lead member must have sufficient corporate sense to make up for the shortfall in the smarts of the other members. This concentration of wits in the lead member may not make the ascendancy of the lineup as fast or easy as the collective smarts of the master's lineup. But corporate ways allow less than efficient use of lineups. Granted that they are likely to be slower and encounter more difficulties, but they do eventually push through to occupy the apex of the corporation in far greater number than their individual wits and skills merit. (Please see Chapter 20, Conclusion: Efforts vs. Wits).

One reason masters have rapid ascendancies is because they get off in each position to a fast start and do not stay long enough to make career-limiting mistakes or allow adversaries to get them in their crosshairs. They obviate the perverse rule that usually operates among climbers—the longer you stay, the more mistakes are apt to be made and the more adversaries and resistance accumulate. Take managers with momentum who slow their pace to stay more than three years in their next position—their mobility patterns indicate little chances of regaining their momentum in the near term. They may eventually get promotions, but they are no longer expected to be pulled up quickly by their superiors. The longer they stay, the more difficult to regain lost career time.

Now, let us go back to your coming to work one morning and finding yourself in the midst of a primal maneuver. Let us assume that you are the operations vice-president rather than sales vice-president of the division. Your supportive general manager has been promoted to corporate vice-president. You expect to be promoted, but instead, your peer, the sales VP, passes you up and your job has been downgraded to division manufacturing vice-president. You never once figured your peer would be the preferred subordinate. But then, you never expected that the new chief would shake things up and make orphans out of a lot of members of emergent or established lineups who thought they had the right relationships for getting ahead, as perhaps you once thought. Now you must rethink your career and devise strategies and moves to prevent being left holding the bag again. You are not the first or the last to be bypassed by a peer or the only one without someone or several to turn to for sharing and gaining wits about what it takes to climb. If you are as private about managing as climbing, you will probably lose on both fronts.

You made several mistakes typical of ambitious people who fail to make a realistic distinction between managing and climbing. The major mistake is to allow your superiors to become more promotable than you. This gap is common, but you failed to close it substantially as to become almost as promotable as your superior. Second, you did not appear to your superior to be able to gain and keep favorable judgments about your promotability. In other words, you were not in control of your superior's mind. Third, you midjudged the wits and skills of your peer to preempt your promotional opportunity. You failed to see how and when your peer became more favorably aligned with the career interests of your common superior. If a lineup did not exist, certainly the semblance of one did. Close relationships may approximate a lineup with practically the same consequences.

While your records of achievements as the former vice-president of operations may have been better on paper, they did not give you the necessary edge to beat out your peer. You know now what you have long suspected—achievements are not sufficient. The gap between you and your superior is too wide. You lost by losing judgments about your promotability. You do not know how to gain promotions to and at higher levels. (Please see Chapter 12, The Promotable Manager.)

You can never tell what awaits when you go to work the next day, but it is no more hazardous than the day before or the day after. No one has the right for continued advancement just as business has no right to expect success forever. New chiefs give business new opportunities by which to succeed, and they trust that by invoking the primal rule, managers will show the agility, flexibility and adaptability to find and exploit new opportunities. To minimize the chaos, chiefs bank upon the exceptional mobility of key managers to make smooth transitions by separating from people, ideas and positions and attaching to new or different ones with as few as possible unintended consequences. In other words, you do not make things more difficult that are already difficult enough.

So you must adjust and adapt to your new boss, your former peer. Do you know why your new boss is more highly valued than you? Do you know how to become more valuable to your new boss than your present peer? Primal restructuring and restaffing may give people second and third chances to remain in the business or to leave for better opportunities elsewhere. And if you remain, what is the one thing you need to work on next to prove your future worth? Read on. You may face other aggravations, when out of nowhere, a controller becomes the general manager of your division.

10

THE CRUCIAL SUBORDINATE

If you are looking to get ahead, which way are you looking? Are you looking downward as a superior over a staff of subordinates or upward as a subordinate under a superior? Of course, as the manager in between, you must look both ways. But as a climber, you cannot have it both ways. Superiors promote, subordinates accomplish. You know this, and that if you want to get ahead, you must not fail to make your superior look good. You figure that the best way to serve your superior is to become an ideal superior to your subordinates. Your strategy is nothing new or novel. It is used every day among all levels of superiors, managers, and subordinates. Each would be happy to have their subordinates approximate the role of the ideal superior, since so few even come close.

You proceed to extract from your subordinates' exceptional accomplishments for which they, your superior, and you take proper measure of credit. Everybody seems to win; you do because you eventually gain a reputation for being a reliable, valuable, results-based superior to your people and a vital asset to the business.

So you may ask what went wrong. For all your effort, you still do not get promotions that reflect your record of performance. You may be tired of changes in assignments with no change in title or changes in title with no increased responsibilities. These dry promotions bring you no closer to the higher level in the hierarchy toward which you aim your career. So you and many peers join the chorus today, pleading "how do you get ahead around here?"

It is difficult not to get locked into a mentality to excel at being an exceptional superior to your staff. The rewards, raises, promotions are all pitched toward high performance management. The formal ways of most businesses dictate that no one should get ahead without contributing demonstrably to the business. From day one, novice managers are fed a steady diet of perform, perform, perform.

Their annual evaluations press upon them that exceptional performance is the norm. They must always do better. Improvement must be continuous. Training programs and seminars are provided with a wide and sometimes wild assortment of techniques and work processes to help managers become ideal superiors.

As if there were not sufficient pressure to excel at managing people, managers may add their own self-imposed variety. It is need for job security. There seems to be so little of it. Because the penalty for being a poor superior is severe, they may attempt to minimize the risk of termination, demotion, or transfer. Even if they do become a well-respected, high-performing superior, there is no guarantee of promotion. So they minimize risk without assurance of maximizing gain.

This strategy puts many higher performers on a treadmill whereby they work harder and longer than ever and still feel no more secure or valuable than when they were novice managers. Meanwhile, they see and hear of managers moving up rapidly around and above and feel pressed from below by ambitious, youthful people to get moving or to get you out of their way so that they can advance.

If this is similar to your situation, perhaps it is time to look another way, adjust your perspective about what it takes by noting that your present focus places your career ahead of your superiors. The implicit premise is that if you want to get ahead, you must perform as an ideal superior to your subordinates and that you will be rewarded accordingly. You have made *you* central to your career.

But you have done more than that. Notice the reciprocal flow of credit. Superiors give managers credit for their achievements who, in turn, give credit to their subordinates' achievements. Credit works also in reverse. The achievements of subordinates add to the achievements of managers whose achievements summate into the achievements of superiors. Credit goes down to the doers and up to those in authority. Notice, also that this arrangement is based upon an achievement perspective. You help yourself by becoming a high performing member of your superior's staff. The natural tendency is for you to pay close heed to your results and credits. The better the results are, the better the credits. However, the question is, credits for what, your achievements or advancements?

If you center your ambitions on achievements, you are committed to overperforming to gain credit for advances. Just as your staff of subordinates each contest in varying degrees for promotions, so are you one of several peers competing for promotion from your common superior. Among all three levels, superior, manager, and subordinate, many peers attempt to outperform each other to gain promotion. This is great. Your section of the hierarchy has solid winners.

However, your premise is false if your superior knows the facts about what it takes to climb. What happens when two people, ambitious to gain promotions, have different strategies? For example, the superior's ambitions are directly tied to advancement and the manager's are directly fixed upon achievements. One is a dedicated climber at heart, and the other, a dedicated practitioner of managing. If you are the latter and your superior the former, you are not apt to gain the potential advantages that your superior offers. Both of you will be on separate wavelengths. And if you are not aware of how some superiors make a distinction between climbing and managing, you will not know that the two of you are not optimally compatible.

You may not be faulted because you have the mind that the formal ways of the corporation prescribe. You are a high achiever who is typically given more responsibility than others. You give more to business than you get and are cheap at any price. Overloaded with work, you have little time to think about climbing let alone suspect that your superior has avoided the trap that has caught you up. Furthermore, your superior may not be seeking simply one promotion. The climber's strategy is to figure out what it takes to get to a predetermined level, say division manager, officership, or chief executive.

Masters do not climb directly to positions, but to interim checkpoints. They know several things. One, they need more assistance than what is needed to get a promotion. Of course, climbers will take every promotion they can get. They are not timid opportunists. Two, they know that achievements, however extraordinary, may not be sufficient to compete for fewer and fewer positions as they ascend higher. The fewer the competitors, the tougher the competition. Three, climbers need potential successors whose quality enhances their competitiveness. Fourth, this quality is measured by how well

THE CRUCIAL SUBORDINATE 77

climber and successor may work together at higher levels. Once again, compatability is key.

So far, these four ways of master climbers may be generally known and respected, but there is a fifth way, silent and implied in their perspective. It is a mutual understanding that superior and potential successor will more or less connive to develop strategies and moves that will give them a competitive edge. Both master and successor agree that the link between achievements and advancements is too tenuous. For this reason, they seek something more certain over which they have more direct control of their ambitions. So they rearrange the formula of ambitions, achievements, advancements with a different perspective. This is the sixth way masters view climbing.

Now there you are, working as a subordinate to the manager who is the preferred successor to the promotable superior. You may be aware of ways one through three, even four, but you cannot be directly aware of the fifth and the sixth ways of climbers. You might be able to read the signs and logically deduce the fifth and sixth ways. If you decipher all of the masters' ways, you may adapt to their way of thinking. Simply put, all the results and credits in the world will be for naught if your superior and manager and you cannot compete successfully. To compete successfully require skills separate from producing managed results.

Some people know how to make the most of their achievements for gaining advancements and to make the most of their advancements to gain more advancements. This train of thought may eventually lead you to turn your focus 180 degrees away from *you*. You put your superior's career ahead of yours. Now you focus intensely upon becoming an *ideal subordinate*. Instead of being dependent upon your superior for promotions, your superior becomes dependent upon your promotions. While your aim now is to become decisive to your superior's career, you also change your focus downward. Rather than have subordinates dependent upon you, you become dependent upon them. All eyes look upwards and away from themselves.

Now you have changed your way of looking to get ahead. In the first perspective, you focus most intensely upon performing the role of superior, and in the second case, upon performing the role of subordinate. You become focused upon promotion rather than performance. Not your advancement, but that of your superior becomes your primary focus. Now your formula is to advance faster by getting faster advancements for your superior. You hope that the one who provides this assistance becomes rewarded by promotion. In other words, you seek the ability to become promotable rather than wait around for credits for achievements to finally auger promotions.

This is what promotability means. You make yourself more promotable by making your superior more promotable. This formula so contrived really aims at speeding up getting ahead. It is a fast-route maneuver demonstrated most conspicuously by masters. Notice the ambition is directed away from being a good practitioner of managing toward becoming a better climber. Hopefully you will be good at both climbing and managing.

At first blush, you may believe this change in perspective will make no difference in getting unstuck from stalled careers or for continuing progress upwards. Perhaps you may not be aware of how managers become chiefs, particularly the masters of the climb. They excel at roles of both superior and subordinate, but they recognize that they cannot get ahead faster than their superiors. If they want to go faster, they have to help their superiors to go faster.

While this may be evident to seasoned managers, what is not apparent is the close-working, informal relationship masters develop with their superiors. Their relationships are based upon certain enterprising practices that make them crucial subordinates to their superiors' promotability. These practices answer the questions, what can you do for your superior that your superior cannot do that will make both of you more promotable. (Please see Chapter 18, The Sponsor.)

While you were thinking about performing well beyond your responsibilities, you realize also that you have a full plate of challenges that offer little spare time for plotting about how to make your superior more promotable. You visualize time constraints but another doubt protrudes. How do you serve interests of both your superior and yourself without coming out on the short end of the stick? What is the benefit if you risk being a good superior to your subordinates? If you let up on achieving exceptional results, a peer may jump in and take the promotion away from you, or a conniving subordinate may set out to displace you. These things happen among ambitious people who will do anything to get ahead. You dare not leave your flank or rear unprotected.

Furthermore, how do you put your superior's career ahead of yours without appearing to play up to the boss? Enough of your peers do it anyhow. In fact, one of your peers may appear to have a favored status because of it. You can see the worst scenario. You help your superior get a promotion who then promotes your lackey peer. Where does it get you?

You may have another reservation. Suppose your superior is unpromotable to begin with, or suppose credits for your achievements have not been passed upward by your superior. Suppose extended superiors consider you to be too light to succeed your superior. Also, you may have overestimated the value of your results or the credits given toward promotion. These considerations aside, you still face the question of how to distinguish yourself from your peers with your superior.

Masters work through these same doubts and concerns. It is not a matter of a lot of time and effort expended that provides your service to superiors, unlike what is required for managing. You are not doing things for your superior, although that may be occasionally necessary. Your assistance is more intellectual. You share your corporate sense to help your superior develop strategies and moves for achieving and advancing.

Some people might be intimidated by the idea that a subordinate needs to be smart enough to advise superiors for other than managerial reasons. This concern is legitimate. Your counsel and advice must pass the litmus test; it must be judged both smart and welcomed by the superior. Smart people cannot be helped by unsmart people. Apropos to this idea is the old saying that paupers cannot bring gifts to a king. Managers short on corporate sense cannot advise superiors long on it. If you are not smart enough to help your superior offset the downward forces that arrest careers and optimize the upward forces that advance careers, you do not have much to offer your superior. What you should have available are some realistic may do's and may not do's concerning translating achievements into advancements without which you have limited value to either your superior or yourself.

As for superiors taking advantage of you, you probably are being taken advantage of anyhow. That is the name of the climbing game.

Climbers helps climbers to climb to help themselves to climb. You must be smart enough to gain an implied mutual consent. No words are spoken and none are needed. You read each other's motives. Each respects the other for having a different, but wise, sense of the corporation. At any time one is going to take more than give. If you can help your superior think through difficult career problems, your services will be judged by their consequences. If your superior accepts your help without intending to return assistance, you simply have failed to establish the terms of the implied relationship. Your signal has not gotten through that the two of you can advance faster than either one of you in the traditional role of members of a formal hierarchy.

However, if you still feel that you are being taken advantage of, it is probably because you have no advantage to offer. No one can use you if you are useless. This overestimation of the value of your wits is the prime cause for superiors to pretend to accept your "gifts" with little in exchange. You may not be as smart as you think.

This lack of comity of smarts may extend to incompatible perspectives. Masters must deal with many superiors who believe climbing is a product of good managing. They are smart in every way but climbing. They make it easy as possible for their staffs to manage and for their superiors to manage them. Insofar as their collective results help their superiors to gain credits for promotability, their efforts may be valued. But if their superiors are takers and not givers, masters cannot expect their superiors also to make it easy for them to gain promotions. Their superiors have an unrealistic perspective about what it takes to make the difficult climb less difficult for both of them. If masters fails to notice this conflict between different perspectives, they risk not having their assistance returned.

However, other masters maintain that most managers do not have a climber's perspective toward their superiors. In most cases they lack the desire to be keen students of how their corporations work. The reason for this ignorance is that a user approach is often at work. It assumes that if you can use something, you do not have to understand how it works. This approach is nothing new; it is not because of the technology-driven business of today. The user approach is at least as old as the Mobility Study of how managers become chiefs. It is common to achievement-driven people. For example, you do not need to understand muscle reflex action to walk or be a psychologist to work with people or how MRI works to spot tumors or how a computer works in order to get on the Internet. You just need to know enough to work whatever you are doing. Similarly, many managers do not believe they have to understand how corporations work to work them. They only have to know just enough of the sphere in which they manage. Anything else they will pick from any source that happens to be available. In effect, they browse rather than map their corporate environments.

User-type minds attempt to make up for their shallow corporate sense by latching onto the popular lexicon of the day. They join the old game of making the new ideas familiar and familiar ideas new. Often they cannot be taken seriously because they do not know what half of their words mean and they do not mean the other half.

Corporate sense has always been a rare commodity. As one master said, "Show me someone who has been to the county fair and knows how to avoid stepping in the doo-doo and coming home with smelly shoes, and I will find my successor." Metaphors aside, you have to have a keen sense of corporate ways or you will not be able to move in and around difficult and conflicting situations. You will continually lose your room to maneuver and bring discredit to your superior's judgment about your smartness. You may be a superior's delight in the sense that if you stick to what you know, you will produce reliable results. But you are not the material that masters look for to sustain themselves at higher levels. You simply are not a good enough observer of the ways of corporate life. You lack the wits to be crucial to your superior in spite of your ambitions to put your superior's career first. You have the correct perspective, but your words are powerless because your wits are shallow. If you cannot be smart enough, at least be a smart superior and avoid becoming an ersatz subordinate. Many managers eschew the crucial subordinate role because it is demeaning. Often the real reason is they simply are not smart enough. Smart people cannot help being smart with their superiors or anybody with whom they may become connected.

There are other reasons that the rule that climbers help climbers to climb may not be commonly or effectively practiced. There are too many people who are greedy, immature, or mentally hobbled to take wise advantage of the implied reciprocity in the climbers' rule, which is why masters stand out so well. Masters demonstrate ideal subordination without having to be encouraged. Their mind is on the ready, including anticipating the needs of their superiors. Their sense of priority tells them where to place their best wits and skills for the most telling effects. Thus, masters avoid becoming gofers. Because of their contributions above and beyond the call of managing well their staffs, they make it advantageous for their superiors to pull them up at promotion time. They are simply too valuable to be ignored.

High achievers are more common than subordinates who have keen corporate senses. There are many ambitious but ignorant climbers out there who succumb to the pressure to excel at managing and who have little else to offer their superiors. They do not have the wits to aggressively manager their own careers, let alone help superiors with theirs.

So what is your perspective? Does your mind serve your superior half of the time or half serve your superior all the time? You need dedication to be an ideal subordinate. That is the price of a ticket on the fast route. If you are always watching out for number one, you will not be able to gain the judgments to assure that, compared to peers and other contestants, you are propitiously positioned and sequenced when vacancies and promotions occur.

Granted the climbers' rules depend upon a lot of ifs, but not as many as those that you must cope with if you lack the smarts to be a vital influence in helping your superiors devise strategies and moves to protect and enhance their opportunity to advance. What better do you have to offer them if you already excel as a superior to your subordinates?

When do you start to climb smartly? There is a difference between dumb and stupid. Dumb is ignorance and stupid is ignorance about being dumb. Smart is to be neither.

11
BYPASSING LEVELS

You will eventually become a corporate vice-president two levels below the chief operating officer, your sponsor. This scenario opens when you and a peer are aggressive competitors as the preferred subordinates of the division vice-president. The latter offers you a major add-on assignment that will include working closely with the division general manager and several managers in other departments who outrank you as well. Your peer continues to give you advice, which in no small way contributes to the success of the project. A year later you are promoted two levels ahead to replace the general manager. As the division president, the division vice-president is now your direct report. Two years later, as a freshly minted corporate vice-president you pull up the division vice-president to be closer to you. Subsequently, this new division president brings up your former peer whom you beat out for the major assignment, completing a lineup of capable and trustworthy members. You are forming another lineup from one of your six other direct reports, but it may never be more favored than your present and most senior lineup. But you cannot tell. People surprise you.

One day you ask your former division vice-president why you were selected over your peer for such a powerful opportunity. The former superior draws a thin line across a sheet of paper with a pencil and writes, "edge." It oftentimes takes just a thin margin of difference to separate winners from losers. Judgments concerning promotions, promotable, and promotability are often hair-thin. Not even masters overwhelm their opponents. The fine edge is not simply a matter of difference in skills. Climbing is a game of wits. Nowhere is this fact more demonstrable than on the fast route to the top. Small differences in wits can make for big advancements. Big advancements include skipping a level or two ahead of managers who outrank you. You may be on the fast route because you have quick promotions but for masters fast also means to jump up a couple of levels. In fact, masters seldom do not leapfrog a time or two in their ascents to the top.

Now about the general manager whose vacant position you filled when you jumped over the division vice-president. It was this division president who used the vice-president as a proxy to select you for the major assignment. This GM eventually moved up to chief operating officer with still two levels above you and in line to become the next chief executive officer. You have a lineup of potential successors that the COO is depending upon to fill key vacancies when the next series of promotions occurs. But the COO has acquired also at least one other lineup. The outcome is never certain when lineups compete with lineups.

In between you and the COO is a group vice-president who the COO inherited during a bypass promotion but who is ineligible for the COO position because of imminent retirement. The informal responsibility of the group vice-president is to "mother hen" the COO's lineup. In effect, the GVP becomes the acting lead member of your lineup and two other lineups that the COO has developed. But your lineup is the oldest and most proven. You work very closely with the GVP to show proof that you can work with the COO. You know that relationships count and comfort levels are often the deciding edge.

The COO becomes CEO and you leapfrog the GVP position to become the next COO with your lineup in tow and a couple of other crucial subordinates. Four years later you succeed the CEO. Your successor apparent, however, is not your former division vice-president, who served as your and your peer's superior, but a lead member of a more recently formed lineup who has a better sense of how to make things work at higher levels. As usual, it is a close call, with the edge favoring a crucial subordinate with more corporate sense. In less than ten years, you move from two levels below the division manager to the top of the corporation. At forty-two years of age, you number among the master climbers who sparsely dot the business landscape.

After completing an eight-year hitch as CEO, you are asked to describe what it takes to go from the bottom to the top. After exhausting your first sessions with the usual management language that gives credit to your noteworthy achievements and their impact upon the business of the corporation, the second set of sessions gets to the wits of climbing. The word "opportunity" continually flows out of your mouth as though it were what climbing is all about. And it nearly is. You recall the major assignment that precipitated your sequence of promotions, including two instances where you leapfrogged the level above. Bypassing and opportunity are not coincidentally related. You cannot be on the fast route without opportunities that allow bypassing. Even slower routes call for opportunities to maintain promotions.

The bypassing maneuver comprises a set of moves that involves discovery. By chance, investigation, or experience, powerful superiors become aware of your achievements, particularly the smartness and crispness of your moves to attain them. While powerful superiors are two levels above you, your immediate superior is vital to your gaining this advantage. If smart, your superior will help you. Fast climbers make more vacancies for promotions than slow climbers. Masters are more apt to move up former superiors with whom they are familiar. The study of the staffs that masters assemble at each level of their ascent shows at least one and two former superiors. Climbers climb together.

For purposes of gaining promotability, there are three types of opportunity. One is to prove yourself equal to your special assignment. The second is to prove yourself superior to your peers, and the third is to prove yourself equal to your superiors. Masters consider the latter opportunity to be of the first order. A promotion is more likely if your moves portend the smarts expected at the higher levels. The rule is that to become a superior you must act as a superior.

In order to be proven authoritatively equal to your superior, your work must be seen eventually by extended superiors. Such observable performance is called "exposure." Your superior assigns you an opportunity that requires you to work with your extended superiors above your lineup. The ultimate exposure is when powerful extended superiors value your performance because of the advantages they gain by it. You have been discovered by people beyond your lineup, and you showcase your immediate superior in a favorable light, whose initial discovery of you has been confirmed at higher levels.

However, you will not likely be given first-order opportunities if you are not trustworthy. The members of the lineup are confident that you will continue to make all the smart moves at higher levels that you made in the past. They trust that you will not act foolishly as to bring discredit to their judgments. If you do, you hurt their future as well. Foolish moves represent judgments that your behavior is all too representative of your pay grade or level of responsibility. To prove yourself equal to your superiors, your moves must reflect wits equal or better than theirs. One way to gain elevated wits is to be given opportunities normally accorded your immediate superior. But you may not be granted these opportunities if your superior does not believe you are smart enough to make the most of them. The starting point of being discovered is to show that you may hold your own with your superior.

Obtaining sponsorship is more difficult the higher the extended superior. What usually happens is that someone closer to your lineup will be asked to give you a try. Usually it is your superior who has standing akin to a member of a higher lineup. The superior may be wise enough to know that you may be discovered to be good enough that extended superiors may want to pull you up to them. This possibility is no threat if your superior understands it, has received the benefits of a lineup, and may have already leapfrogged. In such case, the superior, being a dedicated climber, understands the climbers' rule: People climb fastest who climb together.

Suppose you do succeed with this opportunity and are given additional opportunities to prove yourself further. As a consequence of doing them well and believing that they have discovered a real find, these extended superiors may proceed to give you even more quality exposure. They may place you on important committees or projects that span several levels of superiors or give you special add-on assignments to your present position. These extended superiors may even augment your staff with special assistance or completely remove you from regular responsibilities and place you on loan to them with, of course, permission and support from your immediate superior. After a while, your extended superiors conclude that you might as well be promoted. You are practically doing work at that level anyhow or something comparable.

Of course, you may appear to leave your superior in the lurch, but what lineup would not want another pair of ears and eyes to spot how corporations work at extended levels of the hierarchy. Sharing of information and ideas among the members of the lineup allows sharper perspective of what is valued at higher levels. Your lineup gets secondary visibility.

Because of your special opportunities, you acquire heady amounts of power with people above or outside your sphere of authority. Also, you have become uncommonly mobile, as though transported into another world. In this different environment, you must make decisions that will test your mobile mind, including what old ideas and skills are not useful, what different or new ideas and skills are necessary. Then you must make the proper separations and attachments in a timely and appropriate fashion to exploit quickly your power to prove yourself. You must do well with whatever regular assignments you have remaining and with those opportunities with extended superiors. You will mentally move back and forth, in and out of these two levels of existence. Mobility allows you to be in two places at once. You can be at one level and think about the other level, and if you leapfrog two levels because an extended superior wants you closer, you must let go of those ways of thinking that are appropriate at the lower levels and attach to those at higher levels. Opportunities are both cause and effect of mobility.

In short, you need the power of mobility to acquire quickly what it takes to perform among people who outrank you and drop all the other stuff no matter how valuable it was to past performances.

From these opportunities, you may gain an additional, valuable benefit; it is *visibility*. Because your assignments span several levels of superiors, you are able to see higher authorities, to note how they think, how they relate, what they value regarding performance, and what they credit toward promotability, etcetera. You will become aware of them, not simply as they occasionally drop down to appear before you, but how they appear to you at their work level. This visibility has inestimable value. For one thing, it allows for vision, which is the acute sense of the possible. You see opportunities to nominate yourself or which you will bring into your lineup, or which you may refer to extended superiors. All of which are possible because you gain exposure and visibility to exploit opportunities normally unseeable or unavailable to others.

If you have several highly valued performances in a short period of time, you gain *momentum*. Momentum allows you to appear more promotable than if you had the same performances over a longer period of time. Several opportunities sequenced at the right time can maintain your momentum. Superiors want to take advantage of your momentum. It indicates that you have a pattern of quick, effective moves and accomplishments. They want those presumed wits and skills. Speed and quality are important values. So you may have your momentum expedited.

If by now, you are not sure that you are on the fast route to the top, you must be completely blind, and if you are not aware sufficiently of what is happening to you, arrestment of momentum is likely to be imminent. Speed will not tolerate anything less than acute awareness, both local and distant.

Of course, you also make sure your lead superior wins, who would like to receive credit for finding and developing a manager crucial to extended superiors. All the words spoken or written by members of your lineup about your exceptional performance will never be as loud or credible as the actual deeds made under the klieg lights of high exposure and visibility.

Furthermore, extended superiors will see something far more important than your performances. They observe firsthand your wits to move smartly in higher circles. It is not performance that you carry forward; it is smartness. While managers scramble for positions, climbers seek opportunities. While managers seek credit towards achievement, masters build the wits needed to enhance their promotability.

You may be concerned about passing over your lead superior to a higher position. You may ask, is not that a betrayal of the relationship of assistance your lineup has provided? Is such a move abandonment and disloyalty? I have not seen such allegiance to a lineup that has for its purpose getting promotions since I discovered master climbers in the 1950s. The mistake is to confuse loyal with trustworthy. Two evil people may trust each other even though they are avowedly disloyal to each other. Of course, I am not talking about rank immorality because lineups are formed to be self-serving, as is true of business. You are invited into a lineup because you are trusted to act smartly as long as you are in it. You are not expected to compromise your ambitions. Any member expects to accept any chance to get ahead. After all, the lead superior may suddenly leave for another company or a subordinate may accept a poacher's invitation to join another triplet or lineup in another part of the company. Masters will reach down and pull up a former superior even if it means passing over more recent superiors or subordinates.

If members of a lineup cannot see the future advantage of using each other to go to a higher level faster, they lack the wits to form or stay in them. The lineup prospers partly because by getting one of their members placed at higher levels, the other members have a "cap in Rome" to whom they may go for representation, support, and counsel. Yes, it takes a degree of emotional maturity for members of the lineup to assist someone's career only to have that individual succeed beyond them. Without this maturity, lineups will work.

But to live strictly by your own wits is to die prematurely. You must give in order to get. However, wits are not simply for the giving or asking. They are most apt to be shared in a relationship whose purpose is to gain mutual advantage for getting ahead. You are invited into and will remain in that relationship because you subordinate your interests to that of the superior who has formed the lineup. You cannot prove yourself equal to your superior and undercut or detract from the status of your superior at the same time. If your superior does not want you to have an opportunity, you probably will not know about it. Or your superior may use the lineup to discern what member can make the most of the opportunity. Likewise, you may visualize an opportunity for which your superior should have the first consideration. The whole idea of a lineup is that the members use each other to maximize their achievements and their advancements.

The test of a lineup's durability is how well they can support a member with an opportunity that could very well preempt their chances of advancing. A lot of this durability has to do with how well you conduct yourself. How strong is their trust and respect for you? How much have you given to them? "Takers-only" do not get opportunities. More importantly, how much have you been a catalyst for closing ranks and becoming a tight-knit group? How much have you made possible the easy flow of the exchange of wisdom? Have you helped to make it easy for the members to offer their very best?

When members of a lineup combine wits to find and exploit ideas that are potential opportunities, a sense of mutual dependency develops, forming the sinews of strength and stability. If extended superiors realize the productivity of this informal organization that formally does not exist, few among them would not want to use this lineup or any member of it, even if a member may eventually leapfrog others to become a member of an extended lineup.

You must become discovered by extended superiors, or you will prove yourself equal only to your superior and go as far as your immediate superior will go. Of course, you will try to be the ideal subordinate to your immediate superior but your efforts are not limited to one superior. You may practice good subordination to extended superiors when the opportunity becomes available.

Far-fetched, you say? Not any more than anybody reaching the point of the corporation, let alone getting there in record time. How do you think masters make fast climbers? Take one position at a time, go upwards no faster than their immediate superior? Why do masters who become chiefs reach for people they leave behind to become their officers if it is not to maintain and enhance their advancements?

Business is no more rational than it needs to be. People are not in lock step to a hierarchical order permanently. If superiors can determine your fate, you can determine theirs. If business can use you for its best interests, then it is no less wise or moral for you to use business for your best interests. Why not conceive of opportunities bigger than your superior's capability? Why not intentionally go for high degrees of exposure and visibility? And yes, you may gain the support of your immediate superior to prove yourself equal to extended superiors. Masters do this all the time. It takes clever wits.

Later, when you call former superiors and subordinates to join you at higher levels, you may be sure of their trust and respect to practice crucial subordination. As long as they are members of your lineup, they will serve the interests of the lineup ahead of their own. For these reasons, it is valuable that lineups help members to leapfrog. It is better to have one of their own upstairs than to be stuck with a superior whose promotability is at best questionable or at worst nil.

Now let us return to the point where you are a direct report to the division vice-president. You will benefit from several lineups. But what has not been said is where your first major opportunity originated. You now know your division vice-president authorized it with the urging of the general manager. But it never originated with either of them. You thought of the opportunity, suggested it to your vice-president who you expected would manage it. The VP took it to the GM, and the three of you discussed it. Later your vice-president gave you the GM's decision. Then a four-way discussion occurred involving your peer so that both of you may continue to counsel and advise each other about strategies and moves regarding responsibilities and opportunities. Your peer will be given a few opportunities but not with the equality of exposure and visibility of your first major assignment.

The point is that the peer did not extend assistance because of unselfish motives, nor was your assistance given unconditionally. Both of you knew that your best chance of getting a promotion was to help rather than fight each other. Your moves more or less were to compete to cooperate and cooperate to compete. The GM understood how adroitly the two of you helped the GM drive the business through the VP position, while at the same time each of you rose to the status of crucial subordination. If the peer had come up with a major opportunity that could position the division better in the eyes of corporate staff, the consequences might have been different. But your visualizing how a problem that plagued several levels could be isolated and resolved gave you the edge.

Opportunity makes subordinates crucial to their superiors and, at the same time, helps to prove themselves equal to their superiors. You do not wait for opportunities to fall into your lap. You aggressively seek them out. By such diligence in the service of your superiors, you best serve yourself.

For all of your achievements and credits for promotability, one more made at the right time essentially exploded into a series of spectacular advancements. Your case is not uncommon among masters. It illustrates how a few achievements may generate more than their share of advancements, which is exactly what the fast route is all about.

INTERMISSION: A QUIZ OF YOUR CLIMBING SMARTS

You may benefit if you stop reading for a moment and take a short quiz. Ask yourself the climber's questions. What will you do if you suspect that your achievements, no matter how splendid, are insufficient to compete to gain a promotion beyond the position ahead? What will it take to get two or more promotions?

You need not be concerned with this question if you do not have the ambition strong enough to want to advance as quickly as possible and if, in your judgment, your achievements have already merited sufficient advancements and will likely continue to in the future. Do not make yourself unhappy. Rare are managers who live in harmony with their corporations. Besides, if you really are comfortable, it will take more pain to make you unhappy than pleasure to increase your happiness.

But if you find yourself working harder and giving more to your business and getting less in return, call time out to examine what you need to do differently from what you have done in the past. Reach into the walls of your mind and separate out the humbug that clouds your vision, diffuses your focus, and infects your self-confidence. Reformulate a new perspective using different ideas that may be related to managing but in practice work out to have better consequences for climbing.

Masters maintain that corporations create their own intellect. What they mean is that the formal, informal, and silent ways of their corporations help to frame and predispose their minds to form their wits to manage and to climb. So take care to include your corporation's unique ways, especially those that allow you to distinguish between getting one promotion and a progression of advancements. Of course, implied in a progression is what it takes to gain any one promotion. But gaining one promotion will not likely produce a series of them. If you want just one more promotion, forget about changing your perspective. Masters offer you little help. Because, you see, their wits are not aimed at the position ahead but what it takes to sustain the whole trip or substantial sectors between checkpoints.

In a way, you have already put yourself under test. Having read the first half of this book have you shown the mobility to separate from old ideas and attach to new? What ideas seek control of your mind? If you chose to take this quiz, list the old and new ideas. Self-examination is hard work. It means giving up friendly ideas for which you have much affection. As they say, love is blind. If you like what you see, it is probably because you see what you like. So challenge yourself to see things for what they are rather than what you believe they should be. Be clinical and suspend judgment until your diagnosis has been completed.

Most of the climbers' rules have already been insinuated in previous chapters and will be more directly exposed and described in the following chapters. After the concluding chapter, give yourself the same quiz. How different are your answers as a consequence of reading the last half of the book? You have turned pages, but have you turned over your mind as well? In short, what new or different ideas have replaced old ideas, and how much credibility are you prepared to give them for gaining a new perspective about climbing?

The ideas of the masters usually challenge people who assume responsibility for their careers, while they seek quick fixes from others less qualified than they to diagnose and prescribe what it takes to get ahead. In contrast, the masters know. They have been there, there at the top and there where you are now. They too recalibrate several times what it takes before they confidently move ahead. When you are ready, read on. Masters will stay with you until the end.

12

THE PROMOTABLE MANAGER

Hitch your wagon securely to a strong horse to stay the trip. On the farm, I knew what this adage meant, but what about climbing is comparable to a strong horse, and how securely do you hitch yourself. At the start of your career your superior may not be promotable and you may not be an ideal subordinate. But how would you know the strength of your superior to draw a promotion and to pull you along and for what distance? You will be faced with this uncertainty during your entire climb unless you figure out the difference between promotion, promotable, and promotability.

Most superiors are honest, but they are also private about their future potential and often they are mistaken. Others pretend to be promotable when, in fact, they are not. In any case, if you are going to invest in a superior for any length of time, you'd better make a good guess as to the actual terms and potential returns.

The higher you go, the more difficult to diagnose the promotability of superiors and the greater the stakes for being right or wrong. Your best bet is to assume your superiors are not promotable, and then prove it otherwise. The reason is that more than half of all superiors are not promotable and that many or more of their managers are not promotable, and half of those who are promotable have at most one more promotion coming. If there is a way to predict before the fact, it is the quality of their present or previous promotions. So the questions become, how do you identify the quality of promotions, and what is the price for being wrong?

Managers left behind in the wakes of master climbers illustrate the penalty of misidentifying promotable superiors. They usually misidentify two features; the power of masters to sustain their fast climbs and their power to pull others up with them, immediately or later. Of course, had those "passed over" followed the moves of ideal subordination, their careers may have turned out differently.

They most likely thought that the young whippersnappers would fall flat, and not a few hoped they would, and some obsequiously encouraged it. But promotability of masters is difficult for anyone to read. They play it down and disguise their ambitions. They seldom talk about their past accomplishments or what they know concerning vacancies and prospective moves and movements of people. They practice the informal rule of climbers; never talk about what it takes to climb. Masters keep their wits private except with members of their lineups.

Managers who stand by as masters pass them make a first-order mistake, they are not adequately aware of the signs of promotable. Also, they make a second-order mistake; they ineffectually serve promotable superiors. These two mistakes account for plenty of reasons to be left behind.

In a world that is governed by reality sense, the lack of wit is a greater deficiency than the lack of skill. People do the wrong things because they believe they are doing the right things. They do not know the right things to do because they have a deficiency in knowing what works. This lack of corporate sense is seen every day among people who hitch up with unpromotable superiors who are going nowhere, and neither may know it. Their tight connections prepare them to move in unison with their unpromotable superiors. Of course, these managers are disappointed when they discover their mistake, but not all is lost. They have acquired experience that may serve them well with future superiors for whom ideal subordination has a high payoff. Since many managerial positions turn over every two years or less and new ones are created or replace old, climbers continually have chances of drawing promotable superiors.

Masters may not be as promotable as their fast climbs make them out to be. They often benefit from the luck of the draw, which is to be assigned to superiors who are promotable. While fortune cannot be predicted, it tends to smile on fast climbers at one of three checkpoints, when made first-level manager, when nearing division management, and when elected corporate officer. Climbers will disproportionately benefit, whether lucky or not, when they draw promotable superiors at each of the points providing they make solid connections with them.

However, these levels are also chokepoints because they take the heaviest toll on climbers. As has been indicated, less than 50 percent of first-level managers ever get another promotion, as herein defined. Less than 20 percent of direct reports of division of management become division or subsidiary heads, and less than 10 percent of division or subsidiary managers become corporate officers (i.e., elected by the board). The faster you get through each of these chokepoints, the less likely your ascents will be interrupted. The more promotable your superior, the better the chance of getting a pull up.

The word "promotion" means to go forward, to advance toward a higher level, to close the gap between where one is and where one wants to go. Promotable means to be worthy of an immediate promotion. Promotability is the ability to gain future promotions. Each of these ideas represents judgments. Promotability is the skill to win favorable judgments about promotions and promotable. The *complete climber* benefits from quality promotions, is judged worthy of higher responsibilities, and knows how to win favorable judgments about the value of performances and credits toward staying promotable. By such practices, high promotability means managers have secured a long-term future or at least a future beyond the position ahead. They make it is easy for their superiors to sell their promotions to extended superiors.

If you get hitched to a complete climber, you have the least risk of being left behind. Because masters' personalities are usually centered upon mobility with momentum as their ideal, they dread the thought of staying long in a position and being left behind. For them, arrestment is akin to premature death; it happens but not to them. For this reason they are probably the most aggressive at developing relationships to make it advantageous for superiors and subordinates to support their careers.

Of course, the words "*complete climber*" are mine, but the ideas are inferred from the practices of masters. They excel at winning judgments favorable to enhancing their promotability. They usually know how to make their presence at any time appear to be bigger than their accomplishments. They effuse competency and confidence.

Climbers sometimes attempt to utilize the Barbie-Doll effect. The doll is practically given away, but the clothes cost a bundle. Many ambitious people know how to dress up their results to make them appear more valuable than their actual contributions to business. They even can cause their mistakes to be discounted. But if the *clothes* do not match the size of the doll, their machinations may become transparent. As some masters have learned the hard way, if you exaggerate in order to enhance your promotability, you may appear to exaggerate in other ways as well and lose all credibility. Masters may become hitched to practitioners of the Barbie-Doll effect. What at first seems to be a gifted superior turns out to be a practitioner of magnificent doo-doo.

To assess the various kinds of promotions, you first need to be aware of the idea of *stretch*. Stretch means to become extended by exertion or skill. You must work harder or smarter or both. The difficulty is of the magnitude that exceeds your available resources. You must learn new wits and skills or apply creatively and ingeniously old capabilities or both. It is not difficult to see a superior with a stretch promotion, what with the obvious total concentration and effort required.

Stretch is integral to a developmental promotion, the success of which brings an irreversible experience. You will never be the same again. For example, once you learn to read you cannot return to the status of a nonreader. Hence, a developmental assignment or promotion stretches you out of your usual mode of managing. Your change is visible to those who knew you before and after.

Opportunities to prove yourself superior to your peers or equal to your superiors may be developmental regardless of how much they may lead to advancements. Sponsors may arrange a series of promotions or opportunities in the present position to develop your resources to ensure success at higher levels. Such a sponsor may be several levels above with a keen eye toward assessing talent. Or the lead member of your lineup, with more direct experience forecasting your future capabilities, may sponsor you.

Talent is your potential for acquiring a skill. The proof of your talent, say for reading, is your level of skill. If you are developmental, it may be you are judged to have a large reserve of unused talent. This practical distinction between talent and skill allows a sponsor to promote you not solely because of your skill but, also, because of your personal talent. Thus, you may be promotable because higher responsibilities will make better use of your talent. You have proved to be such a fast learner that there appears no limit to how far you can go. However, when talent and skill are comparable, little room is left for growth. You may be left behind even though your record of performance is exemplary.

Knowing your large reserve of talent, your sponsor may decide to test it by giving you a developmental promotion. In fact, it is a make-or-break opportunity to prove yourself equal to superiors. Sometimes this stretch promotion may not be your next promotion but one thereafter. Your sponsor wants first to position you properly. You must take care not to be misled by this preliminary promotion, as it may not seem to carry much value either to you or your business. It is simply a takeoff point from which the rest of your career may soon ensue.

There is a plausible but fallacious idea that people move up to their highest level of incompetence. It is not their lack of competency, as some would prefer to believe. People are successfully promoted into developmental positions for which they lack ready skill. What stalls their careers is the lack of self-confidence. They lose the inner strength to face courageously their difficulties and exploit wisely their options and appropriate moves. The fear of mistakes causes them to make mistakes. Both talent and skill become immobilized.

Self-confident managers know what they do not know and know how to get what they need and are not easily dissuaded because of the degree of difficulty. The more the stretch, the greater the challenge. For this reason their self-confidence helps to extract from superiors the judgment that they are promotable. This is the value of lineups. Members may more intimately assess their levels of confidence and competency and helps to raise them when necessary.

A stretch position or opportunity may not be your superior's intention. It may occur because of a faulty assessment of the requirements of the assignment and your talents or skills. This mismatch may occur because of rush to judgment or inability to size up people accurately. Nevertheless, as in all too many cases, your difficulties may be attributed to you rather than your superior. In this case, the value of the assignment when finally performed successfully will augur fewer credits toward promotability than the achievement merits. Exertion, however extraordinary, is no substitute for clever moves that reflect superior wits and skills. Still, you may work your way out of the jam and hope that your improved skills and confidence will have a salutary effect upon your future worth.

Masters will experience several developmental promotions, each of which stretches their available and latent resources. Their climbs are made by these stretches. Because of enhanced promotability, they either gain access to lineups or become confirmed members of them, with the lead member their likely sponsor.

But masters, as well as climbers, experience or observe other types of promotions that may have developmental powers to a lesser degree. One such promotion is a *performance* type. Performance promotion means execution of a plan or opportunity for producing specific results. An existing position may be modified or a new one created, with your capabilities in mind. You are considered the perfect candidate for the job. Depending upon the critical value of the performance to the superior, you may be accorded an unusual amount of discretionary judgment by which to optimize your results. Your peers will be alerted, and their cooperation requested to a degree that leaves no doubt as to the value of your position or opportunity. This promotion is also a potential fulcrum for leveraging higher responsibilities.

Performance-type promotions are easy to detect. Your background and record of achievements appear perfectly matched. It is a closed-ended assignment with precise time frame and well formulated objective. It is this promotion from which the slogan is formed, "results count." In contrast, developmental promotion usually has an identifiable problem that requires your formulating an objective and a plan for a solution. It is more open-ended. That is part of its stretch.

While the end result to be achieved drives a performance promotion, the known skills of a manager drives a *functional* promotion. You have skills that are not being optimally used. This promotion is not expected to be a stretch opportunity. Your skills are such that you need little preparation in the arrival stage to get to the performance phase of the APD triad (arrival, performance, departure). One of the values you display is mobility. You can instantly drop what you are doing to move smartly in a different environment.

Mobility is not to be underestimated as a valuable quality for all promotions. Masters call this being at the "ready," prepared mentally and physically to pick up and go without hesitation or regard for what is left behind. When you consider the number of managers who have problems departing from their jobs and arriving expeditiously in new positions, managers on the ready are invaluable. They allow superiors to move managers around to gain the optimal mix of talent and skill.

In this regard, a functional promotion serves a greater purpose than the move itself. It primarily serves the superior's larger responsibility of moving talent and skill into key positions to better drive the business. When mistakes are made, they are not about assessing your capability, which is fairly well known, but unrealistically assessing the new responsibility. Nevertheless, the need to balance the workload is detectable. You know whether you are working below your skills or others are in over their heads. A functional promotion does not carry the weight of a developmental or performance promotion. It is better than no promotion, but it is not a sign of how promotable you are beyond your new position. Still many managers misread this promotion. The vacancy is not created to position you for higher responsibilities or to help you prove yourself superior to your peers or equal to your superiors. You are not considered to be a preferred subordinate or potential successor. In this restructuring move, others may have received developmental and performance promotions or assignments, but you are moved up simply because you have ready-made skills to do the job. Nothing else should be read into the move. Of course, you should not let this fortune determine your fate. You can use this new position to revitalize your career. Future chiefs have catapulted from functional promotions.

Another type is an *availability* promotion. It is not that you are loitering in the hallway and your boss steps out and gives you a promotion on the fly. "*Available*" means that you are present for immediate use. In this sense you may be on the "ready," but what you are promoted to is not on the upper end of your superior's scale of valuable responsibilities. It is not a development, performance, or functional promotion. You may not be the ideal candidate, but for this position, no ideal candidate is needed. You may not even be the best available. More qualified candidates may not be available because they are so perfectly matched to their present jobs that superiors cannot afford to forego such productivity. In fact, you may be the least worst, but you have the necessary training and experiences that watchful superiors may find acceptable. The key word, "*acceptable*," contrasts with "*ideal*" that fits performance promotions. Perhaps others may be equally qualified, but you may have been pressing your superiors for a promotion and so the superior accepts your "readiness." In almost all availability promotions, you are not expected to expand the position. In fact, your superiors may drop off parts or assign them to other people or replace some of them by lesser responsibilities. Unlike functional promotions, no vacancies are created to balance workloads. The skills required are mundane and interchangeable with others that may be used at lower levels.

Your new position may close the gap between you and your checkpoint, but it does not assist your superior's major responsibilities or your peers. In other words, the work has to be done, but it is not a fulcrum for leveraging higher responsibilities. You may not be considered before or after to be promotable material. The nature of this promotion is not difficult to detect. It is just difficult to swallow. It is not exactly a tribute to your self-regard. For this reason, you may elevate the promotion in your mind to be more valuable than it really is.

Often confused with availability promotions are *reward* promotions. You have done such an outstanding job that you are rewarded with a higher responsibility. It may be a matter of fairness or equity. Superiors may want to show managers that hard work and honest diligence on their behalf should pay off. Notice the wording, "on their behalf." They pay for loyalty for such managers not to cross them or take advantage of them in a scuffle or when they are down. This favoritism smacks of ideal subordination, except there is no preponderance of ingenuity directed towards advancing the interests of the superior's career. In this sense, a reward promotion is largely a scheme to protect the rear of the superior.

In other words, a reward promotion has no more value than the potential to protect the position, person, and status of the superior. Reward promotees seldom augur respect in their own right. To satisfy the superior, their performances need only be acceptable because it is their loyalty that is bought and paid for by the promotion. In fact, superiors who indulge in reward promotions are apt to take credit for the manager's achievement while they muffle and discount the latter's malperformances. Extended superiors have a difficult time discerning the manager's true accomplishments and wonder at the few reported blemishes. Why? Because the most adroit at protecting the superior is chosen for reasons dressed up to serve the interests of business. However, a lineup based upon exploiting loyalty, as distinct from trustworthy, cannot be expected to compete with lineup based upon conspicuous achievements. Eventually weakness may cause favoritism to flounder. Still, climbers move up behind their superiors because of reward promotions. However, they are usually confined to staff positions.

The superiors with the weakest pulling power are those who have gotten to where they are with availability and reward promotions. They are the dromedaries with more motion than forward movement. All corporations have them, and they are more numerous than their descriptions herein suggest. As their superiors, masters are less concerned about what to do with them than to see them for what they are. Then if they hitch their wagons to them, they know the limitation of their connections. It is overestimating what superiors can do that needlessly fritters away career time and delays, assuming other career options.

The superiors with the most potential pulling power have gotten performance or developmental promotions. They need help and will seek it from the most competent sources in order to live up to the highest expectations of their superiors. Because members of a lineup know that the difficult developmental and performance assignments are dependent upon their seeing a few ways to make them less difficult, they combine their wits to help each other at their respective levels. With availability and reward promotions, superiors have less need for finding and using such wits. It is an unwritten rule of masters that a subordinate may be no more crucial to a manger than the manager to the superior. The pulling power of the lead superior is magnified through and by means of the efforts of the other members of the lineup. In the framework of opportunities as herein defined, choice opportunities go to members below upon whom members above depend for their accomplishments. These opportunities may reside in present positions or outside of them and may lead to promotions, including bypassing levels or a progression of advancements.

It is important to climbers that no members of the lineup misdiagnose the stretch potential inherent in each opportunity or promotion. As in the adage "it is the unloaded gun that kills," it is the seemingly easy assignment that stalls and destroys careers.

The point of this analysis of types of promotion is to describe the possible varieties of superiors that climbers must be prepared to work for. Also, it is important that climbers diagnose their own types of promotion. To be frank, most managers do not give a hoot for the fine distinctions of promotions and promotability. Some are fatalists, believing they cannot do much about their superiors in the first place. They lack the wits to diagnose their superiors and themselves accurately enough to devise moves to improve their superior's promotability or get relief from the uncertainties and vagaries of superiors with available or reward promotions.

Also, they may be unaware to visualize opportunities to prove themselves better than either their peers or superiors and how such moves may attract the attention of extended superiors. Instead, they simply attempt to do well with what they are expected. They usually have a survival perspective, where the smartest learn to perform just enough to ensure their security. In other words, they lack the corporate sense of the subtle ways their corporations treat promotions, promotable, and promotability.

In contrast to the survivor's mind is the master's. Their perspective directs attention to the following questions, which are prompted by wanting to know just what they are up against that may impede their ascents. You might say that their questions serve as a magnifying glass to bring up close the not-so-apparent nuances that otherwise escape scrutiny.

When you think of a promotable manager, what do you see, an individual or a relationship? Are you aware that the recent promotion of your superior may bring career-limiting moves for both of you, or that your new superior is on a developmental assignment and that you may be required to put your own career on the line and that of your subordinates? Are you prepared to accept the risks of failing and falling with your superior? Or are you prepared to serve but avoid becoming tightly connected to your superior? Will you avoid failure at the cost of gaining promotions?

What quality of promotion have you received lately? Is it one that you got because you were most available? Does your recent promotion require few additional skills? Is your promotion key to driving the business or secondary? Do you feel you are being parked in a position to make room for someone to pass you up or as preliminary to a more important position?

Do your moves invite confidential discussions with your superior about the latter's promotability? Do your moves show support for your superior's promotability? How well do your moves open up the superior to receive your advice? Do you seek opportunities for improving your superior's promotability or your own? How much exposure and visibility do you or your superior have? Does your superior attempt to block your exposure and visibility? How sure are you that your superior is passing to extended superiors credit for your achievements? What is your standing with extended superiors?

Do you understand the symptoms of momentum? How many fast promotions have you or your superior had in the past? Did they occur with one superior or several? How many extended superiors have passed through your or your superior's position? Lastly, is your superior worth saving? Does your superior consider you worth saving? Is it possible that both of you are unpromotable or, at best, eligible for availability or reward promotions?

These questions are the most predominant in the minds of managers with a master's perspective. The ideas circulate in their minds and are available at each level of their ascents to decipher the formal, informal, and silent ways that affect climbing.

So give ideas of promotion, promotable, and promotability their due respect. Hopefully you will not be one of those managers that masters at the point look back and say, "You could have helped me, but you failed to see what was in your own best interests."

13
THE RIGHT MOVES

The first rule of climbing is to make it advantageous for your superiors to promote you. The second rule is to make it advantageous for your subordinates to succeed you. The third rule is to use relationships to make it easy to gain the advantages of rules one and two.

With your relationships intact, you are ready to prove your future worth. You are prepared to accept opportunities, make opportunities, and exploit opportunities. You estimate the benefits and risks. Get on the right side of an opportunity and your future opportunities multiply. Get on the wrong side and you have trouble. Stay on the sidelines and the action passes you by. If you snooze, you lose.

These vagaries of corporate life place a premium upon acute awareness. Ambition without awareness is dangerously myopic. Awareness without ambition is undisciplined and erratic. Of course, being aware is not the same as being in control, but the former must precede the latter.

With your corporate sense, you recalibrate the power of this or that opportunity to gain advancement for you or your superior. Your record to date of exploiting the right opportunities speaks well for your promotability. You expect and await another promotion to gain or continue your momentum.

Your promotions usually come sooner rather than later than expected. But this time, for some strange reason, the usual cues of your imminent departure from your present position are not forthcoming. You are at the ready, mentally prepared for higher responsibilities. The silence seems deafening; the duration seems forever. You are six months overdue an expected promotion. Something has gone amiss. You wonder but dare not ask. With the momentum you have gained, one does not display any variety or lack of self-confidence. But you remain optimistic that, if you play your cards right, you could be a future chief in the making. So what is this thing called "stalled momentum" all about?

You are puzzled because in spite of your alertness, you must have missed something vital at this point in your career. What you may not realize is that your very success has become suspect. You have momentum because of good exposure from three very quick and noteworthy promotions. However, now your superiors have to be certain that your record of performance is sustainable. One more promotion on the heels of several others may make your progression difficult to stop and embarrassing to your superiors if you fail. Your extensive exposure will reflect badly, not only upon those who promoted you in rapid-fire order, but also upon the competency of extended superiors. They may fear that you may be what they call a three-seat performer. You may be good for several promotions, and then it is downhill from there on.

A time comes in many managers' careers when everything falls into place. By skill or circumstance, you produce some very enviable and valuable contributions to your superiors and to the business. It appears that you are an exceptional manager. Superiors are quick to want your skills, sometimes too quick, so they give you a promotion to see if you can work your magic at higher levels of responsibility. You do well, although the effort seems more forced than before. But your results are still admirable. So you get another promotion, your third in less than three years. Now you feel queasy, as though you are in over your head, but your ambition to succeed at all costs has been whetted and your self-confidence set to exert prodigious effort, and by dint of hard work, you finally come through as your superiors had hoped.

With this momentum, you unintentionally come to a fork in the road. Superiors have to make a judgment. Are you really as good as your record of performances? Can you keep this speed up? They have already advanced you at the expense of other managers. But your next promotion will pass over some managers who have stronger records of performance. Are you worth losing their good will, frustrating their ambitions to achieve or to advance or hazard losing their services altogether?

There are all kinds of superiors out there. One set of superiors is not willing to pay the price for your continued momentum. For them it is a matter of comparable worth. They believe in growing their own stars. These superiors may already have a key player or two upon whom they can depend for their advancement, who have been with them longer and although less spectacular, they are known quantities. They developed them. A second set of superiors knows that occasionally star performers fall into their laps, and they will somehow make room for them regardless of the quality of their key performers. When properly used, these exceptional managers can substantially help drive their future advancements. Both sets of superiors know that they are no better than the people they depend upon.

A third set of superiors are disbelievers of the idea of "stars." They believe that a well-rounded staff of reliable committed managers will outperform a staff with one or several stars. A balanced, well-coordinated staff, pulling together will win every time. This third group of superiors will not even attempt to bid for wunderkinds' services. While many superiors agree with this latter perspective, it is an achievement, not an advancement approach. It puts managing as the end-all of climbing. This third group of superiors looks for managers with ambitions to achieve, who will take their chances on advancement. If the wunderkinds were working for them, they would never have gotten such fast promotions. If by chance they were assigned to them, these superiors would make sure to arrest their momentum, put them in less essential work, and cool their egos off quickly. If they have the right stuff, they will show it without throwing out of whack a finely balanced staff.

In contrast to these disbelievers in the "star" system, the other two sets of superiors are firm believers. While the first set has their lineups in hand, the second set is most apt to bid for the services of wunderkinds. The internal market for managers always exists to some extent. No superior owns a manager or has exclusive rights. All assets, including human, are the province of the corporation. Bidding is the euphemism for downright poaching. Hot items such as momentum managers are always susceptible to be taken from their superiors. Unfortunately, they may not know how to use them and will allow them to lie fallow. In any case, superiors with a climber's perspective seldom pass up an opportunity to bolster or complete their lineups.

It is obvious that you are in a predicament. Your superior believes in the "star" practice but hesitates, and you wonder. You may not know what your superior knows. Several fast promotions more often than not break managers. If it is not the third move, it will likely be the next one. No superior wants to be responsible for breaking a "star."

However, loss of momentum is not inevitable. A kind of erraticism occurs in the layout of higher responsibilities. Generally, the higher you go, the more difficult the responsibility, either because it is more wide ranging or less related to your previous experiences. But exceptions occur, such as two performance promotions that may be taken well in stride without the manager being stretched or incurring marginal self-confidence.

It is lack of self-confidence more than competency that breaks managers. Unbeknown to you, you may be perceived as being at the margin. Your superiors may not want to break you and lose your future value. They may have deliberated among themselves about their concerns but have not chosen to discuss them openly with you. So there you sit; waiting and waiting for some sign that you are on the parapet for takeoff. Undoubtedly you do not understand the unfortunate course of most momentum managers. If you did, you would realize that you have entered an entirely different arena for winning judgments. The standards of performance and promotability suddenly change for you, seemingly right underneath your nose. Perhaps you are not as alert about corporate ways as you should be. One thing for sure, you are going to learn about some of them the hard way.

First of all, to maintain your promotable status, you must show some sort of proof of endurability. Generally, superiors are very particular and masters even more so. They do not allow even one turn in their lineups without some degree of confidence of their members' trustworthiness. Of course, past performances do not always predict future performances. Because initial success does not guarantee future success, masters rely upon a more reliable basis of judgment. They look past your much-heralded achievements to note how they are made.

How smart are your moves? Do you overwhelm the objective with prodigious amounts of efforts and resources, or do your moves approximate the economy of effort rule: Use no more or less effort than necessary, leaving few unintended consequences. If your moves are sufficiently economical, such that the probability approximates coincidence that fortune is at work, you may be judged to have high future value. If you continue to delight your superiors with exceptional results based upon smart moves, you offer a more valid way for your superiors to forecast future performances. In fact, your results may occasionally be less than expected, but you may lose little credit toward promotable if the moves are smart. The belief that "results count" skews observations that high-performing managers are smart. However, it is not their results that prove smartness. No major effort can succeed without a consistent and careful focus on finding the correct, well-timed, and skillfully executed move or moves.

Managers do not do objectives, only the acts that are needed to reach the objective. Moves are acts tied together that when properly launched can initiate or reverse the course of events leading ultimately to the results expected. One well-timed move followed by others carefully sequenced has the cascading power to offset a multiplicity of errant activities. Key moves unlock the potential of a plan or program, much as keys unlock doors. The trick is to find that first right move. It cannot be your first mistake.

It is a simple idea really; moves make the climber. They are the fingerprints that certify the ingenuity of smart managers. As masters rise to become chiefs, they learn to plot wisely the minimum moves required to gain maximum leverage in critical situations. They attempt to use no more or less effort than required to perform the task, at least such is their ideal.

Of course, keeping an eye on the big picture and avoiding micro-managing require concentrating on the in-between elements, key moves. This is not easy in a mobile world that easily confuses the means and ends. Activities easily distract some managers, and objectives overly preoccupy others. In either case, efforts may become scattered, lots of motion and little direction; everyone works hard but goes nowhere important. A scatter pattern of activities is a certified formula for disaster. If managers fail to produce expected results, it is because among the myriad activities involved in a major effort, they fail to group a few of them into well-keyed moves capable of carrying more than their share of success. The lesson of managers is that while their efforts are measured by results, their wits are measured by their moves.

The scene facing all levels of climbers is often unstable or even volatile, with ever-changing markers into the future that yield few reliable pointers toward success or warnings of failure. Moves work because of the confluence of special circumstances. They depend upon the why, how, and when of each situation, which is why mobility is an art, the expression of highly individualized judgments. The making of smart moves is an eminently creative expression although elementary in nature. For this reason, the moves cannot be bottled and sold by contemporary alchemists as elixirs that magically transform climbers into promotable managers. This capability cannot be taught and still do service to the peculiar, often subtle, ways of the corporation.

This quality of smart moves is often summed up by the word "*judgment.*" As important is this skill of forming an opinion objectively and realistically in matters affecting the moves of the manager, judgment is difficult to define. One manager's judgment may be often as good as another's, which is exactly why business is filled with "Monday morning quarterbacks," why superiors retain the right to evaluate judgment of the manager, and why performance may not equate with promotability.

The augmentation or intervention to make a plan work invariably presents choices among which several moves could potentially work. If it were not so, the manager would not need judgment. The preference for one move over another leans heavily upon experience and skills acquired in similar situations. If successful results occur, these experiences and skills become reinforced. But judgment may not grow proportionately to experience, due to overreliance upon these heavily reinforced skills and experiences. This hazard is to substitute habit for judgment.

A relatively stable economy and business practices allow many experiences and skills to become transferable from one position or assignment to another. But in a mobile world of radical change, you can find yourself employing different skills and moves, risking the chance that they may be counterproductive to making the program work. So judgment is more critical as change outmodes present skills and moves and opens up the possibility of new forms of mistakes.

In general, managers do not efficiently learn from mistakes. They learn from what works better than what does not work, owing to the tendency of practical minds to fill the breach of failure quickly with effective moves. Practical minds burdened with the necessity of getting things done speedily may not take time to analyze moves any more than to conclude that they did not work. "Forget about them; move on, and don't second guess yourself" is a formula for disaster in a world that offers more opportunity to make mistakes. The effect is that managers accumulate wisdom about what to do more than what not to do. Their judgments are unbalanced, overly reliant upon reinforced wits and moves. By running roughshod over negative experiences, failed moves are less understood than moves to correct them. Thus, continuous improvement may become continuous correcting of failed initiatives.

If you examine managers who make difficult work more difficult, you see that their judgments lack sufficient mobility. Agility, flexibility, and ingenuity are the enablers of judgment. Managers without these qualities use fewer novel moves to meet unprecedented problems. Furthermore, they are more apt to force old skills and moves upon unreceptive situations. The lack of novelty restricts self-confidence, thus limiting correct moves to those done correctly in the past. This is like a dog trying to run forward with the tail in its mouth. In other words, running in circles.

This lack of adaptability may contribute to a failure spiral so deadly to careers. A manager makes a bad move, and in the attempt to correct it, makes another mistake, and then a third or fourth, until nothing seems to work. Then, in desperation, the manager makes an irreversible blunder. What was meant to be an intervention becomes an interruption, concluding with the possible replacement of the manager or abandonment of the program altogether, either of which could provoke a career-limiting evaluation by superiors. Managers are paid to make imperfect plans work and to save faulty implementations. Because they earn their keep by such moves, there is no escape from being smart about them.

While the needs of business press for action, in the thick of it all is the manager who possesses the relevant facts at hand, who has direct view and involvement, and has access to advice from superior and subordinate who now must make one key move that will restart a failed initiative, refocus skewed objectives, or restaff several critical assignments. The potential for the failure spiral awaits, as do plaudits for success. Penalties or rewards, the stuff that evokes mobility from earliest years of life, weigh heavily upon careers. If managers cannot move wisely, what is it they need to do better?

It does not take a goodly amount of corporate sense to know that practioners of the smart move are in high demand or that moves make the manager or that lineups thrive on sharing the wits by members needed to help each other make the smart move or that if they do not live for and learn from smart moves, they will bring little wisdom to the other members.

Given two managers judged to be fairly comparable in their records of achieving expected results, the one known for smart moves will invariably win hands down. There really is no contest. And now you know why masters pass over people with good or better records of performances and why your momentum may be under review by your superiors. You may be as good as your results but not as good as your moves.

From here on, your smart moves must power your results. Each level above does not increase responsibility in an arithimatic progression. As has been noted, the next promotion may be twice as difficult as the preceding position. If you have to increase your effort as much as the increase in responsibility, you are going to become exhausted. It is for your own good as well as that of your superior that your moves in the past be carefully examined. When your superior offers you discretionary judgment about the means to achieve your goals, stop and think when you hear, "It's your move." It sounds compelling; it should. It may be the breakpoint of your future achievements and advances.

So drop the walls of your minds and reach for the humbug that says performance drives promotions. Such oversimplification that yields the "results count" slogan must now be carefully but not cynically examined. What kind of superior do you have? Who knows but that yours is a superior who gets the best out of people before they break and then throws them onto the ash heap of diposables? There must be some reason why you are wondering and waiting. You see, you have a move to make, and even a no-move sends a message.

You have been waiting six months for your superiors to make a move. You decide to break the apparent stalemate. But before you make your move, ponder the answers to more questions about which climbers should be concerned. Why did you not see this arrestment of your momentum coming? Why were you blindsided? If you were as valuable as your achievements suggest, why did your superiors not take you into their confidence? Why are they hanging you out to dry? Is it possible that you are smarter about managing than about climbing? Is it possible that your relationships make it difficult for your superiors to support your promotions? Do your moves suggest the possibility that you are more interested in making yourself look good rather your superiors? Maybe your moves with them have not given them confidence that you will be able to handle superiors at a higher level? Maybe you have the arrogance of many "flash in the pans" that encourages your superiors to teach you a lesson. Maybe this is the move that they are making. If it is, how can you be sure that your next moves will be less clumsy than your past ones?

There is some reason why your relationships make it difficult for them to open up. Maybe they would rather keep you ignorant to see if you can read the reasons why you are blowing in the wind. Maybe they think you are smart enough to catch on without having to be told? If you think you are, then what are your answers to the next set of questions?

Have you made the right moves to align yourself with your superior's future or to align your preferred subordinate with yours? Are you using your potential successes simply to get a promotion and are not concerned about the future worth of your subordinate afterwards? Perhaps your subordinate is a little weak to succeed you but that as the boss you can make up for any of your successor's deficiencies. Are you one of those all-wise superiors that subordinates should depend upon? How much do you depend upon them to be independently smart? Are you muddling? If so, the cure is to get unmuddled. It starts when you realize that you may not be as smart as your record of performance. You may have exerted more efforts for managing than wits for climbing. (Please see Chapter 20, Conclusion: Efforts vs. Wits.)

How would superiors let you know that your moves are not smart enough to endure the pressures of higher responsibilities? Or that your managerial moves are smart enough but your moves for climbing are quite dumb? What kind of moves would your superiors make to let you know and what moves would you make to reply to them? Of course, your first moves must be to determine what is happening to you. But those moves must not prejudice your next moves. So what is your plan?

Keep in mind that you will not be the first wunderkind who has more advancement than corporate sense or who has gone about as far and fast with managerial achievements without realizing that smart moves are as important as the results they achieve.

Bear in mind that the above questions are not speculations. Each of them happens to be one of several reasons that climbers are ditched on the fast or slow track. Now and then, climbers need to take time out and comprehend what has happened to them and what is ahead of them. Otherwise, they will be big on effort and small on wits. Just as there may come a time when everything falls into place, a time may come when nothing makes sense any longer. You are there now. You cannot afford another move without first increasing your corporate sense.

If by now these questions do not help you to gain a hunch why your career has stalled, then read on. Before you make your move, be sure it will be compatible with and efficient to expediting your career. Is your objective to have your superiors explain why you are stalled, or how to get unstuck and start advancing again, or is it more fundamental, such as simply to unlock the wisdom of your superiors regardless of whether it relates to or enhances your promotability? Suppose you need to know a lot of things that you missed in your frenzy to rise quickly. Turn yourself around. Would such an objective by your high performing subordinate impress you? Would you have enough wisdom to help your key subordinate get out of the fog? Maybe if you look closely at the moves of your subordinates you will see that many of them are already at the margin. Neither they nor you may know it. In such a case, your successor, were you to be promoted, could fail miserably. Is it possible that your superiors suspect this potential tragedy and hold you back because neither you nor your preferred subordinate is prepared?

In other words, you have not made it advantageous for your superiors to promote you or for one of your subordinates to succeed you, and your moves may have made it difficult for both superiors and subordinates to hitch their careers to your future. Remember that one right move may start the process of confirming your worst fears or your fondest hopes.

At any given moment, you will make the right move or the wrong. That is the risk of the moment. You never know for sure when it comes until after it goes. Whatever it is, you will learn about the power of the one right move. It is during lulls like yours that masters prove their wits to climb. It is your move.

14
BASIC MOVES: AWAY, WITH, AGAINST (AWA)

I usually ask chiefs to agree or disagree with the old adage (Confucius) that a journey starts with the first step. Chiefs unhesitantly agree. I explain that by such agreement, they have performed one of the most elementary acts of human behavior. It is a move in *support* of an idea. By this explanation, we are able to take additional steps in the interviews to discover the other moves that the glitter of big business achievements tends to hide, including the moves that win judgments of their promotability.

Elementary behavior carries forth the practices of management. It is ordinary moves that culminate in exceptional performances. It is the rudiments of mobility that show agility, flexibility, and adaptability. Wit is not something carried special in a container to be opened and used when circumstances require. Smartness is expressed in everyday behavior or it is not expressed at all. So when corporate managers decide to do something big in global consequences or small in local effects, what are their choices?

All behavior, whether at the bottom or top of the corporation, is limited by the directions available. You can move *away* (avoid, abandon), *with* (support, promote), or *against* (attack, oppose). There is no other direction. Some believe that basic moves should include going around or over, but they are simply creative expressions of the three basic moves. Others believe the best move is to do nothing. Indeed, that is sometimes very wise. But a no-move is not without potential direction. It may ultimately affect consequences the same way as one of the basic moves. So take care, your target will tend to categorize a no-move as having some direction even though you may despair because of this unfortunate misunderstanding.

BASIC MOVES: AWAY, WITH, AGAINST (AWA)

All moves are related in some way to people, ideas, and positions. By positions, I mean more than rank in the hierarchy. I include standing as when we say the "manager is in a position to make a decision" or "in a position to take advantage or to exert preference," etcetera. In this sense, managers occupy locations and take positions. Moves must always take into account that people in positions usually take *positions* and to note the nature of both is necessary and wise.

By ideas, I mean actionable thoughts, in contrast to intellectual ruminations, whimsical notions, sundry expressions, and gabby speculations. Although these seemingly frivolous communications may be reacted to by any of the above moves, the moves that count are about ideas that when acted upon have serious consequences to both climbing and managing. Therefore, do not fritter away moves upon things unimportant. The instance when wit is a pejorative is when it indicts people for being clever about what requires no cleverness.

By people, I mean those now or in the future who can help or hurt your ambitions, achievements, and advancements. In this regard, much of the text describes people who form and join lineups, including their peers and extended superiors. For climbing, the most powerful people are sponsors. Without them, lineups cannot exist.

When you decide to do something substantial with people, ideas, and positions, in or out of lineups, your moves start with openers and end with closures tied together by transitional moves. Whether an action takes a year or more, such as a strategic plan, or a few minutes, such as a telephone conversation, moves, away, with, and against (AWA), will always occur. It is difficult to behave without an implicit or explicit direction, intentional or otherwise.

Smart moves may be so subtle that no one is aware of their direction except you and the intended targets, or they may be clumsy as to be obvious to all. To express a generality is exactly what it is. Unless there is directionality, it is not an intended move. Of course, expressions of a general nature may be interpreted mistakenly to mean away, with, or against, which is why you should always keep in mind how the message may be interpreted. People take things personally by reading themselves into messages. You can unintentionally hurt people who sometimes are the very ones you intend to support. Likewise, you can unintentionally support your adversaries and enemies. These moves may be called accidents.

I could parade in front of you the large number of managers who have been irreparably harmed by accidental moves. Their most common explanations are, "I did not mean to" or "that was not my intention." Some people always make the worst of your moves or the best. Others read more wit than intended or less ingenuity than the moves merit. But they will tend to judge moves for personal relevance and focus upon the most telling move that arouses them. The against move is usually the most unforgettable or unforgivable, except for a few adversaries for whom avoidance of them is the worst sin.

It is well nigh impossible to avoid accidental, mistaken, or plainly dumb moves. Chiefs do not always move smartly. At times, they appear exactly like amateurs. They may be clumsy at opening and have no terminal facility for closing. They often spend as much time recovering from dumb moves as anyone planning smart ones. I have many times seen board meetings where chiefs got off to a bad start and only made matters worse or had the winning hand until the final move when they lost it all.

As in the home, so in corporate offices, I have seen faulty moves spark an internecine war and one well-timed move start the peace process. I have seen average minds outmaneuver superior intellects, and I have seen superior intellects move successfully by gut feel while their well-thought-out moves fail miserably. Moves seem so simple that they hide their power. For this reason, all climbers benefit from the advice to know what they are doing. If you do not, no move may be expedient and less consequential until your sight clears.

All moves are judged by both their consequences and the behavior involved. They have the potential to affect people both ways, help and hurt. The demise of many chiefs and managers may be traced directly to this double-edge affect. To avoid future regrets, they may trace their behavior. Invariably their mistakes started or augmented their double-edge moves. They never had the good sense to correct one or the other misinterpretation to minimize their losses. They succumbed to the deceptiveness of elementary moves. They are easy to make, much as saying yes or no without thinking.

Masters are often seen as quick and decisive. But what many people do not see is the time taken to prepare their moves. However, masters are not exempt from becoming caught up in whirlwinds of action and pay a dear price for loss of time and blemish to their reputations as do slow route climbers. No one is smart enough to be always in control of oneself and the situation, and almost anyone is smart enough to make one appear foolish. It takes fewer wits for others to bring one down than wits to maintain a successful career. Small minds often destroy big minds.

However, the directions of moves cannot be prescribed in advance of knowing the circumstances that the managers face. Careful diagnosis must front load and shape every move. Moves that are intended for a subordinate or superior may cascade up or down the hierarchy. People talk, misrepresent, pass unfounded rumors, and the manager loses control of the move. Because few moves do not have consequences beyond the actions taken, you need bifocal vision. Far sight is the awareness that notes and makes sense of people, ideas, and positions beyond your immediate sphere of moves. Near sight is to be astutely aware of the near-in and immediate consequences, potential or real, of your moves.

This next fact may not surprise you, but what most often trips up masters is not what lurks in their immediate vicinity. Yes, they make some near-in mistakes. For example, they may underestimate the difficulty of their assignments and opportunities, overestimate the capabilities of their staffs and key performers, let things go too far before correcting, or their moves are made without regard to the realistic diagnosis of the above faults. They will augment (with) a faulty plan or program when they need to intervene, and abandon it (away) or remove people who are blameless (against) and support (with) people who contributed directly to the fiasco. They may eventually avoid disaster by mustering every ounce of skill and commitment available to them and their staffs. Now they attempt to substitute effort for wits, always the sign of desperate minds. They have given up on making few, clever, telling moves. This crisislike effort may take resources away from other programs as vital to their superiors.

Malperformances may occur without any distant awareness of corporate events and affairs involved. Masters simply stumble over what is in front of them and then muddle their way out. Of course, most seasoned managers caught up in these circumstances know that this stumbling is not clever use of wits. On the other hand, no one can tell what are exceptional moves either except perhaps superiors watching closely. But this panoply of mistakes may be fully offset by moves that were missing or ineptly used in the first place.

The more serious circumstances that trouble masters lie beyond their immediate spheres of managing. They fail to read the different priorities that extended superiors place upon corporate ways and the special twists they make in judging promotions, promotable, and promotability. Each level and each superior has peculiar ways of using and judging people. For one thing, extended superiors may be on the lookout for unusual and invaluable talent and skill, including potential "stars." While others want solid, reliable, high achievers, some want ambitions strongly displayed to set the competition. Others want ambitious people because they are more manageable. Whatever their priorities, the differences among levels of superiors are numerous enough to fill a book.

Suffice it to say, the one thing that climbers usually lack is sufficient wits to scope out the larger picture relative to climbing. To aid this mapping, exposure and visibility may yield much sense about extended superiors, their ideas, and positions. This sense allows climbers to express in the presence of extended superiors' competency through moves that, for example, wisely avoid superiors who carry no weight, forthrightly support ideas that they value and adroitly oppose strongly held positions that are necessary and proper. You cannot be a cipher or a know-it-all. Your moves must not embarrass you or your extended superiors. Nothing is quite as deleterious to careers as moves based upon faulty diagnosis while under high exposure.

To be considered naive and immature by extended superiors is probably the worst sin of commission, and to be immobilized by fear of mistakes, the biggest sin of omission. It is not easy to move smartly. Few people will help you become smart, and many will help you stay dumb.

About far sight, masters have a recommendation. Extended superiors several levels above, including chiefs, may make ordinary moves and mistakes occasionally. It is not their greater authority that makes them smart. It is their wits to know when to move away, with, and against, the same moves that you will be expected to make wisely when you are discovered. So take heart. Superiors, including chiefs, are as ordinary as you. Do not be intimidated. Relax. The one thing superiors look for is emotional maturity in the form of self-confidence without arrogance.

You know who you are and will make the greater attempt to understand your superiors than you will expect them to understand you. When you live in their world, you are the immigrant and they are the natives. You are not expected to know as much as they. It is how fast you learn that counts. When you do not know something, you will be inquisitive and gain what masters call the ignorance bonus. You are honest and not afraid to be. You will receive credit for not being something you are not, an immigrant with the wisdom of a native. But you cannot stay ignorant very long. And your quest for good sense cannot convey naivete about things you should have learned at lower levels.

One may be somewhat forgiven for a sense of the corporation that does not extend as far out and above as needed. But one cannot be forgiven for faulty diagnosis of things that can be read and comprehended. You need to attempt to know at all times what is knowable in your immediate and far surroundings. Just this good sense could help you avoid the vast majority of accidents that stall careers. You are more than likely felled by things near and far that can be seen but ignored than things ignored but are not self-evident.

If you study the self-imposed encumbrances that make corporate life more difficult than need be, they would include the basic moves. You avoid, support, or oppose the wrong people in your work-a-day sphere and beyond. You simply connect to, and disconnect from, the wrong people or the wrong way to the right people. You can see how relationships have a double-edged sword; they can expose you as witful or witless. (Please see Chapter 16, Relationship Sense.)

AWA moves rely upon some simple mechanics universal to all productive relationships. One of these is to break communication down to include a sender, message, and receiver.* You are the

---

*I am indebted to a former colleague at Michigan State University, David Berlo, for this anatomy of communication.

sender of the message, but the meaning of it is in the sender and receiver. In other words, meanings are not in words but in people. If your move elicits a meaning in people that you intend, you have communicated. But if your move does not elicit your intended meaning in the receiver, you have not communicated.

Smart managers are receiver oriented. For this reason, if they fail to communicate, it is their fault. Sender oriented managers believe that if they have not communicated, it is the receiver's fault. Managers live in a world that uses such flowery, elliptical, and invented words that senders and receivers may not communicate well at all. They pretend to understand but, in fact, do not, and no one may be the wiser. When it comes to AWA moves, this lack of understanding should be avoided. You must switch from popular language to the most basic and universal, or your moves will be poorly understood. You can pretend to be semantically flowery and obtuse as so many managers are today, but do not be careless with explaining and justifying AWA moves. Use simple, everyday words that keep you in control of your meanings.

I have seen managers careless with their words who are also careless with their moves. Their casual and impulsive language makes difficult things more difficult to understand. While they may imagine themselves to be among the movers and shakers, their moves seldom approach the level of power and grace expected of managers reputed to be in control of their words and wits.

Managers may be able to visualize opportunities to prove themselves but fail to make the right moves at the right times. They simply fail to understand the power of one well-timed move, or if they do, they fail to follow through with others properly and timely. They may get a giant of a problem on the ropes but fail to issue the final blow, or lay out a scheme of actions without the power to overwhelm the opposition or adverse circumstances.

Usually these managers lack a sense of priority that dictates moves crucial to the outcome. They may be called foolish or stupid, except when compared to others, they are not any better or worse. However, they leave the field of contest open to the few who know and value the power of a well-timed move to avoid, support, oppose people, ideas and positions that can help or hurt them to manage and climb.

This reaching for the ideal standard of smart moves is a tall order for even the sharpest minds. The fact is that masters do not move smartly all the time, nor does anyone. As masters say, do not let others know when you act dumb, because they may not be smart enough to know the difference.

15

THE RULES OF MOVES

The best that masters have to offer concerning the proper use of away, with, and against moves are rules of thumb. Since anything passing as smart is situationally sensitive and responsive, these rules must be approached with keen corporate sense about their purpose, form, and timing. As masters say, "We may teach you the rules, but no one can teach you how to use them exceptionally well."

First of all, do not try to do everything in one move. Success is more than a single move. Failure has more than a single cause and more than a single cure. The imperfectability of human behavior and the law of intended consequences make success and failure a multiplicity of conflicting moves. Still, moves are not equal. One move can start to reverse the course of events leading ultimately to success or failure. Thus, do not make your first move a mistake or fail to have planned the second or third moves to follow through as required.

Timing is everything. There will be a time to move away, with, and against. When propitious, a move should be insinuated into the course of events as though it were naturally and not artificially contrived, reasonable but not expedient. Nothing affects the power of a move more than the past events and future expectations justifying it. Do not allow others to press you to move when it should be done anyway. Be ahead of what may be expected in order to gain respect for initiative and vision.

When deciding to make a move, sharpen its focus and effects upon the target, leaving little potential for collateral damage. Use a rifle and not a shotgun to avoid unnecessary spray. Moves should involve as few people as necessary to avoid losing control. However, all who have a stake in the outcome of a plan or program augmented or intervened by a move should understand its importance to them even though only a few people will be key to the success of the move.

THE RULES OF MOVES 125

Do not oversell a move. Be aware that if you unintentionally promise too much, others will expect too much. Commitment (*with*) to the plan must not be gotten on the cheap. Overselling oftentimes creates more disappointment than the failure of the move itself. Additionally, you will lose your credibility for future moves.

Any move must be delivered impersonally. Moves must be directed toward ideas rather than people, toward the positions they take rather than the rank they hold. In return, do not take personally other people's moves. Keep your ego at bay. If people can cause you to become personally involved, they can control you by their moves.

Be more suspicious of *with* moves because people are less apt to be honest about them than *away* and *against* moves. Accept support at face value, but keep a wary eye for who stands most to gain, especially those who take your support for granted. When your support of them slackens, they are apt to become frustrated and read the move as avoidance (away) or opposition (against). For this reason never allow your support to be automatically given or expected. Make the targets of each *with* move earn every ounce of your support. Support freely given is commitment seldom returned.

Never change the direction of a *with* move having once made it. If unforeseen circumstances require that you do, take care to give well-thought-out reasons based upon observation or logic or you will become perceived as wishy-washy. In fact, all moves must be designed with a precise purpose in mind.

Use an overarching reason for all moves, and if such logic is not available, release your moves separately between sufficient intervals of time. Never allow a move to interfere with options to make a different move. When you support something, you usually avoid or abandon something else (away) or oppose and destroy something else (against). Where justified by the efficiency of any one move, anticipate what of the other two basic moves may be necessary.

It is best that when a move is positively positioned to enhance a plan or program that all negative attributes be fully accounted for. Thus key players know the upside and downside and will not be misled. Because all moves cost opportunities to make other moves, be sure that you know and explain what opportunities are being forfeited. Those forfeited (away, against) are as much a move as those favored (with).

Moves that are arbitrarily planned and issued will usually carry an information deficit either by their nature or their explanation and understanding. All moves that require the benefits of organization should be front-loaded with relevant information. Arbitrary use of authority in the past will shape the quality of information available for ascertaining the present right move.

Permissive use of authority is just as dangerous to making the right move. Deficiency in firmness and control begs people to indulge in their fanciful discretions. While some of these expressions will be creative, the discipline to commit to a move (with) should always be available regardless who is the authorizer of the move.

If key players commit to the move only because they are involved in formulating it, they have insufficient discipline. You cannot always move with members to gain their commitment (with) as though it were their own move. Key moves are made ineffective because of the lack of such discipline. If information and advice is freely obtained before the decision, no one has the right to withhold commitment (away) once the decision has been made. But they might do it anyhow. This intransigence should be noted and interpreted as a sign of untrustworthiness.

The options available to a key move are seldom those immediately apparent. Single option thinking should be disallowed. Key players who combine moves based upon one option will not be alert sufficiently to the best option. If incorrigible, they and their narrow mindedness should be avoided at all costs (away). Group think should also be avoided or opposed, as should any process that closes off multiple option thinking in the preparation or implementation of a move.

In devising and executing a move, creative discretion may be necessary, but whether the move involves an individual or group, the results of such creative efforts must be held accountable by the requirements of the move. While authority may legitimize such creative processes, no one should be without accountability for the results or the failure of the key moves. No one should have a free ride; nor should everybody. In the latter case, the chain of command will splinter into pockets of self-serving interests and moves. The manager should know how and when to support freedom, avoid too much of it, and oppose it when it serves personal rather than business interests. Freedom is just another expression of authority. This being the rightful move of superiors, they should never relax their authority even though they must be circumspect about its proper use, especially when it comes to planning and making key moves.

Insubordination (against) destroys the power of a key move. So does malicious compliance (feigned *with*) when well into the move, people realize the move is incorrect but do not give the superior timely heads up. They perform exactly as the move requires with the intent to show the superior to be wrong or to embarrass or defeat the value of the move (against). Vengeance is theirs on the quiet.

A move that is incorrect should be discovered as early as possible. Faulty moves discovered early can be more easily corrected by other moves. But when discovered later, the consequences are far more difficult to reverse no matter how wise the correcting move.

As soon as the fault is seen, the parties necessary for the correction should be given immediate and unmitigated support. It may be necessary to remove some members (away) and appoint new members (with) to gain the correct mix of wits and skills. The mistake is to stay *with* some members too long or discount (away) others too soon.

Regarding once again the proper use of authority, people who discover and immediately inform the superior of the fault in a key move should not be penalized (against). The messenger should not be shot. The function of authority is to gain lead time to see as early as possible the fault in the move.

Just as any plan is not perfect, any move also will not be perfect and needs correcting as soon as possible. People will cover up and thereby cut down the superior's lead time and become blindsided. If the perpetrator of the mistake or the malperformer quickly informs the superior, then they share a problem to be solved (with).

If a cover-up occurs or continues, then the perpetrator should not go unpenalized (against). If the fault is both caused and covered up by the same individual or group, two mistakes have been made rather than just one. Full accountability should be extracted. It should be understood that people make mistakes, but if they inform the superior properly and devise clever moves to clean up their messes, they should be credited (with) with such diligence and self-discipline.

People who move wisely to correct mistakes gain self-confidence, which becomes to the superior more valuable in the future than the corrected moves. No amount or kind of moves should destroy self-confidence. Moves exist (away, with, against) to insure that the plan or program is completed without intentionally destroying self-confidence. Even the extreme move of terminating an employee (against) may be done so as to avoid destroying the employee's confidence to gain a living elsewhere.

While this prescription may seem touchy-feely nonsense, it is intended to convey and ensure the primacy of the implicit contract between employer and employee—that the subordinate will dutifully obey a command and the superior will ensure that it serves the common good. When this understanding is sufficiently compromised, the plan or program and the key moves will fail for lack of commitment and discipline. This effect is called friction.

The power of a move is not in the authority that legitimizes it but rather in the spontaneous willingness of people to drop less essential things and pitch in without friction or regard for their sacrifices. The favorable results are the function of key moves made possible by the wits of superiors who know that all plans and programs are subject to failure unless augmented or intervened by key moves. (Please see Appendix E for a summary of the general rules of AWA.)

Smart moves make valuable contributions to lineups. Each member as a manager is prone to form or issue plans and efforts that require correcting. Each member has the opportunity to gain the combined wits of the lineup for assuring smart moves. The reluctance of many people to open up and reveal and admit their faults and mistakes is as common as their desire to push through difficult times alone. It is a form of weakness, including arrogance or smugness, to believe that one is self-sufficient when it is obvious that one is not.

Self-sufficiency is admirable but not when it hazards the achievements of others or your own. But who will you trust to understand without judgment or prejudice your problems and mistakes and take the time to help devise correct moves when it is obvious that you are at a loss for helping yourself? Who but those with ambition to climb need help from people they trust and respect; who do not act as superiors, managers, and subordinates, but as cohorts infected with the common need to relieve their ignorance; who knows that the route to the top is incredibly difficult and are prepared to ease the burden by making as few mistakes as possible; who by combining their wits in a lineup make exceptional achievements and fast advancements more likely. Smart people know where smart help is, and it is not always among members of a lineup. At least they can use the lineup as a backboard against which to test whatever help they get. For this service, members of an effective lineup measure carefully their moves among each other. A careless, crude move against a member, the improper abandonment (away) of a member in need, the careless or artificially contrived support (with) of a member's promotability represent the ineffectual ways of most members of a triplet taken at random across the length and breadth of the corporation.

This is not to say that lineups have little tolerance for wrong moves. Because of the degree of trust and respect, members discount occasional episodes of stupid moves, especially those made with good intentions. In fact, the tolerance is such that masters often define a lineup as "where you can make a fool of yourself without feeling like an ass."

What minimizes crude and rude self-serving moves is the selection of members eligible for a lineup. The members are smart to begin with about how to move away, with, and against each other. They know how to oppose by reason and experience without *ad hominem* attacks, to avoid discussions for which they have no wise contribution, and to support when they have firm convictions. Their affairs may be as rough and tumble as any other group but they are directed against a common foe, how to beat the hierarchy that is stingy about promotions.

Some move more smartly in lineups than out of them. To some extent all managers put on their best behavior with superiors. However, the test of eligibility for lineups is smart moves made in both managerial performances and membership in the lineup. The reasoning is that if you know how to focus your wits upon making key managerial moves with telling effectiveness, you will probably do the same with members of a lineup and with extended superiors during opportunities of high exposure and visibility. In other words, your choice of moves offers maximum effect regardless of their venue.

This pattern of mobility is substantially smarter than the all-too-familiar scenes of a manager walking into a superior's office all dressed up for the right presentation and presence. The manager may show the superior the right amount of support when expected, just enough opposition (against) to appear not to be a sycophant, and clever avoidance of blame (away) to keep from being held accountable or blemished. Now who is crucial to whom? Who needs one more than the other? Now suppose this: The superior may be tolerant of these dumb moves because they are the best that the manager can offer. Also, the manager does an acceptable job and does not occupy a key position, and the superior has a successor on the parapet ready for advancement. With a lineup at the ready, the superior can well afford to be supportive (with) of reliable, productive managers, such as this one, taking care to avoid misleading the manager about promotability.

Suppose also that in the office or cubicle next door to the manager sits a peer who is a member of the superior's lineup. Suppose the peer is younger, less tenured, say a master in the making, one who "rents" every move as though it was an investment with a handsome return expected. When the master passes up the manager at promotion time, how will the manager act with the peer who is now the new boss of the department or division or corporation? Will the manager offer allegiance to the new boss? Given careless use of moves, will the manager be believable? Will the new boss neither condone (support) nor condemn (oppose) nor simply ignore (away) whatever moves the manager makes or has taken in the past?

Masters often describe versions of this scenario about managers who attempt to gain favoritism with moves as transparent as their motives. In some way or fashion, managers whose ambitions may be stronger than their moves are wise, violate the overarching rule of elementary behavior, which is to make no moves that are not earnestly contrived, well prepared, and wisely issued. In other words, be smart about directions. Do not get caught moving *with* when you should be moving *away,* or *against* when you should be moving *with* or *away.* What stymies climbers are moves in the wrong direction. Worse is to have your moves misinterpreted. Your attempt to support becomes misinterpreted as against or avoidance, etcetera. As masters demonstrate, you cannot move in the wrong direction and hope to find the fast route to the top. Make every move count.

This ideal of mobility is worth striving for. Moves make managers both effective and eligible for lineups. In this way, basic moves tie together climbing and managing.

16
RELATIONSHIP SENSE

Face it. Relationships count. How can anyone fail to exploit the advantage to be gained from this universal medium of business? How can ambitious managers expect to be judged promotable who are clumsy and crude at forming and maintaining productive relationships? It is through organized relationships that wits may become extended and accumulated greater than that of the individual contributors, which is another reason why masters form or are invited into lineups.

Knowledge and experience are expected to be easily shared. Managers may get by with less skillful relationships with subordinates and peers in performing their accomplishments but not as members of a lineup. It is knowledge and wisdom forthrightly offered and responsibly received that make a lineup more valuable than any other triplet.

Some managers are a bargain at any price. They relate well, effuse the expertise, trustworthiness, and helpfulness that quickly impresses and disarms people with whom they are trying to communicate, associate, or affiliate. When they terminate temporarily or permanently for whatever reason, they leave a residue of desire in the people to repeat the connection. One never knows when such a legacy will be needed to further future relationships. The welcome mat is out to people with the mobility to glide in and out of productive relationships easily and efficiently. Some of the most difficult people to relate to have the most power to help or hurt careers. The absolute must is not to make these difficult people more difficult. Powerful people, however difficult to deal with, may not personally help or hurt you. Their smartest moves are made through relationships. Even when they directly address you, they are using a relationship with you, however temporary or opportunistic. Power by any other word spells relationship. Neither may be avoided, and both must be used. Still, people are often ignorant of both; especially those who believe great achievements will get them everything.

Moving among emergent and developed relationships is not easy for many managers. They may talk well but not relate well. They find it hard to open up to people and to open people up. These managers cause the mind guards to go up wherein people play mental gymnastics. Because they have to work at the relationships, their ability is handicapped to get quality information, expertise, and support quickly and reliably at low cost in time and effort. The rule of thumb of most chiefs, including masters, is that crucial subordinates should not have difficulty with relationships. If they are rough around the edges with their relationships, masters will help them approximate the ideal of effortlessness. Otherwise, they do not travel on the same route with them.

In other words, people who feel comfortable with you will value that relationship almost as much as the information and knowledge exchanged. When you have to work at exchanging information and expertise, you will not get their best, and they will not give their best if either of you have to tiptoe around strong egos and pry open rigid, immobile minds. If masters have two subordinates who weigh in as equal contributors to their accomplishments, they usually will take the one with whom they have most accessible relationship. Furthermore, masters will upgrade their favored subordinates' achievements and downgrade the less preferred subordinates because of their relationships. These moves may be made without any intent to be unfair. Relationships seldom hover around neutral or bland. They eventually elicit motives to move away, with, or against the people involved. When these judgments change, it is most likely that relationships change.

Because masters are strong advocates of the ideal of effortless relationships, they cannot understand that when the medium of business is obviously relationships why many so-called adult people are so poor at doing what they have done since children, separating and attaching to people easily and wisely. The reason is that people become so involved in relationships that they may not be aware of their critical importance. As with mobility, they take relationships for granted and are not aware of how relationships help to prevent and insulate them from mistakes and their consequences.

A master asked a subordinate manager with straight A's in engineering and MBA courses, "If you are so intellectually bright, why are you so people-dumb?"

Of course, the master was not as rude as it appears here. The question was delivered with the correct mixture of frankness, humor, and good will. The manager nevertheless protested.

"I have very good people relationships. Somehow you got this idea in your head, and I have never been able to disabuse you of it."

"Do you think that your reply deals effectively with my question?" the master asked.

"Well, I am not going to roll over and play dead if I think you are wrong," the manager replied.

"Suppose I am right?" the master said.

"Well, you're not!" the manager protested.

The manager is doubly dumb, unaware of the value of good relationship sense and unaware of any personal deficiency. Instead of moving *against* the master's suggestion, the manager should have moved *with* it and asked where and how relationships could be improved. After all, everyone can improve in something as universally important as relationships. If the manager had used the AWA moves effectively, the master would have noted the start of an improved relationship. Usually the consequence of such a discussion improves awareness of both parties and has the potential to get the master on the manager's side. Needless to say, the master does not get on the manager's side of the desk nor is the manager ever advanced. The last time the master looked (four years later), the manager had not made any substantial improvement in level or position. By just flitting from assignment to project, the manager traveled laterally through the American dream, dragging poor relationship skills. What a waste and what a common handicap.

Of course, managers who become chiefs are not perfect. They all drag with them imperfections. These weaknesses may be blind spots in their corporate senses, incorrigibly bad habits or a propensity for knee-jerk moves or whatever. Their defects are usually more than adequately offset by their strengths. But if you have a choice of a "drag," make sure it is not a deficiency in relationship skills. There is not much you can do to adequately offset poor relationship smarts.

Integral to relationship sense is the basic element of mobility, separating from relationships and attaching, that serves as a test of maturity rather than simply intellectual capacity. How many times have masters seen intellectually gifted people without the wits or skills to reach for and gain help and advice effortlessly. Sometimes it is because they believe that they can think better than others, which is worse than if they could not, or that they don't need help from others to figure out the do's and don'ts of surviving and ascending, or they are afraid to take advice because it may make them look weak. Actually, it is strong people who seek and gain advice and support. It is weak people who try to go it alone. In effect, they ignore or deny the efficacy of this powerful medium of business, relationship sense.

In all the years of studying and counseling managers who become chiefs, I have heard repeatedly that business is not an intellectual exercise. Unlike mathematics or physical science, business does not tap the higher reaches of thought and reason. As they say, "If it were not for people, business would be a snap." They clutter up their relationships such that no amount of higher intellectual capacity may aptly clarify and resolve. Poor relationship is no respecter of intellectual power. The brightest and the less intellectually gifted may be just as bad or good at relationship skills.

Nowhere is the quality of relationships more productive than among the fastest climbers. Masters are the fittest to engage people and to disengage after reaping mutually beneficial results. If they are not, they do not stay in the fast route for long. Without good relationship sense, mobility is akin to a vehicle without a steering wheel; it goes in any direction. Likewise, many people move around a lot, make many connections, but never get big payoffs. They are mobile without good sense. The function of relationships is to open minds for direct accessibility and to keep them accessible for the next engagement. Behind the skills that serve this function is a practical sense that determines with whom to connect and at what level.

There are three levels of relationships. First is when people come together because of their personal qualities. They are fun, exciting, or relaxing to be with. This quality represents the affiliative motive. A second-level relationship is more intellectual because of the information and knowledge gained or exchanged. This skill is not simply to satisfy curiosity, although that may be an incidental by-product, but rather for people to gain a practical understanding of how things work or how to work them or to know and understand events happening near and far or to know the various ways that their corporations work at their present levels of responsibility. Increasing the parties' corporate sense is not to be minimized at level-two relationships. The third-level relationship is for achieving results from shared responsibilities or to gain voluntary assistance from people who are not formally required to help. Here the achievement motive is most prominently engaged.

While the skill to motivate is implicit in all levels of relationships, it is most valuable at level three because of the direct effects upon performance and potential for promotions. The current trend admonishes that "results count," but it seldom affirms as loudly that without relationships, results will not even be possible or how relationships help to determine what results count the most and who counts them.

The three levels of relationships may be keyed to the qualities that managers have, personable, knowledge, and competency. In reverse order, the ideas include fitness and skill to work and achieve. Knowledge, which is more than information, is also understanding gained by clever discernment or actual experience. Personable is more than being amiable and pleasant, but also respectable because of virtuous qualities that people generally value and would like affirmed in those with whom they associate.

The rule of thumb is that you cannot assume that any one level will transform into any of the others. While personal amiability is the lubricant of all relationships, it will not guarantee that people will open up their kits of knowledge or offer their tools of competency. This is the mistake of glad-handers who excessively practice tricks of getting along with people or of those who believe the adage that who you know is the key to success. In fact, it is what you and others know or can do that determines the quality of relationships that most affect the matters of climbing and managing.

Each relationship taps different areas of the mind, and any relationship may involve all three levels. However, generally there is an entrance fee of sorts. Most people do not want to be easily made. They do not open up just to anyone who wants access to them. Even level one requires some form of "courting" that includes warming up to each other no matter how mature the relationship. Levels two and three require even more preliminary care and skill. People do not offer their best knowledge or effort because of a need to inform or work with others. First of all, they may not know that what they know is valuable or how critical their efforts are to their own future.

But as important as relationship skills are, sense of who knows what and who will do what is far more valuable. Once masters find knowledgeable or competent people, they latch onto them as though they discovered a gold mine. As masters move about, they map out who knows and can do what, who will inform and who will commit.

For example, when they arrive in new positions, masters proceed to map the qualities of their new subordinates to derive from them knowledge and prepare them for key positions. After all, people "native" to their positions do not have to disclose what they know when the new boss, the immigrant, so to speak, does not know what they know. It takes considerable skill for the new boss to open up subordinates in order to assess accurately what resources are available and how best to use them. The right moves, including away, with, and against, are absolutely critical for the boss to get off to a good start. Of course, it does not hurt to be personally affable, which is the lubricant for getting to the other levels of relationship. But enjoying each other's company, ways of relaxing, disarming people, and making them feel good are considered by masters as the lowest level of relationships. No one is invited into lineups simply because of these personal techniques.

There are relationships that masters value because of their contribution to crucial subordination. They are peer relationships. Each member of the lineup has peers, people who work for a common superior. All managers act as both superiors and subordinates. They want their subordinates to cooperate to achieve the greater benefits of organization. This means all three levels of peers work effectively together to share knowledge and competency.

As superiors, managers, of course, have the primary responsibility to encourage their staff to develop and use productive peer relationships. However, this task is not easy and may be made considerably less difficult if a subordinate steps forward to become the catalyst for encouraging productive relationship among fellow peers. However, peers may be clumsy at forming and maintaining productive relationships. If among a dozen peers, at least a third will be either clumsy at forming relationships or clumsy at keeping them. Even if others have good relationship skills, they may tend to put their responsibilities ahead of their peers, making for difficult horizontal relationships.

Suppose a manager attempts to be the catalyst for bringing peers together into a tight, productive relationship, something that superiors cannot easily do unaided. And if the subordinate does the same for the manager, the potential of a triplet to produce exceptional results becomes increased tremendously. Note the powerful stirrings of a lineup. The manager becomes vital to the superior by forming qualify horizontal relationships. For the same reason the subordinate adds value to the manager. Vertical relationships assist horizontal relationships and vice-versa.

Let us assume that you are the manager in the swivel chair. You develop relationships with your peers that help your superiors mold a very productive staff that shares knowledge and competency. You have helped to transform a collection into a group with a common purpose, to achieve greater results collectively and individually. Of course, you realize that because of their increased productivity, some of your peers may gain more credits for promotions, but that risk may be offset by the credit you will get as the catalyst. The way masters look at this maneuver is that when you succeed your superior, you will inherit a high-performing staff with which you have already developed productive relationships.

As the manager in the swivel chair, you are becoming productive and secure between a powerful superior and a valuable subordinate with a group of peer managers that you have helped to work well together. All seems sweetness and light except for one risk that will never go away entirely. If you can become a member of a lineup, why cannot one of your peers? The peer who attempts to develop an alignment with your common superior knows what you know, that to cooperate to compete and compete to cooperate, some degree of jostling among ambitious managers is to be expected. Crossing boundaries freely to assist each other is encouraged. The stage is set for possible collusion among a few aggressive peers to freeze out other peers, to narrow the race, to set up the final contestants.

Chances are one of your more aggressive peers is coming right at you. As the catalyst, your power to dominate your peers is apparent, as may be your preferred status with the common superior. As the struggle for dominance tightens, mistakes are apt to be made. Moves that avoid risks, gain support, oppose adversaries may be clumsy, ill timed, and fractious. Innocent bystanders may get caught up in the struggle. Some will get hurt and react to protect their own hard-earned gains, only to make the struggle more intense and complex. Now you have peers choosing sides. These peers have subordinates who may get caught up in the struggle. Now, two levels below the superior, sets of people struggle to make sure that their hard-earned achievements are properly recognized or credited toward promotions. Others are striving solely to use everyday relationships to garner a secure status with their superiors without any thought of promotability.

Of course, the struggle, while intense, remains low-key and focuses upon who will dominate and who will be dominated. Who will have the most power to influence the common superior? Who will speak, be heard, and be followed? Eventually, it may come down to a pointed struggle between you and the lead peer. If you or the lead peer fails to get sufficient support, becomes desperate for power, or loses perspective, the interests of the common superior may become sacrificed. As much as you try to remain on the sidelines, you are caught smack dab in the middle between the lead peer and your superiors. Of course, you try to keep yourself accessible to all peers to help contain the struggle and ameliorate the conflict. Your lead peer does likewise. Two sets of peers armed with their supporters look at each other as adversaries.

What happened to your smooth-functioning peer group, to your superior's well-coordinated staff? With whom does your superior become aligned? Are you still a member of the superior's lineup, or do you just imagine your favored status? Has the lead contestant been taken into the superior's confidence? Are there now two lineups? Have you lost your competitive edge?

Look at it from the superior's perspective. Perhaps the lead contestant was correct. There was room to doubt your promotability. Everything seemed normal until you decided to become a catalyst for encouraging more productive peer relationships. But was that move intended to help your superior or to help yourself? Your superior may have decided that your moves were a blatant attempt to gain power. You already had a sufficient edge to compete for successor to your superior. You got greedy. You wanted total support of your peers. But one of them saw you coming and decided to take you to the mat. The struggle dulled your edge just enough to throw into question your own promotability.

How would you know if you were still favored, with relationship skills so clumsy that you provoked a power struggle among high performers too valuable to be removed? Maybe you misread your superior's attentiveness and obvious personal regard for your future worth to the business. When the superior saw your efforts to dominate your peer group, you overplayed your hand. From your superior's perspective, your moves had the wrong motives. If this condition is true, then welcome to the most common power struggle among climbers. So let us take a close look at what is in play.

The first point of this analysis of the case of the catalyst illustrates how relationships are the carriers of power. Power is acquired and used through relationships. Out of the best or worst intentions, your edge can be made or destroyed through relationships. They require more wits than many people assume.

The second point illustrates a lesson about power. What often makes power struggles disruptive and counterproductive is that the contestants are not evenly matched in wits. Among two determined contestants, if one is clumsy and crude in the acquisition and exercise of power, the outcome will be messy. But if the two are equally smart about power, the outcome will more likely become mutually satisfactory and have fewer perverse consequences.

Note also that peers have no authority over each other. Power is strictly an exercise of mind over mind. But when peers find that they cannot dominate the wits of others whom they consider a threat to their status and careers, they may appeal to the common superior. They do not go begging, hat in hand. If they do, they will betray their personal naivete and weakness. No, they resort to collective power, to relationships. Several collude to make apparent that their ideas about managing the business need to be better heard. When several high performers begin to challenge each other's ideas that obstensibly have the best interests of the business at heart, the superior has potentially the best and worst staffs. The best in the sense that open, honest conflict may upgrade decision making. The worst because the conflict can pit strong egos that aim to protect and enhance their power base.

The third factor at play in the illustration of the catalyst points out a common mistake of aggressive climbers. Masters only need to make this mistake once, and they will have learned the lesson. Never be misled by relationships. In the actual case from which this illustration is drawn, the superior has exceptional relationship skills. The superior moves in and out of relationships with the lightness of a butterfly. Staff members believe that they are individually something special. Each staff member enjoys a relationship with the superior at all three levels. The superior is personable, informative, and competent and shares these attributes fully. In return, the staff members reciprocate in kind. Yes, there could be improvement, as you may expect. However, the staff members are jealous of their presumed favored relationship to the common superior. To preserve their status, they tend to hold back from their peers. Silent walls are built around their departments and responsibilities. The superior keeps prodding them to cooperate better. One of the peers decides to become a catalyst, and you have the beginning of the story but not the ending.

Members of the staff may assume that because of their close relationships to the common superior, they have an edge over the others. It is easy to misread relationships. By their very nature, relationships can be disarming and deceiving. One does not have to be naïve; some of the sharpest minds may be taken in. You see this skill at work among scam artists. When their victims awaken, they almost uniformly express shock because of the credibility of the scammer. Masters are not sleezicks, but if they excel in one skill, it is to disarm and make people vulnerable to their intentions and advances. It takes a mature mind not to be overwhelmed or flattered by relationships or to be biased or adversarial because of them. For masters, the lesson is not to allow your feelings to interfere with your sense of reality. You may keep your judgments to yourself, but do not be fooled by appearance. Yes, relationships are crucial. They dominate judgments about promotions, promotable, and promotability. But do not assume that your relationships do just that because they are productive or enjoyable.

Lastly, the case illustrates that you may be good at relationships when the sun shines and poor when it rains. The catalyst initiated some good moves, but unfortunately, they brought a storm too. A power struggle represents relationships requiring a different order of wits and skills. If you do not know your limitations, you may get in an embroilment over your head and lose. On the other hand, if you avoid all of them, you may also lose. During your ascent, there will be struggles you cannot avoid and must not lose. Thus, throughout the course, you need a sense to know when to avoid some struggles (away), join some (with), and oppose some (against). Knowing what moves to make, when and how, is part of your maturation as a climber.

If your moves only make matters worse, you may embarrass your superiors. If you are clumsy in your own struggles, how can you be of any value during your superior's struggles? How can you give advice and counsel if you lack relationship sense? If you cannot help when your superior is fighting for turf or career, how better may you serve? If your relationships are most productive when the sun is shining, your relationships are not very productive.

The sun never shines on the whole mountain at any given time. Half the mountain is unpredictably drenched in unintended consequences. The implied ethic of ideal subordination is "do no harm." Do not make more difficult for yourself and others what is already difficult enough.

The catalyst may have been undergoing testing for a formative lineup. It has not endured enough stormy weather to be operational. Lineups, regardless of their degree of seasoning, do not formally exist, and when they dissolve, they are not formally dissolved. They are as phantoms that disappear in the darkness. If you cannot be sure they existed, you cannot be any more sure that they will continue to exist.

The harm the catalyst does to the superior may never be singled out. Managers are allowed to make the mistake, "do no harm," once. Nonetheless they will be held accountable. The peer competitor made sure of that by swiping the edge from the catalyst. Now they both will be tested. Can they regain their productive peer relationships? Can they put aside their personal interests? Can they subordinate their careers to their superior's? Will they use their relationships with their superiors to keep or regain an edge or use each other, much as two contestants probing and sparring to take advantage of each other's weakness and mistakes? Which of them will deliver the knockout punch, or will one of them voluntarily withdraw and concede the field to the other?

In one respect, the superior may become the winner. Better to know now who can handle power struggles, because plenty of them lie ahead. Whose moves forecast better smarts at higher levels? Who will be able to defend themselves in a power struggle without mangling the relationships needed for climbing? In short, who will misread and misuse relationships? They are to be treated as coin of the realm and must be earned, saved, and spent wisely, especially when it rains.

17

THE POWERFUL SUPERIOR

There at the point, the apex of their ambitions, a few officers and their chief preside over the jagged mountain below. Getting there means one final step for one of the officers. A few may not want the chieftainship or expect it. Others will accept it but will not fight for it. Some officers will fight intensely to redeem the inexorable personal costs paid for the arduous trek or because getting there is a logical extension of their ambitions to climb, set early in their formative careers.

Among officers at an arm's reach from the outgoing chief sits one predestined to take the point. While not born to become the chief, this officer demonstrates skills in climbing that assure the final act of getting there. This climber may not be the best manager but has the total, unwavering trust of the departing chief.

This successor has a lot in common with other early-arrival chiefs. Their fast climbs are often shrouded in mystery and provoke intense jealousy. Speculation is always rampant. Their many observers and critics seldom guess correctly. Masters are not usually sycophants, ring kissers extraordinaire, excessively greedy, or ruthless to climb over the backs of others. As a group, they are no more these things than chiefs who make more leisurely climbs.

Sitting around the departing chief are the losers, at least for this time around, who may not be accused of the same things as youthful, fast climbing masters. But the older, more experienced, and tenured officers are apt to know how masters get there ahead of them. They have been contestants for most of their climbs. They know each other's moves as the back of their hands. They play the game of winning favorable judgments. Just because they lose the final in favor of the master does not mean they do not understand how to command the attention and respect of their superiors. They know the smart ways to become invaluable to their superiors beyond serving them with exceptional achievements.

Whether their climbs are slow or fast, officers must require the one resource that is allowed but not granted or provided by business, which is power. Power to help or hurt is the tool of their trade. The officers know how to gain power by helping the right people and maintain it by avoiding or opposing the wrong people. They need not be taught much about basic moves of away, with, and against. In their heads is a combat manual of sorts with appropriate offensive and defensive moves. Obviously some of the officers are better at gaining and exercising power, but the differences are in inches, not yards. But as masters say, small differences accumulate into big differences over a lengthy ascent.

The outgoing chief's lineup has more power to gain the support of the board of directors. The story is found in the directors' and chief's relationships. Directors depend upon their chief to sponsor a successor as part of a seamless transition. Their dependency upon the wise counsel of their chief causes them to temper their right to use their authority at will. This restraint is no trivial matter. Investing the business with competent management is the foremost responsibility of the board of directors. Allowing sponsorship of the next chief represents the board's complete trust and respect for the retiring chief. If the board is going to exert authority, a transition is the opportune time. The power that has checked its authority in the past dissipates with the departing chief. The board is free to assert its arbitrary will. In many other circumstances it may, but not if it has grown dependent upon the superior wits and wisdom of the chief.

This same relationship is played out at lower levels by the attempts of ambitious climbers. Authority, dependency, power is a triad of potentially conflicting elements. On the one hand is authority to be rightfully in command downwards, and on the other power to be effectively in control upwards. Authority unchecked by power or power unchecked by authority may be disastrous for both. Superiors who attempt or pretend to be all wise and subordinates who attempt or pretend to be indispensable frequent all levels of the corporation and make potentially difficult, if not explosive, relationships.

The practical necessity of running a business requires that some accommodation be made. However, the chain of command and the authority it represents must be preserved and respected. Any power must be personally derived and may not stand unless justified by the interests of business and supported by the authority invested in representatives of the chain of command.

In a practical sense, superiors and subordinates need each other. Subordinates need the authority of their superiors to execute their responsibilities, and superiors need the total commitment of their subordinates to perform those responsibilities. Authority cannot force commitment. There has to be a give and take. This is the accommodation made for managing purposes.

However, for climbing purposes, subordinates need the support of superiors. To get their total commitment, subordinates must show proper respect for their superiors' career. This commitment is best obtained by developing relationships greater than what exceptional managerial performance usually provides. This is where ideal subordination enters the picture by which superiors become *dependent* upon their subordinates.

In this most exquisite form, such dependency yields the power to check the superior's right to assert authority. The conditions have been noted that need to be engineered whereby authority, dependency, and power combine to the benefit of gaining ascendency for superiors and subordinates.

The alignment of authority, dependency, and power must be done frequently by climbers as they change superiors and subordinates at each of the many levels in the hierarchy. Each superior and subordinate may have different views of the function and value of authority, dependency, and power. Sitting between superiors and subordinates, climbers require considerable practical intelligence for arranging an advantageous accommodation of this potentially volatile triad. Simply put, most climbers are without the necessary wits and, consequently, horrible messes may erupt that defy rational uses of the mind, as was noted in the case of the catalyst.

The power to check authority at any level of the business has the potential to become an insidious trap. Power may be used to transgress upon authority, to go beyond limits set or prescribed for maintaining the integrity of the chain of command. Powerful subordinates may be accused of insubordination and of becoming an authority unto themselves, and their weak superiors accused of irresponsible use of authority. Extended superiors must step in and use their authority to terminate the misuse and abuse of authority and power. The clear and always present danger is loss of control over work crucial to the chain of command.

Chiefs are often fired because of arrogance. They wrap their boards into their hands in order to be free to work their arbitrary will upon the business. When chiefs go too far, the question becomes how far is too far. Only a final judgment may determine, in which case the board may ask, "Whose company is this, the owners' or the management's?" Of course, boards are reluctant to face this issue when business is doing very well. But when the first substantial dip occurs in profit or competitiveness or business wellness, they may become emboldened to face squarely the issues of their authority versus the chief's power over them and who should be *dependent* upon whom.

The misuse and abuse of power is second only to authority for causing managers to be demoted or terminated. Abusing and misusing either power or authority or both are most demonstrable among climbers on the fast track. They may move faster than accumulation of their wisdom to understand the proper uses of power and authority. For this reason, masters often narrowly avert similar fates. They press their luck, walk the invisible line that demarcates trespass. It is difficult to become a consistently high performer and not violate some superior's notion of usurpation of power or authority. There is too much that authority cannot do that requires the use of power.

Now take a second look at the officers seated with the departing chief. At least a third of them are not sufficiently trusted to use wisely the awesome power and authority acquired or available to chiefs. Of course, truthful explanations of why these officers have been bypassed will not be forthcoming. Honesty becomes a casualty of a litigious world, and failure the victim of success. The ways of the corporate world are as silent as ever, prohibiting the learning of lessons and rules of thumb necessary to avoid the trap set by authority and power. Because many ways are deemed better left unspoken, only the most observable and intuitive may read and comprehend. Others learn about these unspoken corporate ways the hard way.

If masters were to open their minds and pluck out the rules about the use of authority and power, no doubt they would commence with the logic of dependency. Their reasoning has been herein noted, but in summary form, it holds that all managers are dependent upon subordinates to get the work done. A few subordinates contribute more than others to the total effort. They become favored for special opportunities to prove themselves capable of handling greater responsibilities. If the manager is promoted, one of the key subordinates may become the preferred successor. The concern is which one may be depended upon the most to support the continued advancements of the manager. This judgment may not be entirely about the manager's discretion. Has the manager served the superior well enough to be trusted with this decision? To what extent is the superior dependent upon the manager for continued advancements? To what extent is the extended superior dependent upon the superior for the same reasons?

These questions will frame the master's rules of thumb with help first from the idea of hierarchy. From the chief to the first-level manager, superiors are dependent upon managers who are dependent upon subordinates, etcetera. Turn this hierarchy around, and what you have is a power structure. By serving superiors, managers gain power over them and similarly acquire power over their superiors. As dependency flows downward, power flows upward.

The dependency of the manager continues at a higher level, and the subordinate accumulates more power to influence the manager, who also retains authority to act at will. The first rule of power is to make a practical distinction between authority and power. Authority is the right to order the behavior of others and expect compliance. Power is the skill to get people to do what you want them to do without the use of authority or when authority is not useful. Managers may face down a palace revolt where the subordinates connive to displace them. Their superior authority, however used or misused, may come under direct attack. In desperation, it is tempting for managers under such duress to protest, "They have no right to do this." But power is not a matter of rights; rather, it is a matter of what works. It is acquired by serving others. The value of managers is not measured simply by their authority over subordinates, but also by their power to help their superiors. By deferring their interests to those of their superior, they gain more in the long run. That is the expectation and the risk. Power is the consequence of becoming crucial to the achievements and advancements of others, foremostly their superior. Notice again that power is useful when authority is not available or sufficient.

This idea offers the second rule. You do not need authority to be powerful. Source and use of power and authority are not the same. If you violate this rule you may misuse or abuse both power and authority. It is a common mistake to believe that you get your power from your superior and the chain of command or that because of your authority you do not have or need power. You need both, but one does not give you the other.

For example, in the early evening of November 9, 1965, New York City was in the throes of a blackout. With traffic at its peak, the streets quickly became mobile anarchy. In the Metropolitan Club at One East Sixtieth Street, where I belong, a fellow member came in to get a flashlight and proceeded to the corner nearby at Central Park and the Plaza Hotel to direct traffic. This lone citizen, without the badge of authority of a policeman, took charge, and everyone obeyed the self-appointed cop at that corner, and chaos was greatly reduced.

This friend took and held power. It is done every day in every quarter of our land and of business. Note that the traffic controller is using power within an accepted standard, helping motorists to get home in a crisis. Real power—practical, useful power—power to serve, to order, to avoid chaos does not require the attributes of authority or gotten from the same sources. Power is self-acquired. It is earned by the usefulness of your actions, given the circumstances at hand.

Having established the second rule, that the source and use of power and authority are different, the third rule of thumb is that whatever works will be judged by its consequences. If a successful coup brings about changes that are deemed necessary in their own right, the use of power may become sustained. But collateral damage may occur sufficient to prevent future uses of power. If respect for authority becomes damaged, the ringleader of the coup may become penalized without reversing the consequences of the coup. In this way, the use of power to displace authority will not become legitimatized.

Notice the not-so-subtle difference between sustaining the consequences and not making legal the actions. Generally, the respect for authority is to be maintained at all costs. If the coup works, it is likely because the manager who is the object of the coup has misused authority or underestimated the power of the conspirators. This mistake is usually considered more serious than the consequences of the coup. Superiors must judge whether the mistake is an aberration or indicative of the chronic deficiency of wits. Certainly no lineup would want a member who is naïve about power and authority. Whatever is the case, the probability is high that sometime after the scuffle, the manager will probably be removed, demoted, or terminated. Superiors cannot sustain the authority of a weak manager without its reflecting badly upon their own use of authority.

One of the collateral problems is that some peers may be brought into the power struggle who should really stay on the sidelines. They are not smart enough to avoid (an *away* move) being used with little benefit and much risk to their own careers. Climbers, especially fast types, must know what struggles to avoid. There are enough of them going on at any time to tempt them to jump into the fray. If they do, they may lose tight focus upon priorities. A weak sense of priority will expose them to unnecessary waste of effort and career time.

Masters may be faulted at times for being too pugilistic. They get involved in fights that may be either nonwinnable or nonproductive to their causes and harmful to their superiors' judgments of their maturity and wisdom. In some instances, masters have had their momentum preserved by sponsors transferring them to save them from being destroyed. Sometimes they have been promoted out of messes in which they could become hopelessly lost. Other times, sponsors may insinuate themselves into the struggle to buffer masters or, after the melee, to discount the whole affair. Without such forms of protection, masters would go the way of most climbers. As masters often say, some people are smart, some people appear smart, and some are not smart even for trying.

Power can hurt as much as help. It can be used simultaneously for both purposes. This elementary observation may lead masters to offer the fourth rule of thumb. Coercive power revealed is power weakened. The reason is that people do not like naked displays of crude, aggressive power. It makes them feel weak. People would rather appear strong even though they are weak than face publicly the fact that they are without power. So when people who are adroitly and unknowingly maneuvered realize what has happened, they may be angry, but they will usually come to realize that they had no chance to begin with. But if openly confronted, they will fight. The harder the fight, the worse the loss for them. The greater the loss, the longer the resentment because they have an identifiable aggressor to focus and maintain their wrath. Give them a chance, they may get even and weaken or destroy the power of the aggressor.

The fifth rule is that the more power is acquired, the more it is effectively used. Practice makes perfect. You need experience to gain and use power gracefully. People without a proper regard for what you can do for them or against them serve as a challenge to your power. You cannot let an opportunity to establish your usefulness go by the board. Powerful people do not turn their power on and off, as a spigot. Almost anyone who deals with masters goes away impressed by what they can do for or to them. These people know that masters have the minds that they will have to deal with. In this way, masters build up a reserve of power to be tapped in future transactions. The ideal is to be wise in all matters they choose to be wise about and offer credible support for those who need or request it, especially those who can hurt or help them.

Powerful people are careful to use their power in the presence of powerless people. One reason is that seemingly powerless people may be camouflaging their actual power. Or they may awaken to the need for power by the demonstration of it. You can never tell that what passes for weakness may someday become a nasty struggle that portends continued difficulty. Never underestimate the helpless.

It has been noted before about the mobility of masters. How they move in and out of relationships after gaining productive information and commitment. What is at work are minds dealing with minds. The victor is the one who best understands what to give in exchange for what is wanted.

Power inspires the acquisition of it. Masters are known to transform weak people into strong people, who often become major supporters, and also, by the way, potential enemies. Helping people to become powerful does not mean that they will not use it against you. Masters have experienced the pleasure of seeing subordinates grow in stature to collaborate as equals and then, later, feel the relentless sting of their antagonistic opposition. Never discount your friend's capability to become your enemy. With practice, you will discern the value of these aspects of the rules of power.

The sixth rule has to do with confusing power with what it is not. Do not dilute the idea of power with unpowerful ideas. For example, many people think power is force, strength, or affection. Force is the application of effort to move an immobile mind. If perchance you change someone's mind, is it due to your authority or power? How can you be sure how much force to use if you are not discriminating about the sources and uses of authority and power? Both can be used to force change, and together they could produce gross, irrational, totally unacceptable conduct. This is comparable to the use of a sledgehammer when a tack hammer will suffice.

Force is commonly called coercion, which divides into two forms. Seduction is when you say or imply that if you will do as I want, you will be rewarded. Intimidation is to imply or say that if you do not do it, you will be penalized. Now, are you forcing change of mind at the level of compliance or commitment? Compliance is when people change because of fear of penalty or hope for reward. Commitment is when people adopt change as though it were their own idea.

You seldom get commitment from the use of authority unless there is abundant discipline. You are more likely to get commitment because you helped them to reason the need and value of the idea for their own good rather than for yours. Power without force to gain commitment is still minds over minds, but it is a rational exercise in thought and judgment. By the way, these new converts may fail to give you credit for your idea. It is not smart to get into a shouting match over ownership of an idea. Let your power be your reward. In any case, note the degree that force of any kind has been used, if any.

Some people dilute their notions of power with the ideas that it is personal strength. In general, strength is capacity for exertion or endurance. Mental strength is the capacity to concentrate your awareness, to maintain possession of your wits, and the ability to think under suffering and misfortune. Strength is to remain as you prefer when force is exerted to change you.

You may be admired for your strength under adversity, but such respect is not power. Mental strength may be gained by overcoming adversity, including fending off powerful opponents and enemies. Strength may be a precursor of power, but do not confuse strong, willful minds with minds that can achieve access and control of other minds. Strongly opinionated people usually lack the power of their ideas, that is why they take such aggressive positions.

Do not confuse affection with power. People who will allow their affection for you to displace their ability to think are not to be trusted with either authority or power. It is naïve to believe that you can translate affection into power for yourself or assume that highly popular people are powerful. They may be popular because of their power, or they may be popular with powerful people, or they may be popular but weak and require the support of, or are used by, powerful people. But because popular people make unpopular decisions, their power must be based upon something that will not be easily dissipated when popularity fades. Masters are not always popular. In fact, they may be hated by many, but they are powerful with powerful people.

The seventh rule states that you get power by opposing powerful people. As they say, a bull does not become powerful by squashing a toad. But by taking on the king of the herd, the winner may acquire, and show proof of, the ability to dominate the herd. This rule does not mean that power is acquired merely by associating with powerful people. Nothing could be more mistaken. Power is personally earned, but the appearance of power may be transferred. You do not inherit the powerful member you have displaced or replaced, but you do show proof of the wits and skills to use power most effectively in your own right. However, moves against powerful people must conform to the rules of moves, or you will be overwhelmed by the consequences. Use of the seventh rule is not for inexperienced users of power. Yet, masters have had to take on powerful people to show that they are managers of consequence. Timid users of power show weakness, which is a greater handicap than losing out to a powerful opponent. As masters say, "winning is nothing if there is no risk at losing."

The eighth rule flows logically from the seventh. Avoid associating closely with people who will give you the appearance of being weak. It is one thing to use power over them, but masters do not bring them into their lineups. The essence of power is to climb. Suppose you acquire power to check the authority of your superior, but your superior has little power with extended superiors. What is the net advantage to you? If extended superiors do not have confidence in the wits and wisdom of your superior, you become known as having considerable power with a weak superior. Extended superiors are apt to see this relationship as a function of the weakness of your superior rather than of your smartness. They may conclude that you cannot hold your own with powerful superiors, let alone with themselves. This is a common but deadly judgment. It means that you are possibly a high performer without the smarts to assist, advise, and upgrade the plans and moves of a superior considered equal to them.

A way exists to alleviate this judgment: Perform conspicuously enough to be discovered worthy of a better superior. This judgment may result in your displacing your superior or being transferred to another superior in whom your extended superiors have more trust and respect. For this to happen, you had better seize opportunities to prove yourself equal or better to their preferences of a valuable superior, which may not be directly known and only intuited.

Regarding membership in lineups, the ninth rule means that if extended superiors are not dependent upon your superior for their achievements and advancements, they are not apt to include you or your superior in their lineups. As is noted above, your power to command the attention and respect of extended superiors may be no greater than that of your superior. Reverse this scenario. Extended superiors depend upon the wits and skills of your superior to whom you are the preferred subordinate because of your power to influence your superior's plans and moves. Now the flow is logical; dependency flows down and power flows up. The lineup collaborates to increase the dependency of extended superiors upon the superior. By checking the authority of extended superiors, the power of the superior is increased considerably. These moves augur more discretionary judgment for the other members. It also allows opportunity for a four-level lineup with the extended superior the lead member. Or the power may be distributed into two overlapping lineups. One lineup includes the extended superior, the superior, and manager, and the second lineup is the superior, manager, and subordinate.

The primary concern of many climbers is the quality of successors two levels below, in which case, the purview of the extended superior extends to the manager reporting to the superior. In turn, the superior may want to be concerned with two levels below, including the successor of the manager. Generally, the major reason that managers are limited from forming a third lineup composed of subordinate and extended subordinate is the power of sponsorship. But the point to be made concerning the ninth rule of thumb is that if your superior's upward power is limited, your power is also limited. To gain relief from this limitation, members below practice ideal subordination to members below than their respective achievements merit. In return, power flows upwards.

Whether you stop and assist a friend in need or enhance and protect your career, power is self-serving. This is the tenth rule. Do not pretend to be a self-sacrificing hero. This veneer will easily wear thin. People may not be skillful about the use of power, but they can detect a charade when they see it. Just do what needs to be done as inconspicuously as possible and keep your motives to yourself. Even though the rewards of power are not apparent, it is pleasurable to be sought by all manner of people far and wide for your advice and wisdom. However, unlike the wise use of authority, power offers few formal or public credits. Not even your efforts to upgrade the plans and moves of your superiors will be recognized for their inherent power. So let your moves speak louder than words. Remember that you can never have too much power, just the appearance of it.

Besides pleasurable, power is best that complements authority. This eleventh rule means that power does what authority cannot do. Business talks about tearing down walls and opening up functions, departments, and divisions to freely access information and expertise. This requires the use of power because people cannot be ordered to share their very best. In this context, superiors bring people across functions to form task groups to solve problems, find the best practices, but then they build the walls around their minds until someone successfully opens them up again. What did this someone use? The answers will evince euphemisms *ad nauseam*, leadership, change agent, team playing, assertiveness, formational management, etcetera, every word but power.

The closest in sound will be the oxymoron "empowerment," which comes under a hundred meanings. It was introduced to business by populist ideologues who were antiestablishment, antiauthority, anticommand, and control freaks, who pushed the idea of "power to the people." Aside from the odious patronization, the word has become a joke to thoughtful managers. But the very existence of the word, empowerment, shows how naïve people are about the differences between the advantages and disadvantages of authority and power, or they would know the proper term is "authorization."

In all relationships, power does what authority cannot. Knowing where authority ends and power begins and the advantage to be gained by one over the other is what makes smart moves. You cannot be pulled up by powerful superiors if you predicate your moves upon your use of authority over your subordinates. No one has enough authority to offset powerlessness with superiors. In other words, showing proof that you are a good superior will not make you a crucial subordinate. The wits for managing are not the same for climbing.

The violation of the above rules leads to the twelfth rule of thumb. Do not be intimidated by power. Powerful people are not fearful of power. They have the wisdom to see it for what it is. They know why they and others use it. This realism allows them to use it and not be afraid to be used by it. They know when they have sufficiently checked authority of superiors, when to back off and avoid being greedy. They also know when their authority has been checked enough by their subordinates. In both cases, they know how far is too far, where the lines are that allow reasonable and proper amounts of power. If they do not know where and when power crosses the boundaries of propriety and reasonableness, they will surely lose their power. But the whole exercise of power is to get what otherwise they cannot have.

This boldness is most demonstrable in lineups. Members unabashedly give in order to get. They are expected to use superior wits to develop powerful ideas that others will depend upon. If they cannot influence the career strategies and moves of the members, they will be useless. Useless is rank powerlessness. In the course of gaining endurability, a lineup will change its power structure. Some members will gain power and then lose it to others. When one member dominates the others, the others do not feel intimidated. They do not attempt to assert themselves in order to achieve equity. Rather they jump in and out of the discussion or connection because they have something useful to offer. If two members of a lineup are easily intimidated by power and the third is not, then the productivity of the lineup will depend upon a single individual. This defeats the advantages of an informal organization. The lineup is no better than any hierarchy of adjacent managers. The answer is not to assert yourself unless your ideas are smart enough to command the attention and respect of the lineup. Of course, the move requires judgment to know when you have floated a useless idea and when to back off and remain quiet to avoid becoming known as a complete fool.

The objective of the lineup is to check the arbitrary use of authority of extended superiors, which determine promotions, promotable, and promotability the lineup has earned in its reason for existence. What impresses extended superiors are the exceptional achievements and smart moves individually and collectively of members of a lineup, their power to coordinate the actions of their peers, and to control three levels in accordance with the expectations of the chain of command.

The thirteenth rule states that no one should expect to keep power. Power is mercurial. You have it one day and lose it the next. The reason power is unsustainable is because of the mobile world of business. People with whom you have influence are suddenly uprooted. The ideas that you ride to gain power are replaced by new ideas. You may be caught riding a dead horse, such as a project for which you gained much peer power but which is now finished or cancelled. But most importantly, superiors who temper their authority out of respect and trust for you are suddenly transferred, terminated, or unemployed. In comes a new superior who has heard about your power and resents it if not rejects it, and perhaps you along with it. If you understand that power is not permanent, you will not be offended or frustrated when you lose it. You will understand why new superiors are cynical, if not fearful, about your power. However, once you know how to acquire it, you may get power again. Remember that the skills are personally owned and are transportable because of your mobility.

The tragedy is the number of managers and climbers who do not know about the rules of power. Masters do not individually know all of these rules. At best they only know and practice a few, which is more than most people. One reason for the ignorance about power is that power is not in the proper vocabulary of most businesses. Because managers cannot differentiate it from all the humbug, there is no incentive to study it, talk about it, and reach openly for power as a proper resource of management. Represssion creates hypocrisy. People may pretend not to be powerful, when they actually want and enjoy power. Imposters arise who fake clout with others, including their superiors. Pretenders to "power behind the throne" are the worst because they seldom reveal themselves to their superiors. They cannot because they are frauds. In almost all cases, they have such an urge to help and assist people that they have to fake their desire and ability to do it.

Climbing requires power to coax the authority hierarchy to let climbers through. Masters use lineups for power to persuade, if necessary, their superiors to use the members advantageously. Those who are not going higher will not practice self-sacrifice to make way for a lineup no matter how powerful. Business does not lay down its life for another business, managers don't lay down their careers for other managers, and climbers don't give up the climb because they have passed over others.

Business has no traffic cop that tells people when to stop or to move ahead. There is no invisible hand that ensures that competition to get ahead always serves the best interests of business. Whatever power you acquire, you are the beneficiary of it. When you help someone, you help yourself, if only by strengthening your relationships. Relationships are the medium of power. To control fate is why masters use powerful relationships. Without it, business will control their fate. Now, why should a master's control of fate be any less honorable than their superior's control of it?

To conclude this analysis of power without due regard to self-interests would be incomplete. Masters shall not say that they did not climb at the expense of others. Every one of their promotions prevents others from getting promoted; neither will they deny that they thoroughly enjoy power. To have power over others, especially superiors, has a most exhilarating effect, far more than authority, because power is something they earn personally. Masters make it to the top partly because they appear powerful and partly because they are. Some people fear them, a few love them, but they are generally well respected for the power of their smart moves.

No one gets to the top without the wise use of power or without the power to sponsor or without the benefit of powerful sponsors. The rules of power herein described are meant to gain and exercise the power to command the respect and support of powerful people who can help or hurt your advancement. The fast route to the top effuses power of smart moves to become a crucial subordinate to a promotable manager sponsored by a powerful superior.

Powerlessness is for many chiefs a devastating experience. Retired masters report that they miss authority and their CEO perogatives and perquisites. But because of their fast climb, they miss more the power to beat the system, to coerce the stingy hierarchy that resists fast promotions. They miss the power to control levels of the business through lineups, to show members how to get the most out of their relationships with superiors. They miss having power greater than the authority over them. Their businesses throw everything imaginable at masters to deter and stop their rapid ascent, and still they make it with the help of smart combinations of powerful superiors and subordinates in their several lineups. It is understandable why masters seldom serve as apologists for power.

In summary, power is the natural condition of human affairs. It cannot be eliminated. Disguising it by other words does not change it. It can only be used and coped with. Power may complement authority and deter its arbitrary use. It cannot stand alone without the implied or benign support of corporate ways. Conspicuous display of power reduces its effectiveness, as is true also of authority.

Power of lineups extends subordinates' knowledge and expertise to their managers, and theirs to superiors with the accumulated wisdom becoming distributed back down. From this collective effort, members gain a sharper, more realistic sense of the many ways that their corporations affect climbing at their several levels and above.

As the officers hear of the news that a youthful climber will succeed the departing chief, they become aware, if they did not already know, of the key officer upon whom the chief depended the most. The chief may speak in popular jargon about the reason for the promotion of the master climber, but explanation by any choice of words is still power. Besides, power by any other name does not seem powerful enough. At the end of their climb, the final notation in masters' manual of rules of thumb will undoubtedly be "power is to climbing as three parts out of four."

18
THE SPONSOR

The skill of the masters compared to other climbers may be illustrated by the difference in walking the floor and climbing the stairs. Both are acts of mobility. In walking, the forward foot is attached to the floor before the rear foot is released. Separating and attaching also occur in climbing the stairs, except the body is lifted enough to clear the next step. In walking, the movement is strictly horizontal. Some climbers attempt to floor-walk themselves to the top, so to speak. They have no appreciable lift and spend much career time moving around laterally.

Masters get a lift up from the extended hands of their superiors. But their legs must be strong enough to minimize their need for a pull up. Otherwise their superiors will have to pick them up and hold them erect on each new step up. In such case, this assistance becomes gross favoritism toward weak managers who are not promotable in their own right. The manager's strength to gain and take advantage of a helping hand comes from several sources of which the foremost are opportunities that prove themselves equal to superiors. Because managers appear to be one of them, the extended hands of their superiors become as much confirmation as assistance. The superior extending the hand practices the power of sponsorship. In turn, it is this power that managers want to be able to lift up their chosen successors.

What is involved is a struggle between authority and power. Superiors usually want their authority to extend beyond managers to their subordinate staffs. But managers want this control for themselves. After all, what are managers for? For this reason, managers struggle to gain power over their superiors just as their subordinates attempt with them. The matter is more than selecting the manager's potential successor but also the key subordinates from whom successors may be selected. This power struggle flares up most heatedly when a manager fails to get intended performance. Then the superior may press to make changes in the manager's subordinate staffs.

However, if the manager is to be held accountable for malperformances, the manager may want to get control of selecting and assigning all staff members, especially those in key positions. This move intends to check the rightful authority of the superior to take charge of the selecting, assignment, and promoting of all personnel in the levels below.

This struggle between authority and power is played out in different versions and arenas all the way to the top. Even chiefs may be tempted to sponsor managers as far as two levels below or more. The often spoken operating rule that good superiors select good managers and then stay out their way is practiced by some chiefs more as an exception than as a rule. These chiefs may pretend to allow their executives to select and promote at will. They hold frequent performance reviews of their executives and their subordinates with a free flow of information and judgment up and down. But the executive knows the final say will be the chiefs. That is the nature off authority at any level. It is always on duty, no matter how much the superior may disguise it.

It is difficult for many managers to believe that anyone other than themselves is as clever at spotting winners. Masters will even slant their discussion of performance evaluations and judgments about their managers' key players and potential successors. Over time, these managers may use their master's standards for selecting key subordinates and assigning major opportunities. And perhaps such thinking is best for any given doublet. But the ideal is to develop managers who are better at these matters than superiors. With independence of thought, when they agree, it is more likely to be coincidence than contrivance.

This practice is shared by most chiefs and definitely by most masters. For them, managers whose judgments are both as credible and independently derived as their own are the stuff of which lineups are made. This practice requires that managers must be smart about control of their staffs for finding and developing their successors. However, masters seek a sort of test to determine if their managers are ready to assume such responsibility and risk.

Unfortunately, managers may press prematurely for power of sponsorship and make issues of both authority and power. These managers lack a sense of how power of sponsorship is acquired and used, or the superior is confused about the function of it.

Sponsorship is not derivative of authority. It does not show up in the formal ledger of duties and responsibilities. The manager earns the power to sponsor. With it, the manager may form, join, and maintain lineups. Without the power to sponsor, the members would comprise just one of many couplets and triplets that exist throughout the corporate chain of command.

Sponsorship is the top step of an informal, nonspoken hierarchy of power. At the lowest step of power is the credibility of the manager to *evaluate* subordinates, particularly their performance and promotability. Although managers normally have the authority to evaluate their subordinates, they may lack the power to evaluate. This is because power hinges upon whether and how the superior acts upon the manager's evaluations. If the manager's evaluations are merely filed away with little direct actions taken by the superior, as is often the case, the manager does not have much power to evaluate. Remember that power is what power does. Power is impact.

But if the superior acts upon the evaluations, such as to encourage the manager to give the subordinate in question a choice opportunity, then the manager has power to that extent. If the subordinate exploits this opportunity to achieve performance highly valued by manager and superior, the latter will most likely become more dependent upon the manager for future credible evaluations of subordinates. In this way, all three members of the lineup may benefit.

A higher degree of power comes from the manager's effective recommendations. This second level, power to *recommend,* is once again determined by how it is acted upon by higher authority. For instance, the manager initiates advice, untainted by the opinions of the superior, to raise substantially the salary base of the subordinate or to give greater responsibility. Nuances are important here. In evaluations, especially those given verbally, which are the ones that matter, managers may credibly recommend a personal improvement program for their subordinates or they may slant their evaluation to reflect surplus of talent or skill that calls for more important asssignments at the same level or higher. Then the superior may ask for their recommendations.

At this point, the manager will be judged by the superior to see if the manager can wisely match skills of the subordinate to the requirements of the prospective opportunity. Matching based upon predictions of future performances from known skills and results is different from matching observable and evident skills and performances of the subordinate in the present position. Fortunately, most seasoned managers learn early in their careers the difference between judgment based upon observations and judgment based upon predictions. Superiors may say that their evaluations are credible but that their recommendations are not. Thus, they lack the judgment to go from known facts to credible forecasts. They have control of the mind of their superior in one instance and not in the other.

As an operating rule, masters often do their performance and promotability evaluations separately. They make promotability a special case for discussion with their superior. They carefully integrate both evaluations and recommendations of the subordinate with the superior's values of promotability. Managers study carefully the opportunity for their subordinate, making sure the assessment is in line with their superior's. Now they have a four-legged stool; the subordinate's skills and achievements, their direct observations and evaluations, the superior's values of promotability, and the opportunity of vacancy in question. Masters discover whenever they achieve syncopation among these four elements, they have something credible upon which to place their recommendations. By this stool, they leverage power over the minds of their superiors to the point that they move rapidly through the next levels of power to gain eventually the highest prize, sponsorship.

The power to *nominate* is greater than to recommend or evaluate. This third level of power is seen when the manager nominates the subordinate for a promotion. The manager expects the approval of the superior with greater certainty than in the case of recommendation. Most superiors will think twice before they refuse the manager's nomination, owing to the confidence the superior has in the judgment of the manager and in the dependency of the superior upon the manager in matters vital to the lineup.

When you nominate, you put your judgments on the line but not necessarily your relationship to the superior. Ideally, your values and those of your superior's about performance and promotability are in harmony. If they are not, then you cast doubt about your wits to judge. However, it may be necessary to use your power to change your superior's values regarding performance and promotability. But remember, power to recommend is not based solely upon logic and reason but, also, upon the benefits you afford the superior by your total relationship.

Suppose that you are a star performer and a highly respected, informally designated successor to your superior. If you have substantially the same level of quality of performance and promotability in your favored subordinate, you have the key ingredients to be crucial to the promotability of your superior. So you see how the superior is vulnerable and will think twice before rejecting your nominations.

It is smart to use assiduously a four-legged stool composed of what the nomination will do for the superior, for your relationship, and for their nominee, all with due regard to the opportunity in question. A reasonably argued presentation is most apt to display credible judgment, which is to what superiors defer before they will allow managers to check their authority to assign opportunities or to promote at will.

Ultimate power is *sponsorship*. In this fourth level of power, you put more than your judgment on line, but also your relationship with your superior. It is a pledge amounting to a personal guarantee by the manager to honor responsibility for all acts, moves, decisions, results, and consequences now and in the future of the particular subordinate in or out of a lineup. It is best to seek this power when your credibility of judgment is at its peak. Proper timing requires judgment based upon the rule of reality. You must see things as they exist and, likewise, must your superior. Mistakes are apt to occur when at any time the superior is not sufficiently observant and possessed of good judgment.

There is a tough double test. Do you have good judgment, and does your superior see clearly that you have it? Managers with more power to influence than skill to sponsor have too often beguiled their superiors. Managers are difficult to resist who make decisive if not critical contributions to their superior's promotability. After all, as superiors, they wrested sponsorship from their extended superiors. They enjoy the feeling to be in charge of the staffs without someone always watching over their shoulders. The accountability for picking their own people becomes translated into double credits both for promotability and for achievement of exceptional accomplishments.

But the stakes are high. If wrong, superiors can lose vital control of key positions one or two levels below them. Mindful of the potential consequences, masters practice the following two rules: First of all, they never completely relax. They practice oversight in order to step in at the proper time to assert their authority. Second, masters will allow sponsorship only because the manager has displayed as good or better judgment than they have. If this is not the case, the manager must rely upon the lesser powers to win the struggle to countervail against the master's authority.

The fast route requires arriving, performing, and departing smoothly, quickly, and efficiently. There is an irrefutable minimum; know what people you need with what mix of skills for the opportunities at hand. With this wit in sufficient amount, managers may gain great achievements from average staffs. However, if their successors are average, exceptional performance of their staffs will return to mediocrity. In other words, you can have average staffs but you cannot afford to have average successors.

Furthermore, continuity of high performing staffs requires periodic replacement of weak or key members at the right times with people of right skills. Managers are more apt to be alert to this requirement than superiors two levels above these subordinate staff members. They may not be expected to have as wise judgments as their managers directly on the scene.

Because managers cannot be compelled to make wise choices if their wits are insufficient, superiors must remove this deficiency by replacement of the mangers with people who ideally can gain the power to sponsor, have the judgment required, and show the confidence to assume the responsibility and risks. Frankly, few managers come prepared with these skills. Masters never start off their careers with skills to sponsor. It usually takes several levels of experiences with the willingness and patience of several superiors and their cooperation for managers to gain the power to sponsor. Masters may occasionally misidentify winners and losers. But because of their perceived future worth, their superiors discount their errors. They are too valuable to allow the most ideal skill to arrest their momentum. To fail occasionally at the ideal level means that masters still may look incomparably better than others.

The wisdom to sponsor tends to be portable and it may acquire a momentum of its own. Once you excel at picking, replacing, and promoting the right people, superiors will seek to gain your services. After all, you excel with the critical wits and skills that help superiors and businesses become successful. You are a valuable commodity in the marketplace for managerial services.

A highly competitive, volatile global economy values highly your exceptional judgment about the use of the power to build a high-powered staff around carefully selected key players to drive a business, division, or subsidiary. In so doing you sponsor a bullpen of attractive, capable successors, among whom is one that will receive your full faith and credibility. By such wits, you put at ease your superiors, wherever they may be, who value competent continuity of succession? People with the wits to sponsor wisely can write their own ticket.

However, if the sponsoree fails soon after or later, you will be faulted because you guaranteed your successor's performance. You raised your superiors' expectations, lulled them to sleep while they attended to malperforming managers, relaxed their controls and vigilance and careful oversight, and then suddenly they wake up to see that you misled them. Can you ever be as completely trusted again with power of sponsorship?

Power and authority represent relationships among two or more people. Upwards, sponsorship represents power over the superior and downwards, sponsorship is privilege exercised as apparent authority over subordinates. In other words, it is an article of faith that subordinates may rely upon as though it were delegated authority to the meager from the superior. Of course, it is not. Power has merely checked the assertiveness of the superior's authority. The authority of the superior remains intact and at any time may be used to decertify the manager's power to sponsor. To be allowed to do something is not the same as having been authorized to do it.

For that matter, masters do a lot of things that are not formally authorized but for which they may be held accountable. There is no such thing as a free territory wherein managers may roam irresponsibly. Some managers, naïve about authority, would like to believe so. In fact, they practice as though once authority is delegated, it becomes theirs. No one's authority is owned, not even the chief's.

It is derived from owners of the business and is divided and delegated by the chief in decrements to lower levels of the corporation.

It is tempting to want the authority and power to choose your staff members, your preferred subordinates, and your successor. These opportunities represent the ultimate way to show you are as smart as your results, better than your peers, or equal in wits to your superiors. However, to your subordinates, you may become viewed as the "complete boss." This is a trap. Subordinates would like to believe that everything under your control is yours to control. If your subordinates can control you, they can better control their fates without being anxious about your superiors' judgments. If they believe you have the authority to select your successor, they will play up to that expectation. The fine distinction between power and authority may escape them, such as your relationship of trust and respect with your superiors that allows freedom of discretion.

This scenario traps many managers who are inclined to put becoming a complete boss ahead of subordination to their superiors. They enjoy, both in practice and appearance, being superior to their subordinate staff. To them, it is what managers are all about. You have heard their plaint, "If you don't like what I am doing, then remove me. Otherwise leave me alone to do my job." Up and down corporate corridors resounded their lamentation: "get off my back." So these managers press their advantage to become as full of responsibility as possible and an authority unto themselves, if not in fact, then in practice.

This ambition is both common and good for business. It allows for application of creative imagination, initiative, diligence in all matters and, often, exceptional accomplishments; all of these good things, but also the bad things. For one thing, they are playing into an inherent inconsistency. "Complete bosses" may not allow their subordinates the same freedom of discretion. Those who want the most for themselves often offer the least to others. If managers may choose their successors, will they allow the same opportunity for their subordinates? Granting this power is inconsistent with the idea of being the complete superior.

Notice the steps of power, including evaluation, recommendation, nomination, and sponsorship. At any step, "complete bosses" may dominate the transaction over their subordinates. In many instances, subordinates do not have the power to evaluate unabridged by their managers. In this case, performance evaluation becomes a charade, a bureaucratic nicety with little relevance to the way their real world should work.

While masters use these steps to develop people to eventually become trustworthy sponsors, "complete bosses" use them to keep people under control. The difference between what they want for themselves and what they will not grant to others is what many masters call greed. It is the ambition to gain power to check the assertiveness of superiors' authority in order to become boss unto oneself. Suffice it to say these "complete bosses" are not the stuff of which lineups are made. They do not practice in deeds ideal subordination. In words they may pretend, but they do not really serve their superiors for the purpose of enhancing the latter's pro-motability.

From the master's perspective, complete bosses represent thorny issues about power and authority. The ascents of masters are plagued by managers who are not bright about these issues. These issues always lie in wait regardless of level in the hierarchy and are ready to be aroused by climbers not smart about practical differences between power allowed and authority delegated. For these reasons, masters invariably check with superiors about issues as critical to a lineup as sponsorship. It is more than a courtesy move. Masters and their superiors know of their power to sponsor. When they have it, they need not be arbitrary. By discussing with their superior, they are confident that they will not have their power or the independence of their wits compromised. The superior will make it very clear that it is their move. While both will have to live with the consequences, masters are best able to predict them or they should not be a sponsor. But they could be wrong. Just because they have the power does not mean infallibility. A helping hand to lift them up will be all the more forthcoming if they never forget that with all the power at their disposal, they are always first and last a subordinate.

This perspective is easily lost. The higher they rise, generally the more freedom to make discretionary judgments and the easier to assume away the authority that allows the opportunity to distinguish themselves through the choices of their key players and successors. This mistake is both unwise and ill mannered. Among members of a lineup, manners are more important than rights. Besides, the fast climbs do not allow masters many mistakes about judgments as critical as sponsorship of key subordinates and successors. They must take care to be correct, be honest when in doubt, seek counsel when necessary, then put the full weight of their relationships behind their decisions. Anyone less wise and courageous will fail the ultimate test of promotability. If masters are wrong, their power will be checked by their superiors' authority. Until they have been proved wrong, masters will oppose all voices of protest and frustration.

There will be many. The higher they go, the greater the pressure upon masters to make the politically correct choice. Extended superiors far removed from the scene will dispatch messengers to encourage selecting successors whom they prefer because of past commitments. The collective power of a lineup to hold fast will relieve much of this coerceive power.

Still, sponsorship is high risk. You put more than your managerial reputation on the line. Your relationship with your superiors and your lineup are on the line. Also, your power to sponsor puts your own sponsorship by your superiors at risk. If you cannot pick winners, how can you attract and develop winning successors? The game of climbing is winning judgments. You cannot win bigger than to be judged as exceptionally smart about picking successors, especially if they prove to have long-term value. It has often been noted herein that your performance stays with the position or assignment. Granted, achievements may continue to impact the business favorably for some time. But your successor moves up with you and becomes a crucial element of your future promotability. Embodied in your successor are your smart moves whereby you prepared well your successor and acquired adroitly the power of sponsorship. It is because of your smart moves that you gain your lift up.

No doubt your successor wants to earn the power to sponsor. You will put this crucial subordinate through the same tests as your superior did with you, starting with power to evaluate, then recommend and nominate. When you allow your successor to gain sponsorship, the lead member of the lineup has coordinated smarts for picking winners among three levels. The potential for gaining minimum control of three levels has been achieved. The fast route is at hand. A crucial subordinate reports to a promotable manager who is sponsored by a powerful superior.

In conclusion, you will search high and low for masters who are not reputed for moving with winners, avoiding losers, and opposing those who inveigh against their choices. They demonstrate this wit: If your basic moves of away, with, or against are not wise and firm about your sponsorship, how can you prove yourself to be equal to your superiors in lesser ways? If you lack the confidence to make wise judgments and stand on them, you will do a lot of walking the floors rather than climbing the corporate stairs. What good is mobility without the power of a lift?

19

THE MIND FOR THE CLIMB

The mind for the climb may be summarized by a review of the fast route to the top, followed by a more detailed explanation and rationale of the masters' rules of thumb.

The fast route to the top is to become a crucial subordinate to a promotable manager who is sponsored by a powerful superior. Each of the major terms represents judgments. First, take the practical meaning of fast route. Route is a means of access to the top or wherever your ambitions lead. This course of travel is determined largely by your superiors. In most cases, you do not select them, they select you. You are chosen because they depend upon you for their continued advancements. The route includes climbers pulling up climbers, many of whom are aligned three or more levels deep. Strings of climbers dot the corporate landscape. The most common are triplets. Some are doublets just forming. Others are quite mature lineups that have passed the test of a promotion or two.

Corporate climbing has a certain affinity to mountain climbing. Several people are strung along the face of the incline securely tethered by pitons and lifelines by which they leverage themselves until one of them finally reaches the point. Who arrives first is sometimes in doubt. Luck may determine the order of ascent, but more often, they have a lead member who has the greater skill for climbing. Likewise, corporate climbers must not be intimidated by the steepness of the slope or pixelated by the risks or predisposed to esteem themselves higher than the tall mountain they are climbing. They must compete with other strings of climbers scattered over the corporate face above and below who have their own independent perspectives about how to arrive on top first.

Lineups of corporate climbers move at various speeds, depending upon the difficulty of their circumstances. Fast means to move up working with fewer superiors and positions or less career time at each level than usual for managers who become chiefs. Fast is regulated by your superiors' judgments about your mobility to adapt readily to changing corporate ways and circumstances, to be agile to move harmlessly through a myriad of obstacles and traps, and to be flexible and tractable to deal with arbitrary and unreasonable demands upon your time and efforts. In effect mobility becomes a vehicle of sorts that provides transportation among, over, and through corporate ways.

In regard to these, you will be judged by your wits and skills of mobility needed to sustain the fast route. Winning favorable judgments offers evidence and credence that you have this most basic skill for the climb. You must win and continue to win these judgments because they allow you to capitalize upon your mobility to move quickly and easily until you reach your destination.

If you have the climber's perspective, you will probably favor focusing next upon the idea of *powerful superior*. Powerful superiors are climbers who have the power to pull up other climbers behind them. They will tap the most elementary form of power, which is the ability to get people to do what they want to do without use of authority. It is most succinctly expressed by successful efforts to help or hurt people. Powerful superiors can help in ways that their authority cannot. For one thing, they can form lineups. However, superiors cannot use their authority to order you to align your career with theirs. Lineups are extraterritorial ways that silently exist outside the authority and other formal ways of managing, as do almost all ways of climbing. No invitations are sent to join lineups, no words are spoken, and no penalty inflicted if you do not, and no apology expected. Power is subtle that nudges you to become associated closer than usual with your superiors. Without any exchange of promises or commitments, you are smart enough to read the signals of powerful superiors, to accept association in their lineups, and to know how to gain and share the implied assistance and protection.

What you may not know is the amount of power your superior has to direct and constrain the rightful use of authority by extended superiors, especially in regard to judgments about your promotability. Hopefully, your superior has the power to be the sole judge of your achievements and advancements. Then you have the advantage of having to win the favor of one superior rather than several. The estimate of your future worth to your superior is seldom expressed directly. You are never allowed to take your favored status for granted. This practice is one of the silent ways that superiors use the benefits of lineups without formally recognizing their existence.

Sponsorship gives lineups their special power over higher levels of authority. These extended superiors depend upon your immediate superior for their achievements and advancements, and likewise your superior upon you. However, it is not that your superiors do nothing but depend upon you. They gain credit for the achievements of their staffs of which you are a member. They also depend upon you to help them gain a special edge to compete successfully against other contestants. The difference between fast and slow climbers is often a narrow but sharp margin. It favors contestants who as successors give their superiors vital control over key positions. Also, they provide their superiors with wise advice and counsel about managing and climbing, are trusted by them to make smart moves at higher levels, and to learn as fast as required by their increased responsibilities. They have a special sense about how their corporation works and avoid getting bogged down in all kinds of internecine battles and becoming trapped by others shrewd about climbing. These qualities represent an ideal composite of crucial subordination. In some form or degree, these qualities have the potential to enhance the future worth of both your superior and of yourself.

Now it is your turn to find and develop a successor as crucial to you as you are to your superiors. Some managers find it easier to become vital to their superiors than to find and develop subordinates crucial to them. Others are prone to do the reverse better. You must make both moves acceptable to your superiors. This means that you want to attract and develop subordinates who are high performers and who will cast their lots with your future. However, the wise will be reluctant to hitch their careers unless you are promotable and show evidence of promotability. If you have some control over your own promotions, they will assume that you have some control over theirs. They know that your most favored subordinate will be judged to be your potential successor. Your superior may allow this judgment because together you have developed a relationship of mutual trust and respect.

Subordinates read into your other evaluations, nominations, and recommendations the power to influence your superior in ways important to them. Because of this apparent power, subordinates may become all the more eager to assist your career. The smartest know how to serve you beyond their exceptional achievements without ostentatious display of servitude. This subtlety is appreciated because in no way should the corporate ways pertaining to the link between performance and promotions be openly disputed or offended. Formally, results should always count. Informally, your relationships above and below will help to frame the judgments involved in making your climb to the top.

These relationships have the potential to make your climb less difficult. It is up to you to know how to get the most out of them. The trick is to make a crucial contribution to your superior's career without losing your independence to think and act, to earn the power to handpick your key subordinates and successor, and to work with members of the lineup to multiply your wits about the essential ways that the corporation works and how to work it. Of course, nothing is guaranteed. Fortune may step in at any time and declare all wits and skills to be inadequate or irrelevant or improper, just as bad weather may set in to stop the mountain climbers' ascents or to commence their rappelling.

The above narration, representing in general the closest approximation of the collective mind of master climbers, may be detailed by describing their "may do's and may not do's" concerning the fast route. No one master uses all of these rules of thumb equally well. Prospective climbers should know how the rules work their way into relationships that spawn lineups.

The Climber's Rule

Climbers climb together. Usually, when a vacant position is filled, other vacancies are created. By knowing and anticipating moves and movements of people, you attempt to become a beneficiary of these sequences. It is self-evident that you need more help than your performances allow. Too many contestants who already have been judged by promotable superiors to be their preferred successors have prior claims upon these vacancies. Either you stand in line and take your chances or you adapt the climber's rule and work it assiduously. Nothing intellectually profound is required. The rule simply means that you must become the edge sufficient for your superiors to compete successfully against other contestants for valuable assignments and positions. Putting your career second to your superiors is not a gratuitous expression of self-sacrifice. For climbers, altruism is not a proper way to play the game, nor do corporate ways officially require it. Rather, the climbers' rule is a strategy for expediting your achievements and advancements. There is an implicit quid pro quo. You serve others who best serve you.

Anything done well is difficult and anything difficult may be made less difficult. The ideal superior makes it easy for you and your staff to do your best. This extra effort makes it advantageous for you to make it easy for your superiors to manage you. You do not wait to be asked or told. Your mind is on the ready, including anticipating the needs of the superior. Your sense of priority tells you where to place your best wits for the most telling effects. You avoid laying indiscriminately upon your superior just anything that appears useful. You pick and chose ideas to avoid, to support, and to oppose, using judgment about their potential consequences to your superior's career. Thus, you avoid becoming a gofer.

Because of your contributions above and beyond the call of managing well your staff, you may hit the jackpot. It is to gain opportunities to sharpen your edge over your peers by acquiring quality exposure and visibility with extended superiors. The ideal is to use fewer achievements to garner more and faster advancements. This ideal may be approximated by a proper perspective. As a manager, you focus primarily upon your subordinates. As a climber you focus intently upon your superior. In turn you select and develop key subordinates who will acquire and utilize this double focus for your benefit. The one you depend upon the most becomes your successor. Your superior now has a dependable successor in you and you have one as well. The quality of this lineup in no small way enhances the promotability of your superior. Your superior advances, then you advance and your crucial subordinate advances. Climbers help climbers to climb.

The Mobility Rule

Smart moves promote better than exceptional results. Promotability is not simply about achievements, but the smartness of your moves and movements. How you move among people, ideas, and programs at one level greatly determines if you will be moved to higher levels. Your ideal is to make no more or less moves than necessary to achieve expected results with few unintended consequences. Your consistent, shrewd moves to support, avoid, and oppose (AWA) enable you to exploit propitious opportunities and maneuver through risky and tricky conditions, including the most illusive or demanding corporate ways. Your finest moves will be to quickly and precisely augment a critical plan and intervene in a failing program that is particularly valuable to your superior. Your superior will be the judge of the value, not of some abstract notion of the good of business.

Because your moves and movements consistently put you in control of things, you earn the trust that you have the wits to move just as wisely at higher levels. These same wits make you attractive to lineups to help the members upgrade their strategies and moves for achieving and advancing. Simply put, you rely upon engaging and disengaging in the right way, at the right time, for the right reasons, with the right people, ideas and programs.

Mobility plus power (to be discussed later) represents the bookends of the other three essential ingredients of masters' prescriptions for climbing, organization, hierarchy, relationships. Of course, results count, but they are the symptoms of the smart moves to attain them. Your peers may be impressed by your record of achievements, but you are not as much. You know that you cannot take your results with you, but you do your wits.

If you lack the wits and skills to quickly mobilize your efforts and those of others to optimize opportunities to prove yourself, you may just as well forget about becoming a preferred successor to a promotable manager, particularly one aligned with a powerful superior. Mobility is the entrance fee for getting on the fast route.

The Organization Rule

Smart climbers organize their smartness. Managers use the idea of formal organization to combine and coordinate the efforts of people to produce results greater than the sum of their efforts.

Climbers use the idea of organization informally and silently. Without this skill, a lineup will fail to generate the power to assist the individual and collective careers of the members. Furthermore, the ideas and benefits of organization cause lineups to evolve and to supply the enabling efforts for using the climbers' rule.

Several people may discover or determine that they have a common objective or purpose. They divvy up their responsibilities according to their wits and skills, just as managers practice division of labor. This couplet relies upon each member's separate contributions, the accumulation of which makes for a collective result difficult to ascribe the efforts of either member.

For climbers, their common purpose is to expedite their advancements. They need each other to think through how to use the formal, informal, and silent ways of the corporation and perhaps invent a few themselves. No doubt they already have in place a good working relationship for managing their formal responsibilities. If they do not, they cannot reap the benefits of a lineup. Thus, formal organization used for managing becomes intertwined with informal as climbers attempt to develop their strategy and moves for producing exceptional accomplishments and for advancing their careers.

It is said that two heads are better than one, but only if they are corporate-wise to begin with and know how to extract and coordinate their wits for optimal effect. When done properly, the rule of organization is demonstrated. Several people, well coordinated by purpose, wits, and skills, will acquire a more useful perspective and sense about how to advance faster than people who take sole charge of their careers. Smart people have the smarts to know how to grow smarter together.

Lineups are not tea parties or even comparable to management-oriented meetings and discussions. In some respects, they are essentially informal "spy networks" that gather and share information from many sources. The members analyze and comprehend it for gaining lead time about forthcoming events and happenings, including possible movement of people above and below them, vacancies and probable promotions, lineups and their members, and changes in power, including who currently has the most clout to help or hurt the present and future opportunities of the members. Care must be taken to gather, analyze information, and derive corporate sense unbiased by hidden agendas or spiked by exaggeration or rushed by time constraints.

Lineups break down and become nonessential to the members because their collective wisdom is no better than that of any one member or the members are too preoccupied with their managerial responsibilities or the lead member has lost promotability or power of sponsorship. In the latter case, a lineup may recharge itself to help the superior regain promotability. In the first case, either the members are improperly selected or, more likely, no one member knows how to pull out and tap their individual wits.

This brings up the second case. Members may not manage their time sufficiently well to have the time to assist the lineup. Poor time managers should not be members of the lineup. If they are presently overloaded with poorly managed work, they will be swamped at higher levels. However, in most cases, people always have time to do what they want to do. Usually the problem is that the lead superior has not organized the lineups' resources to justify the time required of each member. Too much time is taken for the results acquired. These superiors may not be the best organizers of their managerial responsibilities. In such cases these and other defects may infiltrate their lineups.

Still, lineups may continue to exist hobbled by the inefficient application of the idea of organization. Compared to other lineups, they may have enough effectiveness to sequence their members for taking advantage of forthcoming vacancies and promotions. Almost all fast climbers maintain that any help members give to a lineup pays far greater dividends than comparable help given to unassociated individuals.

Motives of self-gain put in the service of helping members of a lineup are more dependable than the same motives disguised as serving the interests of business. Where else in this world of rampant hypocrisy may one be self-serving but in an informal organization of climbers openly dedicated to helping each other to gain advancements, even if one of them bypasses the other. If others are left behind, the efficacy of the rule of organization becomes verified. It matters not which member gains the advantage. Of course, you hope it will come to you. But if it does not, you are not in worse condition, and if you feel you were taken advantage of, well you were! You had the same motive as the others. If you cannot celebrate the extraordinary lift up given to a member, you joined the lineup under false pretenses, and if the member who has leapfrogged reaches back later to pull you up, you will probably not accept the promotion, right? Because you do not want to be taken advantage of again? Well, forget about your climbing career, because superiors are always going to be dependent for their advancements upon managers, especially their key performers and potential successors. That is the name of the game; you help others who are best able to help you.

Of course, members of a lineup are not poverty-stricken. They do not need to beg for help. They may have as much coin of the realm in exceptional achievements as other contestants. They just want a superior edge and, to that extent, they depend upon each other. It takes several people to produce a master climber. How wisely they divide their wits and skills among each other to optimize their career strategies and moves has the potential to be the most efficient means of helping climbers to climb.

The Hierarchy Rule

No triplet can outwit a lineup. Now fuse the potential benefits of the informal organization with the idea of hierarchy. A basic unit comprising several people spanning several adjacent levels offers the ideal way to optimize the value of the above rules of thumb. If business is going to use a hierarchy to achieve managerial purposes, you will use it for climbing. In effect, without starting an internal war, you are going to use an informal hierarchy to beat a formal hierarchy at its own game. If the hierarchy functions to hold people down at their highest levels of competency, you are going to use it to prove yourself equal to your superior. If extended superiors are going to make judgments about your promotability, you are going to ensure that your immediate superior moves favorably on your behalf. This means that you must strengthen the power of your superior as much as possible to check the arbitrary uses of extended superiors' authority. Otherwise you will not have optimal control over your career.

A lineup of superior, manager, and subordinate may use its expertise to identify better the key subordinates at their respective levels through whom they may better drive their responsibilities. By working together, they help their staffs to work together. These efforts may occur anyhow without the need for a lineup. What may be more relevant to climbing are their efforts to gain control of the hierarchy above them. Their lead member is in a better position to see and read values and priorities of extended superiors that regulate and influence promotions, promotable, and promotability. Other members of the lineup have extensive connections to pick up those signals and vibrations. Masters prefer to call this perceptiveness, "value sense." It is sensing that is important to important people. Value sense includes reading what is not made evident.

Recall the case of the new CEO and CFO (Chapter 9, The Power of Lineups). The lineup is the division manager, the vice-president of sales, and the controller made division CFO by displacing the previous CFO. By supporting, coaching, and protecting the new division CFO, the lineup shows the flexibility and adaptability to adjust to the implied expectations of the new CEO and the new corporate CFO. Now sales and finance drive the division's business rather than sales and operations. While formally the division CFO and sales vice-president are peers, informally they are not treated as equals. The silent intent of the lead member becomes carefully read to make one of them the preferred successor. This being the case, the peer will assist the successor apparent and thereby assist the lineup devised by the division manager. Each member understands that the best way to break through the hierarchy above is to form and use on the quiet their own informal hierarchy. Any number of moves may now occur, but one thing is certain, the lineup has a keen sense of values sufficient to anticipate changes in the ways that people will be evaluated and promoted. Other people may sense this change in values but may not have the wits or confidence needed to follow through.

As it turned out, the lineup got control of the hierarchy above sufficiently to advance its members. But note that the displaced division CFO did not get tethered to the division general manager's lifeline. This free fall may be explained when technically competent managers believe that wisdom is found in words and numbers and that speaking or writing them should be sufficient to gain the attention of people and control of their minds. However, wisdom is not a unilateral expression. It is framed and given creditability within the context of relationships. The displaced CFO did not know how to overcome what masters often call the "stranger's predicament." It is ridiculous to expect people to believe others if they do not know them and trust their motives and integrity. For this reason, medicine shows contrive all kinds of guileful moves to persuade the gullible to buy their worthless products. It works when a quick bond of credibility is established.

However, buying a bottle of cough syrup and believing in career advice substantially ups the ante on credibility. The displaced CFO did not have the wits or skills to form relationships that invite credibility even before any words and numbers are presented. In a data-rich world, many experts are ignored because they do not know how to make their facts credible and useful to people who could benefit from them. They violate the next rule of thumb.

The Relationships Rule

Relationships form winning judgments. The affiliative motive is a resource as important as the motives of achievement and power. People need to express themselves in the presence of people they trust will understand them. They seek something more permanent than casual acquaintance or professional association. They are most easily disarmed, and their minds penetrated by people with whom they are comfortable. They will memorialize their relationship in notes and letters that recall the pleasant times they had together. Now transport this affiliative motive into the context of a climber's perspective. Relationships become the glue that binds a lineup into a cohesive unit and obligates members to assume responsibility for each other. Simply put, the members want to be together and to continue their valuable relationship at higher levels. There is a certain thrill when people come together to make it together. Comraderie is part of the thrill of the chase.

Members may become attracted to each other at several levels. They are personable and enjoy each other's company. They are informative and depend upon each other for gaining knowledge about corporate ways. And thirdly, they are competent because these three levels transform a formal hierarchy of superior, manager, and subordinate into a tightly knit group whose members may not think of resenting and rejecting calls for assistance from each other.

Without relationships, as used by climbers, a triplet of superior, manager, subordinate will remain a formal hierarchy, and the usual differences of authority and responsibility among the members will infiltrate and bias the exchange of information, knowledge, and expertise. Authority and information are always potential adversaries. The function of relationships is to neutralize or ignore the authority of the formal hierarchy when matters of climbing are concerned.

Moving from their formal roles as superior, manager, and subordinate to their informal relationships requires skills of mobility. Some members may quickly and easily move from their formal, over-under relationships in favor of informal, collegial relationships, and back again as efficient use of relationships requires. Other members may not relate well either way. In either case, they do not help to optimize the benefits implicit in the rule of organization. It is because of poor relationship skills that managers may not be invited into a lineup or may not remain for long in it. They may possess difficult personalities, temperamental minds, or crude, rude deportment. They have to be worked around or moved out because they simply do not fit in.

In contrast, people with skills to gain quick and productive access to each other are most apt to enhance and receive the superior benefits of an informal alignment. The objective is to extend and multiply their wits through relationships. They never know what all they know and experience, and others may know what they do not know. They can never acquire sufficient corporate sense alone.

Wisdom in the first instance is to know what it is. It seldom is personally contrived. Through relationships, members combine observations, intuitions, and experiences to gain a sharp edge for slicing through the clutter and glitter of everyday corporate life. This task is expedited by members who are sharp witted enough to know what wisdom is and who always need more of it and who are not afraid to admit it. Weak minds are reluctant to use relationships to seek the help of others. They are overly impressed by what they know and cannot be impressed by what others know or they are afraid that they do not know enough and fear being discovered inadequate or inferior. Strong minds seek wisdom and respect others who seek relief from the lack of it.

One form of ignorance concerns what is happening at levels above the lineup. Long sight is required of each member, but it has limits. Much of what is relevant to corporate sense is revealed in close, often confidential relationships, both formal and informal, at higher levels just as in the case of a lineup. This is where the value of the lead member comes into play. If the lead member of the lineup has close relationships with extended superiors, then valuable information, knowledge, and expertise may be made available to the other members of the lineup. They do not have to spend so much time reading the tea leaves. In this way, relationships augur well for upgrading collective corporate sense. The practical advantage for the members amounts to redesigning career strategies and moves if necessary.

But there is a potential glitch in this procedure for transmitting and increasing corporate sense. It is about the matter of confidences. Some things are expected to be held in trust within close-knit relationships. This is especially true of certain corporate ways that are in vogue at the time. On the levels within the formal hierarchy, oftentimes corporate ways are practiced differently, and some extended superiors may give these ways a personal touch. They ride some practices and beliefs harder than others, and then, later, other ways become their diligent concerns.

For example, extended superiors may alter their judgments about who are promotable due to unexpected vacancies. In some cases, availability or reward promotions become the order of the day or more substantial promotions, including developmental, performance, or functional. Consideration may be given to going outside for replacements. Preferred lineups may lose to newer lineups. Prime moves may be in the wind or in play that will alter drastically many positions and opportunities. A power struggle may be underway whereby functional lineups, say finance and sales, are competing for ascendancy.

In such cases, extended superiors will play their cards close to their chests with only the members of their lineup aware of these machinations. As noted in the case of the new CEO and CFO, lineups may be reshaped to reflect the change in values and priorities that may affect both managing and climbing. These ebbs and flows may be known only among members of higher level lineups. As a trusted member of an extended superior's lineup, your lead member may be aware of these changes in ways, values, and priorities but may be required to maintain sealed lips. In effect, your lineup experiences a deficit of awareness.

However, this ignorance may be relieved by another informal corporate way. Confidences are conditional. They are not expected to be relayed to anyone deemed untrustworthy. A lineup's relationships are the epitome of trustworthiness. If members cannot be trusted, there is no lineup. Consequently, lineups are usually the first to become aware of corporate happenings above them that they should not know. This gives members lead-time to revise and to get an edge on competitors' strategies and moves. All of which show that lineups and relationships as climbers use them are synonymous.

The Power Rule

Power does for climbing what authority cannot. You should not minimize this muscle-building ingredient of your strategy and moves for climbing. Many people do. In fact, they often fail to make a practical distinction between power and authority. People are often so busy advancing or discounting new jargon that when faced with substantive words, they misuse or ignore them as well. Many businesses are reluctant to use these words for fear that power and authority will represent a throwback to command and control ways. Well, masters of the 1990s have news for them. Authority and power are very much alive today in spite of semantic contrivances to disguise them. It is more than interesting that some businesses use fashionable lexicon this way. Power and authority are integral to running a successful business. Managers could use authority and power more efficiently and constructively if the ideas were part of the language by which they think and communicate. Those who make a useful distinction possess a silent tool for climbing that encourages a form of favoritism far more than any supplicant could expect.

Authority is the right to order behavior and expect compliance. Compliance is to do whatever is required because you must. But power is to get people to do what you want when authority is neither available nor useful. Power is not a hierarchical ordering of superior over subordinate, but rather mind dealing with mind. In this sense, powerful people have the mind that others must deal with. You may avoid, support, or oppose powerful people, but you cannot pretend that power does not exist or assume away the consequences of it. It is always present to be used for good or evil, wisely or crudely.

Managers have power when others judge them to be smart and depend upon them for help. Simply put, it is their wits in particular and their corporate sense in general that superiors rely upon. This is usually the basis of power behind the throne. Superiors seek advice and counsel from those they trust to use their power for purposes rightly earned.

Masters maintain that high performers are less difficult to find than corporate-wise managers. Managers may have abundant skills to become exceptional performers, but not enough corporate wisdom to make a lineup out of them. They may be prone to make mental errors and stupid moves in the area of powerful, extended superiors that reflect badly upon superiors. In short, unsmart managers cannot be trusted to have the edge with powerful people. As masters say, "Keep them out of sight so they can make better fools of themselves in private."

When used properly, your power has the capability of obtaining commitment, which is when people do something because they believe in it as though it were their own idea. Power, as authority, may coerce compliance, but not in the context of climbing. You need to command the attention and respect of your superiors over whom you have no authority. So you practice the above rules of thumb to make your superiors dependent upon you. In exchange, you gain the power to check the rightful authority of them to select and promote at will your key subordinates and successor. Thus, dependency flows downward and power flows upward.

You hope your superiors likewise have power to check, constrain, and modify arbitrary assertiveness of higher authority. The same dependency/power combination may be extended to your subordinates. When this happens, three levels of people have the potential to control key positions. Of course, you and your subordinates have peers about whom your superior may not have the same amount of confidence. But at the least, your superior has the semblance of the minimum amount of support from well tried and tested people upon whom each will be dependent upon high-performing staffs in key positions and assignments at their respective levels.

The key to gaining the power to sponsor is to earn trust and respect greater than and different from the value of your achievements. If you are the lead member, your power to sponsor becomes the power train of the lineup.

These rules of thumb may be used to gain decided advantage over other climbers. Your strategy may be similar, for example, to businesses that gain a competitive edge in the marketplace. Other firms must compete with them to keep up. But businesses may also gain a controlling position. They have commanding share of the market such that other firms must compete among themselves for the remainder of the market. Your ideal for climbing is to secure a commanding status by being judged a long-term contributor such that other climbers will have to compete among themselves for near-in positions and limited promotions. You secure a strong lock on your future. Whatever your achievements are, they will gain for you more advancement than for your competitors.

The judgments you want to win are those of your superior and hopefully several levels of extended superiors for whom you have the staying power to maintain your future worth. In fact, you may be judged capable of doing better the higher you progress. The key to controlling your future lies in your wits to win these valuable judgments. In other words, you make it easy and advantageous, if not necessary, for your superiors to take you with them when they move up or to later maneuver you through a level or two of superiors that they have passed.

You should be prepared to bypass at least once in your career. With the power to sponsor, you have the option later to pull up former superiors or subordinates who have been left behind. They too may leapfrog. These former superiors or subordinates proved their future worth when they were members of your lineup. With such indisputable value observed and experienced first-hand, you would be pressed not to use them. No doubt, staff members already in place when you arrive in your new position may perform just as well. You hope that will be the case because you will need all the help that you can muster. But it is not how well these inherited staff members may ultimately perform, but how secure and comfortable you feel about using unknown quantities versus known.

Besides, you do not have all the time in the world to prove yourself at each level, unless of course, your ability to learn quickly has tailed off sharply and your future worth has substantially decreased. But you do not want this to be the judgment. Out of self-interest, you pull up trustworthy people who have proven wits to help you make the most of your opportunity. Of course, you will need more staff members than one or two but sometimes a few well proven staff members will give you the edge necessary to achieve expected results. Masters are uniformly respected for their keen judgments about their key subordinates.

As you might expect, passed up managers will register complaints against fast climbers and their superiors. Many of these protests will be justified because climbing is not necessarily a rational process. In fact, as has been noted, business is no more rational than it needs to be. Many corporate ways are merely pretenses of business necessity. Rational explanations or logical defenses of business interest allow wide degrees of discretionary judgments. Almost all practices, except the most transparently and flagrantly self-serving, are used to enhance and protect careers in the name of business interests. Business does not lay down its life for a competitor. Managers should not be expected to be self-sacrificing. If they are, it is because of affection or misguided altruism or the absence of incentive to do otherwise. In any case, sincere managers should not be faulted for their good intentions or pitied when they are run over by climbers with more realistic ambitions. Masters do not want subordinates who treat superiors as prima donnas or offer up their careers as sacrifices. They cannot be trusted. That subordinates put superiors' careers ahead of theirs is a frank admission that their own careers will be best served. They are trusted because their motives are the same as their superior's.

Still, these silent ways of determining trustworthy successors must pass the semblance of muster by the formal ways of judging promotable managers. While careful consideration of relevant circumstances and possible consequences of anointing successors may be formally required and displayed informally, circumspection is more often the exception than the practice. Usually judgments about promotions, promotable, and promotability as defined herein are made later, within the silent consideration of endurable and proven relationship of mutual trust.

Notice the words *judgments, relationships, trust*. These ideas are emotional equivalents more than rational considerations. While managers may formally proclaim that performance counts, they do not say what achievements count, past, present, or future. Nor may they admit that among two subordinates with relatively equal records of performance, they will chose the one with whom they have a more comfortable and trusting relationship. Nor will they reveal how they encouraged a stronger relationship with their preferred subordinate nor how their relationship helped them to define up the preferred subordinate's achievements and define down the others.

The one consistent theme throughout masters' renditions of what it takes to go from the bottom to the top is the wits to extract from superiors favorable judgments about their future worth at higher levels. Their most demonstrable skill is mobility, and equally potent, but less apparent, is their use of power. Climbing is, at base, a procedure to mobilize your resources and that of others to gain the power to edge out other contestants for promotions sanctified by the appeal to business interests.

Serving the interests of business and interests of careers may not be mutually exclusive. Masters have to make some tough business decisions, including leaving behind high-performing superiors and subordinates. Even then, few masters will sacrifice their careers one iota if they can show some kind of business necessity for their predetermined choices of favored staff members and successors. In most cases, this judgment is not difficult to justify. But it is the ultimate judgment that needs to be won. The power of sponsorship may be lost, not by discreet favoritism, but by transparent, self-serving motives. As one master remarked, "Favoritism is an option formed by irrational considerations, justified by business necessity." If favoritism is winning judgments for expediting your climb, then you owe it to yourself to sharpen your wits about this emotional feature of the real world of climbing.

You never know how smart you can become until you must become smarter than you are. Dedicated climbing will force smarts that no amount of managing may. The fast route is the ultimate test of what it takes managers to become chiefs.

20
CONCLUSION: EFFORTS VS. WITS

How is the fast route different from the slow route? Who are most likely to be your competitors? The fast route contains progressive promotions. Progressive means a continuance of connected series of moves that advance you toward your goal. You do not want just one promotion. Rather, you seek a promotion that will lead to another and another, etcetera. In other words, you want to gain hierarchical momentum.

If you are on the fast route, you will have an edge over other contestants at the point of each promotion. Now what is it that gives you your decisive edge? It cannot be your achievements in present and past positions. They may take you to the next level, but then, once again, you must prove yourself equal to your increased responsibilities, which is precisely the nature of the slow route. It is plodding and ponderous with little assurance that you can successfully compete.

At any given time, you are no better than your last performance. This judgment means that your potential to advance is dependent upon what positions become available. If vacancies occur that fit your skills, you may be eligible for promotion. But take notice—you are dependent upon the movements of other people, including their promotions, terminations, resignations, demotions, and transfers. When the turnover is high, you are more likely to advance, and when it is low, you are not. In other words, you have no control over your future. However, your potential for advancement is greater than most managers who are not promotable regardless of the movements of people.

But promotable is not promotability. The latter means that you acquire the ability to assure advancements. You successfully assert a claim upon the future beyond the next position. You are the manager for whom superiors make vacancies. You have won their judgment that you are worthy to go all the way until you prove otherwise.

CONCLUSION: EFFORTS VS. WITS

Even if you quicken the pace of advancements or bypass a level or two, you have benefited, compared to others still plying the slow route. You know from reading the preceding text the rest of the story about how masters get off of the slow route onto the fast.

But there is risk; slow climbers may interrupt your progression at any point. Those most likely are ready to pop, to burst forth seemingly out of nowhere with unexpected or overly earned promotions. As the climbs of masters show, it takes only one of these "pops" to preempt your opportunity for continued advancement. The risks of climbing also include people who steal a promotion away from you, who may never get another promotion the remainder of their careers. Masters are irritated by new superiors who have been given availability and reward promotions, who are easily threatened and attempt to slow down their fast ascents.

The fact of the matter is no one's future worth is inviolate. Superiors change their minds; their own careers become jeopardized; their sponsors lose power; suddenly they quit, or lineups are reformed when the prime rule becomes activated. Or you lose that certain something that makes you more valuable to your superiors than simply your achievements. Many of these risks cannot be anticipated or planned for and must be dealt with as they arise. But there is a very predictable class of competitors that can define for you the terms of the climb. They can cause you to lose more than the next promotion and also control of your long-term future.

The contest is not between the masters and you. They may set the fast pace, but they do not represent the largest mass of climbers. Fast climbers are not numerous enough for you to focus upon in your drive to the top or wherever your ambitions may lead. Even masters do not consider their main body of contestants to be on the fast route. This should not detract from the potential advantages to be gained from knowing the fast route. The hierarchy of superiors through which you must climb comprises largely managers plying the slow route. Of course, they are not purposely putting the brakes on their ascents. Rather, they are working the managerial perspective about what it takes to get ahead.

It helps to draw back from the sense of combat and take the long view. Whether you know it or not, what you are involved in amounts to a race between effort and wits. Perhaps in the grand scheme of things, these two factors usually set the terms of any protracted contest. Of course, they are not mutually exclusive. To become efficient, effort requires wits and wits without effort is akin to hands without tools. Still, there is usually a certain emphasis that places one ahead of the other. This priority is demonstrated between early arrivals versus normal and late arrival chiefs. (Please see Appendix A, The Origins of Chiefs.)

The preponderance among the latter, slower climbers is what may be called big effort managers. They stand in sharpest contrast to masters. These managers will be your most formidable competitors, your most difficult superiors, and potentially your highest performing subordinates. Generally you cannot get on the fast route without their support or acquiescence. Because Big Efforts dedicate their wits to understand how to manage more than climb, they are promotable by superiors with a similar perspective. At any time they may "pop" forth to interrupt your progression. Furthermore, these plodding, effort-intensive managers have the gait to slow the climbs of everyone below them.

You might say that Big Effort-types work their way to the top while masters finesse their way. One outperforms in order to gain an edge and the other outmaneuvers. Big Efforts usually link their ambitions directly to achievements, believing advancements will take care of themselves. Masters link their ambitions directly to advancements, relying upon fewer but more valuable achievements. One group seeks critical assignments by which to prove themselves equal to their tasks, and the other uses opportunities with high exposure and visibility by which to prove themselves equal to their superiors. Big Efforts will work for more superiors during their climbs and bypass fewer of them. Masters will work for considerably fewer superiors and rely upon bypassing them as a practical career move. You might say that one shoots for quantity of achievements, and the other for quality.

Where these two worthy competitors depart the most is about their respective perspectives. Big effort managers practice the ideal of becoming a superb superior to their staffs. They will use their staffs to exert unremitting ambition and prodigious effort to achieve the most difficult assignments. They are proud of their records and reputations for always coming through. They hope that their reliability in the clutch will make it too tempting for superiors to turn them down. Even masters may rely upon them to staff their key positions.

These reliable, high performers brook no one on their staffs who are not similarly dedicated. Either their subordinates make it with them or they do not make it with anybody. The exit door is always partly ajar for those who think they can get by with loyal servitude rather than effortful service. When Big Efforts move up, they prefer not to take subordinates with them. They believe that they can find and develop high performers at each level of their climb. Staffs two levels above their subordinates are far more developed and ready for action. But they are known to sneak a few well-deserving subordinates if they become hard pressed. For this reason, big effort managers are accused of using people that their predecessors have developed. Big Efforts reply that their successors reap the same advantage so the difference is a wash.

Of course, they want the power to select the key members of their staffs and their successors. But their successors are chosen strictly because of their past achievements and not for their future worth. They do not consider their successors to move up with them as co-equals, but behind them, much as subjects of a sovereign. Promotions are performance or functional, because the idea of developmental promotion is not in their language of good management. They believe in stretching people to their fullest as a practice of getting the most out of them and not for developing them for higher responsibilities. Big Efforts vigorously denounce availability and reward promotions. Rather than financial rewards to motivate achievements, they favor subordinates who gain intrinsic rewards from their accomplishments. Hence, they believe that ambitions should be directly linked to achievement and not to advancement, contrary to the case of masters.

Big effort managers do not believe that anyone has better wits to direct their careers than themselves. Managing careers is the one thing that people should never share with anybody. They may share almost anything else to become effective managers but not about how climbing may become their lead skill. For this reason, big effort managers will press subordinates for high performance without any discernable obligation to look out for their future careers. They are not sponsors at heart. All climbers are on their own. In fact, big effort managers do not see climbing as a skill separate from managing.

Usually they are revolted by ideas of master climbers. In fact, when faced with the prospect of having a fast-route-type superior, they are tempted initially to seek employment elsewhere. However, when they discover that the master climber is just as demanding, they may settle down if for no other reason than to prove through sterling achievements that they are more deserving of their new superior's job. Displacing superiors is considered fair game as long as it is done through superior performances.

However, their competitiveness may turn to upmanship, where their wits are used to outsmart the superior, in which case their moves become blatantly adversarial. The removal of these hostile but high-performing staff members is a master's nightmare. The moves to convert them or work around them, short of their transfer or termination, require the adroit use of authority and power. Masters take care to solicit the advice of members of their lineup to avoid messy staff relationships or to make heroes out of these well-reputed high achievers.

If anyone at any time is most ready to pop, it is Big Efforts. They have fewer advancements than their achievements merit, and their services are usually in demand by both slow and fast climbers. While big effort managers have different perspectives about climbing and managing, they share their enthusiasm for racking up admirable records of high performances. However, the weakness that slows down Big Efforts' progress is their lack of corporate sense. This shortfall causes them to be outmaneuvered by smarter contestants, including masters with substantially less impressive records of performance. Of course, they blame "politics" and other like machinations. They have a difficult time understanding that no one may take advantage of them without their help.

Because of their myopia or naiveté, Big Efforts must work at gaining an acute sense of the ways that their corporations work, especially at higher levels, and how to be more clever about working them. Masters come by corporate sense more easily and intuitively. But with Big Efforts, this sense is not easily attained, because their focus is tightly upon the more important practices and beliefs that affect the business and their managerial opportunities. Their no-nonsense approach often represents a mental immobility that rejects the way things are in favor of the way they should be. In order to change corporate ways for the better, they may lie in wait to become chiefs. If they do, primal screams will rumble and shake the whole enterprise. The lineups that are destroyed or interrupted may be soon reconstituted or reformed because of the protection required from a chief who uses an ax rather than a paring knife.

Masters will at some time early in their careers cut their eyeteeth on big effort superiors. They must prove themselves equal to their tasks and forego devising opportunities to prove themselves superior to their peers or equal to their superiors. Masters will learn that hard work and reliable achievements have their own reward. At the same time, they will learn a few tricks that managers bank upon who place so much of their advancements upon their achievements.

For example, masters will learn how to avoid or cover mistakes that will reflect badly upon themselves, dress up their achievements to make them appear more valuable, and dress down their malperformances to make them appear less damaging. Because their big effort superiors tend to look for themselves in their subordinates, masters may play their game for the while. This game includes hiding their ambition to go all the way and to collude with others to gain advantages not possible by their achievements. But one lesson that masters learn or have reinforced from their "hard charging, hands-on" superiors is that there must be better ways to turn achievements into advancements.

In addition to these differences in perspectives that place emphasis upon managing versus climbing, masters are more mobile than Big Efforts. Generally, masters are far more agile, flexible, adaptable, and can work better with big effort managers above and below them. In this regard, big effort managers have a soft underbelly. Usually their advancements are slower than they expect for their exceptional achievements. Because they want recognition for their reputations of high performance, they often get frustrated from staying too long in positions. This immobility often occurs because they rely almost solely upon past achievements to push them up. They keep longing for that one big killer assignment that, when completed, will turn all eyes of their superiors upon them. They measure promotable in *feats* rather than in some abstract notion of future worth. Their greatest fear is that they will be used as workhorses for the tough assignments that contribute more to the business than to their advancement that eat up valuable career time.

(Please sees Appendix B for plateau and staircase patterns of climbing.)

The problem of Big Efforts concerns their strong downward orientation that allows little room for ideal subordination. They are not trusted to put their superiors' careers ahead of their own. They communicate best their support for their superiors through the splendid achievements of their staffs. They believe this contribution should be enough. But even this practice may become suspect because they are driven to achieve regardless of their superior's bad fortune. In other words, give them a job to do and they will do it and assume that their superiors will look out for themselves. They are apt to be sponsored by superiors with the same perspective who are similarly confined to the slow route. Big Efforts' careers demonstrate how slow climbers breed slow climbers.

The other problem of big effort managers is their use of too many resources, including the time and effort of people. They are not deft practitioners of the economy rule that prescribes no more or less effort than required to achieve the expected results with few unintended consequences. They often gear up beyond necessity in order to be certain of the outcome. These ways may include radical refocusing, restructuring, or restaffing to make sure everything will go their way. They may not be any better planners, but they often stay the course too long, believing in persistence, rather timely and shrewd moves of augmentation, and intervention.

You would not say they are very mobile. Big Efforts arrive in new positions with the insistence that their new staffs make the greater attempt to understand them than they understand their subordinates. Their use of authority often interferes with gaining reliable information quickly, which often leads to faulty diagnosis of problems. Although they do not intend to shoot the messenger, they, in effect, do so by never taking no for an answer. Most Big Efforts are formula managers, having acquired from previous experiences a set of operating rules and practices to be imposed and made to work regardless of how new and different the assignments and positions. In this regard, they find it difficult to separate from pet ideas and become attached to those that are new, novel, and more attuned to changing circumstances. Furthermore, they are viewed as using people more than developing people, especially with regard to increasing their own promotability over their key subordinates'.

You may ask why do they persistently hew to the managerial perspective rather than the climbers' approach. First of all, it is a mistake to assume that Big Efforts are not convertible. In fact, masters usually start their careers with ambition to succeed as high performing managers. Somewhere in their careers, masters come under the influence of a superior with a climber's perspective who, by the way, is usually a converted big effort type. But the main reason many big effort types may stick exclusively with the managerial approach is mostly due to the powerful ways that corporations continually reinforce it. Also, as high achievers, they thrive on the intrinsic rewards of challenging assignments. Their periodical advancements sufficiently sate their ambitions, at least for a while. In other words, they get enough advancement to bait them to continue their achievement approach to climbing.

Whatever the other reasons for slow climbers, not all of them may be uniformly cast in the mold of big effort managers. You will have other types of competitors, but for practical purposes, you may safely assume that your most likely tenacious competition will be from big effort types.

Because they have the ambition to reach upper levels where their achievements gain more attention and credits, they provide an opportune opening for masters to connect with them. Masters do so through use of their superb relationship skills plus other ingredients of the masters' rules that help to gain Big Efforts' trust and respect. But the most appealing attribute of the masters is their acute corporate sense and shrewd wits that usually exceed Big Efforts'. For this contribution, masters have been known to gain rare sponsorship from them, to succeed them, and even to leapfrog to higher levels with their support, if not blessing. In this regard, the masters' successes illustrate the truth that if you can make it with these heavy hitters, you can make it with all other varieties of slow climbers.

Big effort managers are in high demand if superiors want to get tough assignments done and costs are no major concern, including transferring, demoting, and terminating people. Big effort managers largely account for the massive restructurings of big business during the last two decades. Not a few of them credit each other with restoring big business competitiveness in a global economy.

In contrast, masters attempt to make no more changes than necessary. They have a bias that prevents them from becoming the revolutionaries that Big Efforts typify. Masters are afraid that moving too quickly or radically against corporate ways and wisdom will destabilize the very structure they are trying to climb. But they will, if necessary, make radical changes, but not with the enthusiasm and surefootedness of big effort managers. In contrast, big effort managers believe that all fast climbers thrive upon their successes. As Big Efforts often say, "Sure, we do the hard work that makes it easy for the wunderkinds."

While big effort managers and masters make for an odd couple, they share two strong convictions. They will root out people from their staffs who expect promotions but will not work for them. And they fundamentally oppose the corporate practice of singling out so-called young, high potentials and starting them on a fast track, scheduling and moving them into positions where they may be more easily discovered and developed. Both believe this is corporate subsidizing of undeserving careers. It is akin to socialism, only big business passes handouts to the favored few and, thereby, interferes with the competitive nature of corporate climbing. Of course, you can appreciate why they feel this common bond. Big effort managers predicate their climbs upon hard earned achievements and expect others to believe and practice the same article of faith. They do not like coddling youth. Masters will not allow themselves to become aligned with anyone who is not promotable. If your achievements have not made you promotable, do not expect to be invited into a lineup. Lineups are not to make it easy for managers to advance who have not paid the initial price. Masters are not repair shops for broken-down climbers or counseling centers for witless climbers who don't know what they don't know. Thus, master climbers may be just as contemptuous of so-called high potentials on corporate welfare as big effort managers. However, masters may be more tactful about expressing their contempt or remain silent on the issue.

There are other routes to the top, but none contrasts more sharply with the masters than managers who make the difficult task of climbing just about as difficult as it may become and still make the climb. But from the masters' perspective, Big Efforts give climbing a bad name. They often discourage others from making the climb because they use others at all costs just to maintain their reputations for performing difficult assignments. They pass on their faulty and self-damaging ways that require sacrifice far beyond what is ordinary and necessary. They harm people who feel compelled to mimic their wasteful efforts and who often fall by the wayside because of reduced mental or physical or moral vigor. But masters also recognize that it is the responsibility of climbers to use their wits to protect themselves from the harmful ways of big effort managers. After all, "You cannot have it all your way to go all the way." Besides, the fast route is no piece of cake. Just refer back to Chapter 2, Corporate Sense, to note the ways that the fast route may break careers. Recall the number of managers who gain momentum and lose it, never to be heard from again. Masters have their story to tell, as do Big Efforts. Neither one is a devil nor a saint.

As clumsy and crude as big effort managers may seem to masters, they finally make it to the point in greater number than the masters and illustrate the old adage that hard work counts and climbing the difficult way is still the most common expression of ambition.

The big effort managers invariably arrive at the top much later in their careers. Not a few of them get there as late arrivals just before the time clock runs out on them. They share in common with other slow climbers the tendency to get caught up in a perverse sequence of unintended consequences. The more difficult they make the trip, the more time they will need. With more time, they will make more mistakes and attract more adversaries and enemies. To offset this drag they will need more conspicuous achievements. Big effort managers may arrive at the top with records of performance longer than the masters, but they also may have records of incurring greater difficulty. They are the Babe Ruths of business. The Babe was both a home run king and a strikeout king.

However, reality dictates that the point can accommodate all sorts of people, regardless of their difficulty getting there. Not everybody has the wits to pierce the dense hierarchy ahead using few superiors, jumping several levels, maintaining unbridled momentum, and edging out competitors by the narrowest of margins. This is an ideal that only the smartest and most mobile may even hope to approximate. But the attempt will sharpen their wits and compel them to see and sense a less difficult way of getting advancements than relying upon relentless ambitions and prodigious achievements to overwhelm the wily ways of corporate life.

When the big effort chief announces early retirement at sixty some years of age, the inevitable question is why sponsor a successor who is fifteen years younger, who ranged within the corporation less than one-half as far, had fewer than one-half the superiors and substantially fewer accomplishments. Under such circumstances, the usual public answer is that the young successor is uncommonly capable and is exactly what the business needs or words to that effect. But what may be left unsaid is that the board enthusiastically concurred with the big effort chief. As soon as possible, a new management should take the business in a new direction with a lineup of proven officers and managers that could move into key positions, capture firmly the reins of authority, and effortlessly gain control of the hierarchy and, thereby, make less difficult the difficult things needed to bring the business around to more competitive ways of believing and practicing. They chose a jaguar over an elephant, at least for this time around. But note that behind this early arrival chief lumber the more numerous elephants with weighty achievements that eventually must be given their due. For them, it is only a matter of time. They outnumber the jaguars about four to one.

So you see, you have a choice, effort versus wits. Yours is not an either-or proposition but rather, what priority will you choose to give to one over the other? Do you slug it out the best way possible or find an easier or smarter way to advance? What shall be your formula? Link your ambitions directly to advancement or to achievement? What is your preference, to manage in order to climb or to climb in order to manage? One thing for sure, you are going to make the effort required to achieve an exceptional result, which itself requires no mean amount of wits. But they are different from wits to make yourself far more valuable to your superiors than your splendid record of performance.

In sum, what it takes includes knowing how to get the most hard-headed, hands-on, high-performing superiors to value your future worth greater than your present and past contributions so as to become too crucial to be left behind or passed up by a competitor whose formula for advancement is prodigious effort exerted by dint of blind ambition.

The masters' rules implied in the nature of the fast route are to make it advantageous for your superiors to promote you, make it advantageous for your subordinates to support you, and make it easy to continue to gain these advantages during your ascent.

Some make the climb look incomparably easy, others make it ponderously difficult, and most do not make it any way. It is your move, so make the most of it.

Appendix A: The Origins of Chiefs

Unmindful of mobility and the patterns of moves that give managers access to the top, many observers of the large corporate scene throw chiefs onto one big heap. For them a chief is a chief is a chief. Wrong, no, never. For example, some chiefs use external routes to come in directly to the top of the corporation. They are relatives of founders and former long-tenured chiefs (birth elite), outside lawyers and consultants who serve top management and the board (professionals), representatives of financial houses or blocks of shareholders (proxies), and former members of government and the military (bureaucrats, politicians, and officers). These "externals" average about ten percent of all chiefs.

Their patterns of mobility illustrate the belief held by many boards of directors that chiefs do not need to climb up a hierarchy to acquire the necessary wit and skill for managing a big business, that not all of what managers do as chiefs is dependent upon the lengthy practicing of management, and that many managers find it easier to manage at the top than at lower levels, given all the support available to chiefs, including an effective chain of command.

Suffice it to say that some but not all of these presumptions are at work in the mobility patterns of what I label "hierarchs" (to distinguish "externals" from managers who use a hierarchy to get to the top).

All other chiefs are hierarchs, including managers who use two or more businesses to arrive at the top. The latter are leveragers who parlay their achievements in one corporation into advancements in another or several. Leveragers are outsiders who come directly to the chief's job and represent about a third of all chiefs. Their patterns of using mobility to get the most out of climbing and managing have some major challenges and risks completely separate from other hierarchs.

Many chiefs are pure hierarchs (37 percent) because they go from the bottom to the top of the same business. These "natives," or

THE ORIGINS OF CHIEFS

"lifers," have been disciplined by a single-management hierarchy, unlike the externals, and have certain opportunities and risks not associated with leveragers. Foremostly, they have to live with the consequences of their achievements and failure, sometimes for years to come. Lifers do not flee, as do leveragers, to gain a fresh start or better opportunity. While lifers cannot outrun their past easily, they know better the business from ground up, the major changes that have occurred and who is ahead and behind them during their climbs.

Lifer chiefs span the whole hierarchy of a single corporation. They should not be confused with insiders. Insiders may be either leveragers or lifers. Leveragers who take more than five years in their newly adopted companies before they become chiefs are considered to be insiders. Most chiefs do not consider a five-year-or-more tenured manager still to be an outsider. Insiders account for about 18 percent of all chiefs. Together, lifers and leveragers with inside status account for 56 percent of all chiefs. Outsiders, who come directly to the chief's job and external-type chiefs account respectively for 33 percent and 10 percent of all chiefs.

Chiefs may be further segmented by the speed of their ascents. About 18 percent of all chiefs arrive at the top early in their careers, between 8 to 12 years ahead of the largest batch of chiefs. In contrast are the chiefs arriving late in their careers, after 57 years of age. Late arrival chiefs display different patterns of advancement, parts of which are similar to early arrivals but most of which are idiosyncratic. This report is not about how to *barely* make it to the top, although such a presentation might be interesting about "what not to do and still get there before the grim reaper."

Most managers become CEOs between the ages of fifty-one and fifty-five. These "normal arrival" chiefs form a mixed bag of mobility patterns, with few representing the ideal of what it takes to become chief. Some are better at climbing, others at managing, and a few are passable or superior on both accounts. Each represents an enviable record that offers many examples of "what to do" to get to the top.

Putting early-arrival, normal-arrival, and late-arrival chiefs in the same hopper dulls considerably the diagnostic edge for cutting to the quick of "what it takes." It is akin to averaging out the skills of the slowest and fastest runners in a race. Of course, it is incorrect to say that the average contestant had this or that skill or an average amount of any skill.

This report separates business chiefs another way. It concerns chiefs of the largest industrial corporations. In the Mobility Study of how managers become chiefs, over 300 chiefs in each of five decades were drawn from the 500 largest industrial corporations for each decade. This report does not mix these CEOs with small business heads, entrepreneurs, bankers, public utilities CEOs, and service business presidents, etcetera.

Nor does the report throw together "rookie" chiefs with veteran chiefs. First-time chiefs are different from second-time chiefs in that the latter are invariably outsiders, hierarchical climbing and leveraging are past them, and they do not need to learn what it is to be or become a CEO. Only a few veteran chiefs are called back to head up their former companies.

In short, this study does not use a conglomeration of externals, leveragers, outsiders, insiders, lifers all mixed together with early, normal, and late-arrival chiefs. One cannot find anything common in their mobility patterns by ignoring their differences.

A third of all chiefs never had the ambition to become chief, and many were surprised when they did. A second third did not catch the ambition until around division management. The last third had the ambition during or before employment after graduation from college, and they, too, were often surprised when they became chiefs. The predominant number of early arrivals, our master climbers, belongs to the third category of chiefs. The first group is dominated by late-arrival chiefs. In this report, I focus exclusively upon lifers with the ambition early in their careers to go all the way and did.

This report is about what it takes (wit) managers to climb from the bottom through a single large industrial corporate hierarchy to the top well ahead of the time of the vast majority of chiefs.

Appendix B: The Mobility Patterns of Chiefs

S-Curve: (30 percent). A slow, fast, slow cadence as in the letter S starting with a gradual and steady rise from nonmanager (NM) status to manager of nonmanagers (MONM), hence to manager of managers (MOM), followed by a fast ascent to division or subsidiary levels (DM), culminating in a slow but steady progression to CEO. The path of the S-curve of the route may be wide or narrow as determined by how many lateral and cross-functional assignments. The amplitude of the swings at the incline does not interfere with advancement.

Sleepers: (10 percent). This pattern looks like the letter L. They stay at lower levels for a lengthy time, usually a fourth or more of career time, as an employee (nonmanager NM), manager of nonmanagers (MONM), or at a level above as manager of managers (MOM). Sleepers then shoot up to officer status in another third and then into the COO and CEO in the remainder of career years. Sleepers are most commonly identified by the speed they go from first level manager to officer with little noticeable arrestment, followed by a steep, almost predictable transition to the CEO.

Shooting stars: (10 percent). Their patterns look like an inverted letter L (Γ). They shoot up fast from early levels, past division levels and then spend a third or more of career time before regaining mobility to the chief job. Many stars are identifiable by career arrestment (flame out) in which the lucky ones are given special assignment that will restore their upward mobility.

Staircase climbers: (25 percent). A jerky, staircaselike movement through positions of near equal time from NM to the chief's chair. There may be short delays along the way and side trips with additional special opportunities to prove themselves. This pattern draws a little skepticism and resentment among others.

Plateau experts: (15 percent). Distribution of career time into one or two or, at most, three lengthy plateaus, each level comprising about a quarter of career time. This pattern draws the least resentment, augurs well for reputation as a manager, and develops the most supporters for the manager. The most common variety is to stay at or near division or subsidiary level (DM) for a lengthy time.

Itinerant: (10 percent). Some managers leave tracks that form no discernible design. There is no point in their career that clearly indicates they are definitely advancing toward the top. They may be passed over, moved laterally, taken out of discrete positions, and given special projects that appear casually hung onto the organization chart. They may go up two levels, turn back down one, and then move sideways to perform as situational responsive experts more than as managers. I would ask a typical itinerant, "Let's see, you went over to this job. Why?" "Well, someone thought I could be helpful." "Then you crisscrossed and went over to here." "Yes, I recommended myself. I thought I would be needed." Still, they will get spurts of rapid advancement that clearly show advancement up the hierarchy. They usually arrive later than most chiefs.

Each of these mobility patterns brings its challenges and risks. All depend upon managers maintaining a clear understanding of where they are at any given time. Many skilled managers walk away from a golden opportunity and never know it, often at the angst of their superiors. On the other hand, managers may misinterpret their loss of momentum as permanent when it is temporary.

The most critical smart is to read accurately the hierarchy and your place in it and why. The most common motive is disciplined ambition, and the most common character quality is self-confidence. Almost all early arrival chiefs suffered a position or assignment that tested their endurance and resolve, self-confidence. But they did not give up in their attempt to improve their status either by managing better or climbing more skillfully or both.

The staircase mobility pattern is most apt to prevent flagging of ambition and confidence by the steady reinforcing of each. But ambition is no magic bullet because the two L patterns may kill the chance for continued upward mobility as well as assist it. The appearance in the L patterns of ambition can cause the suspicion by others of looking out only for number one (avarice and greed).

The challenge to sleepers is that they often bypass many intervening positions and are subject to the accusation that they are not seasoned or well credentialed managers.

Shooting stars also have the same challenge. They often fail to understand the why and ways of business practices beyond their limited path to the top. Going so fast, they cannot absorb all that they need to know to be good generalists and gain wide and deep enough understanding of what the business is all about. Also, they often move faster than their mistakes and do not know their weaknesses well.

Managers who experience one or two lengthy plateaus and survive these relatively lengthy periods often develop a gait that is cautious and thorough, sometimes tentative. They actually have to enjoy settling down and making an honest career out of managing. Usually the first plateau is at the level of manager of managers (MOM). The second is usually at or near division level (DM) or at a senior officer level such as CFO, COO, or EVP, etcetera.

These plateaus oddly enough are where careers are often made or broken. Of course, there is considerable washout at the first management level (MONM) but not as great as manager of managers (MOM) level. Roughly 50 percent do not make the MOM cut.

The next critical point is at the division level where managers may not measure up to division standards as a direct report to the division or subsidiary manager (DM). The adequate but not exceptional managers may be plateaued or transferred. The turnover as a direct report to the division manager is over 60 percent, but among those who survive, one out of three division managers (DM) will be eventually promoted to respectable officer status or terminated. The likelihood of either is about equal. The remainders are transferred to other divisions, demoted, or kicked upstairs with staff jobs and never heard from again.

The division or subsidiary position is most critical because managers are measured not only as a peer of other division managers but also against officer levels of the corporation. They may be better than other division managers but not ready to become a corporate officer. It is here that oftentimes the highest performers are passed over for managers who are well rounded.

The most common reason given by chiefs about why they sponsored a candidate for a key corporate officership is, "I assume they have the requisite performance records. What I want are people with practical ideas, smart moves, and strong character qualities, who can be trusted to apply their resources vigorously to become decisive contributors to my lineup."

But sleepers and shooting stars have to be acutely aware of and avoid career-limiting moves and career arrestment. They simply do not have the time to get bogged down and end up nowhere. They must wisely approach each position, perform to expectations, and depart cleanly for the next job. They must make quality relationships quickly and disconnect without terminating such relationships or incurring ill will. As they say, "You may need them on the way down."

Appendix C: The Language of Mobility

I. Basic mobility (S-A)

 A. Separate—*disconnect,* sever, detach, disperse, disassociate, split (see AWA, move away).
 B. Attach—*connect,* commit, join, associate, fuse, unify (see AWA, move with).
 C. Managers make many relationships, but a connection is a special relationship where the parties are wedded "at the hip."
 D. The choice and quality of connections and disconnections determine status in the organization.

II. Management mobility (APD)

 A. Arrival. Smart presence during the approach to a new assignment determines quality of performance.
 B. Performance. The base from which advancement springs is not position but smart moves.
 C. Departure. Leaving smart is as much an art as arriving smart.
 D. The APD is in constant use in all connections and disconnections.

III. Directional moves (AWA)

 A. Away (see 1A)
 B. With (see 1B)
 C. Against—oppose, attack, vie, counter, resist, destroy
 D. All moves, covert or overt, must be made with awareness of their actual or apparent directions.

IV. Key Moves (A-I)

    A. Managerial

        1. Augment—to enhance in some major way the likelihood of completion of a program without major disruption of the core effort.
        2. Intervene—to compel a radical change to save or replace a program.
        3. Gain or regain control of results requires key moves.

    B. Career

        1. Augment—to enhance and accelerate a career pattern.
        2. Intervene—to radically redesign one's career strategy.
        3. Gain or regain upward momentum relies upon key moves.

    C. A move is a series of interrelated acts specifically aimed at a limited objective within a larger plan or purpose.

V. Targets of moves (PIP)

    A. People
    B. Ideas
    C. Programs
    D. Since the carriers of ideas are people, *What It Takes* concentrates primarily but not exclusively on these attributes of people.

VI. People—power to help or hurt careers

    A. Advisor

        1. Teacher—one who imparts corporate "smarts."

THE LANGUAGE OF MOBILITY 211

   2. Practitioner—one who demonstrates corporate "smarts" (they who know, do and they who do not know, teach).
   3. Master—a sponsor who can teach and demonstrate corporate wisdom.

B. Sponsor—No one gets to the top without one, several is ideal.

   1. Evaluator—the power to review and recommend others with qualified support of superiors.
   2. Nominator—the power to assign or promote others with explicit support of superiors.
   3. Promoter—the unqualified power to arbitrarily determine a subordinate's career.
   4. Sponsor—a promoter with long-term interest in the career of a manager, with power to protect and enhance such investment for corporate or personal gain.

C. Crucial subordinate (CS)

   1. Complementary—fills in the superior's voids, offsets superior's weaknesses.
   2. Supplementary—reinforces the superior's strengths.

D. Impostor—people may pretend to be better connected to powerful superiors than they actually are or be wiser or more expert than their experiences justify.

E. Crucial subordinates are likely candidates of sponsorship. The connection between crucial subordinate and sponsor represents the highest quality of mobility effectiveness and relationships skills.

VII. Ideas: Career enhancing or limiting. Performance, authority, power, opportunity, promotability (PAPOP).

   A. Performance—to produce results that are highly valued by superiors (see II B).
   B. Authority—the single resource that distinguishes managers from nonmanagers. The misuse or abuse of authority often spells career arrestment or termination.
   C. Power—skill of influence without use of authority; vital to building personal support.
   D. Opportunity—to prove oneself superior to peers or equal to superiors.
   E. Promotability—to be able to garner promotions or to secure long-term future worth.
   F. PAPOP is a hierarchy of issues, each of which changes in meaning and use as one advances toward the top (performance, authority, power, opportunity and promotability). Please see the book, *How Managers Become Chiefs* (1997).

VIII. Positions

   A. High or low visibility—manager's line of sight extended to powerful superiors several levels above or line of sight limited to immediate sphere of action.
   B. High or low exposure—line of sight of powerful superiors extended downward several levels to manager or blocked by manager's immediate boss or nature of manager's position.
   C. Visiposure (high A&B)—chance of being discovered and sponsored very high.
   D. Dead end (low A&B)—chance very poor of gaining advancement.
   E. Visiposure (positions with high exposure and high visibility) are usually present in the mobility patterns of early arrival chiefs.

IX. Promotion Moves

   A. Long promotion: Physical distance is not the factor. Rather how far a position or assignment exceeds the manager's acquired skills and experiences. "Stretch" promotions require astute APD moves.
   B. Short promotions: The preponderance of skills and experiences required for achievement in a new assignment or position has been acquired already. The need for smart moves of the APD should not be discounted.
   C. Developmental promotion: A long promotion that will inordinately prepare the manager for greater responsibility. Smart arrival is key here.
   D. Availability: An ideal candidate for taking a promotion and doing the job expeditiously because of the availability of the precise skills needed.
   E. Functional promotion: A short promotion in a function that strengthens and reinforces skills already acquired.
   F. Lateral promotion: Any of the above moves but without demonstrable advancement in a status or position in the hierarchy—not to be confused with lateral transfers.
   G. Cross-functional promotion: Any of the above moves that span two functions, i.e., from sales to manufacturing.
   H. Leapfrog promotion: To advance ahead of one or several positions, superiors, or reporting levels beyond one's present status. Usually a long promotion. Smart use of APD needed because of an entirely different environment.
   I. Assignment promotion: A task of extraordinary importance that confers demonstrably superior status and authority without a noticeable change in position and reporting level. Performance will augur high negative or positive exposure, depending upon the value of the results. Local and corporate smarts essential.

J. Dead-end promotion: A noticeable increase in position or reporting level but with less status, authority, and importance to superiors. Usually a short, functional move to make room for other people more valued.

K. Momentum promotion: The attempt to capture the skills of a highly valued manager whose consecutive achievements are expected to continue at a higher level. May be a long, short, or assignment type promotion with demonstrably favorable career opportunities.

L. Bookends promotion: Usually a developmental promotion to a position with high risk of failure substantially minimized by placing the manager between a competent superior and subordinate. Not to be confused with a sandwich assignment, where you are put between two "heavy" people who limit your effectiveness. Excellent APD and local and corporate smarts required.

X. Mobility wits: The ability to do what one sets forth to achieve with no more or less effort than necessary, leaving few unintended consequences. *What it takes* is the following smarts:

    A. Local smart

        1. Acute awareness and comprehension of events and circumstances that occur within one's line of sight, including mobility practices of people.

    B. Corporate smart

        1. The ability to accurately map the terrain, interpret the signs, anticipate the trends and directions and the moves and practices of people in the larger sphere of the business, including extended mobility patterns.

THE LANGUAGE OF MOBILITY 215

- C. Maze bright (A&B)

    1. Special awareness of what rewards and penalizes careers (helps and hurts) and the avoidance of entrapment and loss of room to maneuver.

- D. The above smarts are what upward-bound managers look for in their sponsorees. Sponsors want assurance that their crucial subordinates will not get entangled and lost in intricate corporate affairs. They treat their investments in crucial subordinates as assets with long-term payoff.

XI. Routes (see Appendix B for the basic routes of mobile managers who become chiefs).

- A. Fast route to the top

    1. One of the composite paths used by managers to become chief
    2. When executed wisely these paths become the fast route to the top.

- B. The fast route is composed of

    1. A lead superior, with power to sponsor.
    2. A middle member, called mobile or promotable manager.
    3. A direct report to the above called crucial subordinate.

- C. The above forms a lineup that when performed properly will move the members higher, faster than any known formation of three individuals.
- D. The mobility rule: Any set of managers who so combine to coordinate their wit and skills to form a hierarchy will do more than the same number of people in ordinary superior, subordinate relationship.
- E. The key wits and skills are mobility, starting with the basic moves of attaching and separating.

1. How, when, and with whom to connect and disconnect are the wits and skills making good relationship sense.

F. The power of the lineup is greatly due to drawing upon the medium of business, which is relationships.

XII. Master climbers. These excellent scalers of the corporate hierarchy take the fast route which, in effect, increases their chances of getting to the top.

A. The difficult journey is not made more hazardous, because they know how to avoid the mobility trap, to move faster than your wits can sustain.
B. The mobility trap that slows and stops almost all climbers, save the masters, occurs because the fast route exponentializes risks of failing.
C. Masters use their mobility wits and skills, including forming relationships in the lineup and outside, that will help them to greatly improve their chances of using the fast route effectively.

XIII. The climbers' rules

A. Do nothing to make it difficult for superiors to promote you. Preferably make it advantageous for them to promote you.
B. Make it advantageous for subordinates to help you.
C. Use relationships to make it easy to gain advantages above.

XIV. The above rules are most applicable to gaining and maintaining membership in a lineup.

A. The climbers' rules are based on the idea of smart effort. Whatever needs to be done must be done with less time or effort.

B. Even the most difficult tasks can be made less difficult.
C. Managers are attractive members to line up because of their smart efforts.
D. Masters move fast, need people who do things fast and efficiently.
E. The ideal of masters is effortlessness.
F. They make the climb look incomparably easy.

Appendix D: Wit From A to Z

A. The higher one goes, the less likely one will go higher. This is the rule of the corporate pyramid. Relatively fewer positions with more contestants limit and intensify ascent. Getting quickly out of lower levels carries more value than short tenure in any higher position. The longer you stay at lower management levels, the less competent you become to manage and climb. The exception to this rule is the inverted L (Γ) pattern of mobility (VII E).

B. To resist the gravitational pull downward that keeps the largest body of managers at the lowest levels where most of the work is performed, one must distinguish between the skills of climbing and managing. To make this distinction work, you must be clever about the ideas of mobility (I through IX).

C. The higher you go, the more effortless must become major achievements. If you must exert more prolonged effort with each advancement, mental exhaustion and its attendant mistakes will terminate upward momentum. This is the law of economy of effort that holds that enervation is a formidable adversary of climbers. Efficient execution of APD is a must (II ABCD). Please note: Chiefs may work long hours but their efforts are more concentrated on priorities that have high payoff. Their effort payoff ratio is high. Hence the definition of effortless.

D. Few managers arrive at the top without intentional displacement of at least one superior. This move caries high risk and high benefit. This rule of displacement is practiced most assiduously by early arrival chiefs (VII DE).

E. No one gets to the top or very far up the organization without trustworthiness. Trust is implicit condition of sponsorship and promotability and rules all career sensitive and dependent relationships. Managers unwise about trust make career limiting attachments and separations. The rule of trust is that the less said about it the more it dominates quality connections (IA B).

F. No one gets to the top without sponsorship. To directly seek a sponsor is foolish. To attract sponsorship requires advanced use of mobility skills. This rule holds without exception among early arrival chiefs (VI B).

G. To be discovered for getting sponsorship you must gain assignments of high exposure and visibility. The risk is that malperformance may be seen as far as exposure extends. The rule of visiposure is that it is better for superiors to discover you on your terms than to be discovered on their terms (VIII C).

H. To ease through the organization, you must have fewer malperformances so as to make it easy for superiors to sponsor you. The worst judgment is to be accused of poor judgment about character and capability of close subordinates and associates to whom you are tightly connected (VI B, IX C).

I. Crucial subordinates acquire the power to sponsor their self-chosen promotees because of the former's connections with superiors based upon smartness and trustworthiness. To acquire the power to sponsor, you must first show wise use of authority (I B, VI B).

J. A mistake is the result of incompetence, and an error is caused by human frailty. Crucial subordinates make errors, less favored managers make mistakes. This is the rule of discounting (VI C).

K. A mistake may become viewed by superiors as an aberration if it is gross enough to defy rational explanation. Blunders usually gain special dispensation for the sponsored few, i.e., no one can be that dumb. Most early arrival chiefs make at least one blunder. This is the "beaut" rule (if you are going to make a mistake, make sure it is a "beaut") (VII A).

L. When the manager's malperformance impinges severely upon the careers of valuable others, including superiors, the rule of discounting may be withheld. The perpetuators usually become insupportable.

M. Coaches without power of sponsorship are the least reliable source of wisdom. Mentor is the most overused and weakest word in the lexicon of climbers (II AB).

N. Poor performance usually ensues from faulty arrival in a new position or assignment; hence the rule of the 5 Ps, prior preparation prevents poor performance permeates the APD triad (II, ABC, VII A).

O. All plans are doomed to failure unless they are periodically and smartly augmented or intervened by key moves (IV AB). Moves are the footprints left behind by fast-rising managers.

P. Advancement involves moving through an ever-changing structure of PAPOP, the silent force behind promotion and termination. Managers climb through these issues rather than positions (VII ABCDEF).

Q. Misreading the covert requirements of performance penalizes both achievement and advancement. Important assignments may carry implicit expectations that may never become known even when violated. This is why managers fail to know why they fail (VII A).

R. Misuse and abuse of authority is the most common reason for arrestment of career. The proper use and meaning of authority may vary with changes in superiors and positions in the hierarchy (VII B).

S. Failure to make a practical distinction between authority and power risks making both ineffectual. Power fills the inadequacies of authority, is self-obtained and can never be transferred, unlike authority (VII C).

T. Managers fail because they cannot separate from old ideas and experiences when faced with novel situations. They illustrate immobility. Without flexibility and agility to adapt and adjust smartly, they come from behind even when they move ahead. Clutching their old, worn skills, they attempt to back into the future. They become victims of a mobile world that requires more respect for what is ahead than what is behind (I AB).

U. Many are qualified but only a few are eligible. Knowing and exploiting these differences is to be smart about making a rapid ascent. The difference between qualified for promotion and eligible is the difference between being a candidate for a specific promotion and being generally verified as a valuable, long-term contributor. When you are eligible, your future promotions are assumed or assured. This rule is both cause and result of momentum and sponsorship (VI IE).

V. Among opportunities to prove yourself superior to your peers or equal to your superiors, the latter type drives speed of advancement and is concomitant with eligibility (VI ID).

W. Climbers excel because of quality connections and disconnections. Managers may deceive themselves about the quality of their separations and attachments. They attach to friends who are not their supporters and separate from adversaries who are not their enemies. Climbers see people for what they are or they cease to be deft climbers (I AB).

X. A mobile mind adapts and adjusts with flexibility, speed, and adroitness. The corporation requires mobility more than ever. It is mobility personified and attracts at all levels the most mobile minds and expels sluggish minds that do not move with the events for which clever wits are required (I AB).

Y. Ordinary behavior rather than sophisticated practices are the stem root of achievement and advancement. Moves made by managers are common to all levels of the organization. The rule of universality of managerial behavior holds that the uses of mobility are no different at first-level management than at upper-level management. Novice managers are miniature chiefs (III ABC).

Z. Power is what power does. This rule determines the use of directional moves with superiors (III ABCD).

Appendix E: Rules of Moves

General and Nonspecific

1. All plans and intentions are subject to failure unless augmented and intervened by basic moves.
2. Any move must ring true as authentic representation of honest intentions.
3. Moves are not arrived at casually. They represent positions, not poses.
4. Moves are adopted for purposes greater and other than the moves themselves.
5. They must be efficient in their purpose, leaving no doubt as to their potential to effectuate identifiable and needed results.
6. The timing of their implementation is as critical as the moves themselves.
7. Each move must discount the value of other options available or considered.
8. Each move carries the potential for unintended consequences, which require swift augmentation and intervention by correcting moves.
9. Potentially unintended consequences must be anticipated as early as possible. The aging of faulty moves can create worse consequences for which no move, however wise, may be sufficient.
10. Any lead moves inevitably require use of the others. These secondary moves must conform to the above rules as well.

Special Rules of Away, With, Against

Moves *with* (attachment)

- Know the difference in degrees of approval, support, and commitment.

- Signal people to know when you are performing these values and why.
- Do not allow misunderstanding of the above degrees of attachment.
- Never give any strong value to an emergent idea that is still developing.
- Never go quickly from commitment to abandonment.
- Or make commitment while there is still doubt, or abandonment when there is still hope.
- Going from positive expression to negative quickly will cast doubt about your stability and credibility.
- Do not allow one idea to limit other options. Avoid single-option thinking.
- Make sure the target idea is central to the key move and not tangential.
- Ferret out tangential ideas to prevent loss of focus. Keep your mind uncluttered.
- Make sure the arbiter of ideas is the objective and expected results.

Moves *away* (separation)

- Never show ambivalence about away moves.
- Use more useful ideas to dispel the aura of unwanted ideas.
- Use supporters of ideas to counter negative ideas and moves.
- Use early converts to dissuade others.
- Avoid ad hominem arguments.
- Do not force people into set positions.
- Privately keep your options in case you want to go on the offense.
- Make sure no collateral damage is done to useful ideas.
- Make sure that there are alternative ideas to embrace.
- Do not preempt the opportunity for others to move away first.
- Never use confusing signals to indicate abandonment.

Move *against* (separation with prejudice)

- Attack faulty ideas at their source.
- Prefer to move against the ideas than the individual except when the latter is grossly culpable.

- In the case of a patently unuseful move, achieve closure quickly.
- Once the decision has been made, move out quickly and thoroughly.
- Do not solicit approval from others for banishment.
- Do not be reluctant to express your authority properly and timely.
- Do not implicate others in any move to banish.
- The move must be seen as your decision alone.
- Give people a chance to reconsider.
- Use moves no more extreme than necessary.

Appendix F: Major Conclusions of the Fifty-Year Mobility Study

The *first* observation that has emerged from a five-decade study of chiefs in the largest industrial organizations is that they are as diverse in their managerial skills as managers whose careers top out at lower levels. No pattern or mode of managing precludes anyone from getting to the top. All masters perform differently.

The *second* is that no quality or combinations of qualities of personality, intelligence, or character may predict managers who become chiefs. There is no such theory as the right personality to go to the top. Chiefs are introverts, extroverts, autocrats, democrats, honest, dishonest, arrogant, modest, etcetera. There is no reason for anyone wishing to make the effort to feel inadequate because of personal qualities.

The *third* is managers who become chiefs cannot be predicted from the peers they leave behind. I have many times attempted and failed to predict from division managers who would become CEOs. In particular, masters are not known until they become chiefs (see the eighth observation below).

The *fourth* is that one-third of apparent or designated successors do not become chiefs. No one has a lock on the chieftainship. It is a fluid set of requirements that change with conditions inside and outside the business.

This is partly due to the *fifth* fact that over thirty percent of chiefs are unpredictably selected from the outside and an additional ten percent comes in at the top as corporate lawyers and other professionals (externals).

Because of the uncertainty of making chief in one organization, managers will use two or more. Those chiefs are called leveragers and will be described in one of the sequels to this book. Over one-half of outsiders come directly into the chief's job, and the remainder into one or two positions below, spending less than five years before they become CEOs. Many outsiders are pulled in at lower levels to perform critical assignments. They usually gain an edge over insiders for the chieftainship. Among outsiders who come into the COO job (chief operations officer) almost forty percent do not become CEOs. This is due to the tendency for a CEO who has a number of executives who may have what it takes to become chief.

The *sixth* observation is that lifers who go from bottom to top of a company do not perform appreciably better as chiefs than outsiders. This observation has been discussed in *How Managers Become Chiefs*. When allowance is made for the disadvantages of outsiders and the advantages of lifers, the result is a draw. Most failure at the top is due to a poor understanding by chiefs of business conditions, which is often the result of poor judgment of the board of directors.

The *seventh* is that the speed of ascent of chiefs cannot predict their tenure or staying power at the top. For that matter, there is nothing in the rules of mobility that guarantees success at any level in the hierarchy.

The *eighth* is that changing corporate conditions have as much to do with advancement as the efforts and qualities of managers who become chiefs. The idea that a good manager can manage under diverse and changing conditions is only partly true. Masters do because they have minds geared to mobility that provide agility, flexibility, and adaptability. But other climbers may have mental rigidity and narrowness that disallow them to move quickly and assertively with changing circumstances.

The *ninth* is that managers going from the bottom to the top will work under the regimes of at least three chiefs, each of whom will change the alignment of executives and managers wending their way to the top. Thus, many climbers will be unpredictably sidelined and others unexpectedly given new life along the route to chieftainship. This mobility serves as the background that shows why any position may be temporary and any advancement the first or the last. It is no longer true that promotions offer the strongest indication of security of status or employment.

The *tenth* observation is that any attempt by artificial means, such as tests or inventories, to preselect at any level managers most likely to advance to chieftainship will be for naught. The competitiveness of climbers is unpredictable and requires more than managerial skills. The corporate environment is not a steady state of known or predictable challenges and risks. Further, the marketplace for finding managers who become chiefs is greater than that of a single business because at least a fifth of all managers from the first level to the top come from outside.

All of which yields the summation point that any attempt to predict from any level who will eventually become chiefs is sheer speculation. Whereas I cannot predict who will become chiefs, I can describe after the fact the routes that chiefs take and the wit and skills they use to make their climbs. I can also describe the perspective that organizes their ambitions in relation to career goals and that orders up appropriate wits and skills to deal with conditions and problems on their way to the top. But as to specific moves that are required to get ahead, such is beyond my wisdom. I can offer options available to the climbers, but the most appropriate must be selected and executed to meet the unique nature of the conditions and circumstances at the time. Climbing is an art of applying the rule of mobility by the wit and skills of those who have to live with the consequences.

The readers may question why I separate managing from the wit and skills of climbers. The reason is that I was not getting an adequate description of what it takes to become chief. One day I realized that what is required to get a promotion is not the same as what is required to progress to the top. Many managers got promotions but seldom went very far. A few went part or all the way. Next, I realized that I had to separate these two related but distinct activities that operate in every chief's career, climbing and managing. Without the use of this artificial cleavage, how managers become chief could not be adequately dissected and described.

However, making a practical distinction was not easy and had escaped many an investigator's fine eye. I discovered that using the idea of mobility as an overlay sharpens the features of both. This is reasonable to expect because mobility is universal to all forms of behavior.

The idea is that mobility acts as a magnifying glass that sharpens efforts that otherwise would go unnoticed and that directly contribute to a progression of advancements to the top. Close examination showed that climbers use the same resources as managers, but they combine and focus these resources in unique and subtle ways, such that the unaided eye fails to see the distinction.

About the Author

In 1949, I started the Mobility Study of how managers become chiefs. The Study audited the mobility patterns of chiefs and division managers of over 350 of America's largest industrial corporations in five-year segments until the Study was formally terminated in 1997.

The procedures included analyzing the positions through which these managers passed on the way to their destinations and their acquired experiences.

In 1968, largely due to the successful publication of *Mobile Managers,* I became a personal confidante to chiefs and their protégés or potential successors who for the most part were in trouble with their board of directors or superiors. I have continued this confidential advising to this day.

However, by the early 1990s, I had accumulated enough data from the Mobility Study to alert the business media to some strange happening in the corporate ranks. For example, I reported to the *Wall Street Journal* that eight of one hundred chiefs failed to survive their first year in office, up from one per one hundred five years earlier (*Wall Street Journal,* "More chiefs find revolving door," 10/7/92). I also reported to John Cunniff of the *New York Associated Press,* who had been reporting results of the Mobility Study since 1971 when *Routes to the Executive Suite* was published, that similar mobility patterns identified division managers.

Later in a related report, I showed that more than a third of CEOs came from outside the company (*WSJ,* "Portable CEO," 1/26/98). I also reported that between 1990 and 1997, the number of CEOs staying in their jobs to retirement age fell twelve percent and that of all CFOs, twenty percent failed to stay in their jobs more than three years (*WSJ,* "Heavy Duty," 05/03/99). In the same period the forced termination of division managers had increased more than twofold.

I had documented what was generally known, that managing had become exceptionally difficult and dangerous to careers. However, by counseling troubled chiefs and their protégés and successors, I got behind these facts to penetrate the clutter of plausible but usually incomplete or fallacious reasons for their failures.

In 1997, I decided that any additional information from the Mobility Study and confidential advising would become redundant and decided to commit to paper the point of view that the complexity and uncertainty of corporate life required ambitious managers to separate the skills of managing from the skills of climbing, that those who could perform both skills were smarter about how their corporations work and how to work them. I called this practical intelligence *full smart*.

The title, confidential advisor, is not a gratuitous appellation. In my practice I never visit on the corporate grounds of my clients or practice in public view. My clients usually have an unaudited account to pay my fees. Because they and I value privacy and confidentiality, we were able to communicate more personally than otherwise. None of the names of my clients have ever appeared in publications.

However, a few with whom I have worked on a less confidential basis have volunteered some quotable quotes. I included them as background.